Collins

MATHS FRAMEWORKING

Complete success for Mathematics at KS3

YEAR 9

PUPIL BOOK 3

KEVIN EVANS   KEITH GORDON   TREVOR SENIOR   BRIAN SPEED

Contents

This chapter is going to show you

- how to find the nth term of a linear sequence
- how to describe a sequence derived from a geometrical pattern
- how to find a second difference
- how to find inverse functions
- the limits of some series

What you should already know

- How to continue a given pattern
- How to graph a simple relationship

Sequences

Arsenal had a sequence of 43 games in which they scored in every game. Is it possible to predict how many goals they would score in their next game?

A **sequence** is an ordered set of numbers or terms, such as the positive integers, 1, 2, 3… . Every number or term in a sequence is given by applying the same rule throughout the sequence. Look at Examples 1.1 and 1.2.

Example 1.1   What is the next number in the following sequence?

10, 100, 1000, 10 000, …

It is 100 000.

What is the term-to-term rule for the sequence? Multiply by 10.

Example 1.2   What is the next number in this sequence?

1, 2, 4, 7, 11, 16, …

It is 22.

Show the differences between consecutive terms. They are: 1, 2, 3, 4, 5,… .

The position of a term in a sequence can sometimes be used to find its value. The idea is to try to find a general term which represents the pattern. This is usually written as the **nth term**, or as **$T(n)$**.

nth term of a sequence

A sequence is usually defined by its nth term. Look at Examples 1.3 to 1.5 to see how this works.

Example 1.3 ▶ Write down the first four terms of the sequence whose nth term is given by
$T(n) = 4n + 2$.

The first term, $T(1)$, is given by $n = 1$. Hence, $4 \times 1 + 2 = 6$.
The second term, $T(2)$, is given by $n = 2$. Hence, $4 \times 2 + 2 = 10$.
The third term, $T(3)$, is given by $n = 3$. Hence, $4 \times 3 + 2 = 14$.
The fourth term, $T(4)$, is given by $n = 4$. Hence, $4 \times 4 + 2 = 18$.

So, the first four terms are 6, 10, 14, 18.

Example 1.4 ▶ Write down the nth term of the sequence 2, 5, 8, 11, ...

First, find the differences between consecutive terms. The sequence has the same difference, 3, between consecutive terms. This shows that the sequence is in the form $An + B$.

Since the common difference is 3, then $A = 3$.

So, in order to get the first term of 2, –1 must be added to 3. Hence $B = -1$.

That is, the nth term is given by $T(n) = 3n - 1$.

When a sequence has the same difference between consecutive terms, it is called a **linear sequence**. A linear sequence can be defined by a general term that will be in the following form:

$$T(n) = An + B$$

where A is the common difference between consecutive terms, B is the value which is added to A to give the first term, and n is the number of the term (that is, first, second, ...).

Example 1.5 ▶ Write down the nth term of the sequence 5, 9, 13, 17, 21, ...

The difference between consecutive terms is 4.

To get the first term of 5, 1 must be added to 4.

Hence, the nth term is $T(n) = 4n + 1$.

Check this as follows: $T(1) = 4 \times 1 + 1 = 5$
$T(2) = 4 \times 2 + 1 = 9$
$T(3) = 4 \times 3 + 1 = 13$

So, $T(n) = 4n + 1$ is correct.

Quadratic sequences

A quadratic sequence is a sequence whose nth term contains n^2. For example:

$$T(n) = n^2 + 3n + 4$$
$$T(n) = 2n^2 + 4n + 3$$

When looking for a pattern in a quadratic sequence, the second differences have to be considered. Follow through Example 1.6 to see how this works.

Example 1.6 ▶   What is the pattern of second differences in $T(n) = n^2$?

The first six terms of the sequence $T(n) = n^2$, where $T(1) = 1$, are:

    1, 4, 9, 16, 25, 36

The first differences are those between consecutive terms. These are:

    1 4 9 16 25 36
      3 5 7 9 11

The second differences are those between consecutive first differences, as shown below:

    3 5 7 9 11
      2 2 2 2

Every quadratic sequence has second differences which are the same throughout the sequence, as shown above.

1 Find the next three terms in each of the following sequences.

    a   1, 5, 9, 13, ...   **b**   3, 8, 13, 18, ...   **c**   2, 9, 16, 23, ...
    d   4, 10, 17, 25, ...   **e**   6, 14, 24, 36, ...   **f**   5, 8, 13, 20, ...

2 Write down the first four terms of each of the following sequences whose nth term is given below.

    a $2n + 3$ **b** $3n - 2$ **c** $4n + 5$ **d** $5n - 3$
    e n^2 **f** $n^2 + 1$ **g** $n^2 + n$ **h** $n^2 + 3n + 4$

3 Find the nth term of each of the following sequences.

    a   6, 10, 14, 18, 22, ...   **b**   8, 15, 22, 29, 36, ...
    c   −1, −5, −9, −13, −17, ...   **d**   −15, −12, −9, −6, −3, ...
    e   2.4, 2.6, 2.8, 3.0, 3.2, ...   **f**   1.7, 2.0, 2.3, 2.6, 2.9, ...
    g $\frac{1}{2}, \frac{2}{5}, \frac{3}{8}, \frac{4}{11}, \frac{5}{14}, ...$ **h** $\frac{3}{4}, \frac{5}{9}, \frac{7}{14}, \frac{9}{19}, \frac{11}{24}, ...$

4 Look at each of the following sequences of lines.

    Diagram 1   **Diagram 2**   **Diagram 3**   **Diagram 4**

    a   Find the number of lines in the nth shape.
    b   Find the number of lines in the 50th shape in the pattern.

5 Write down the first five terms of each of the following sequences.

    a $T(n) = (n + 1)(n + 2)$ **b** $T(n) = (n - 1)(n - 2)$
    c $T(n) = n + (n - 1)(n - 2)$ **d** $T(n) = 2n + (n - 1)(n - 2)(n - 3)$
    e $T(n) = 3n + (n - 1)(n - 2)(n - 3)(n - 4)$

6 **INVESTIGATION 1**

    a   Find the second differences for each of the following sequences by writing down the first six terms.

        i $T(n) = n^2 + 3n + 4$ **ii** $T(n) = n^2 + 4n + 3$

    b   What do you notice about each second difference?

    c   Investigate what the second difference will be when $T(n) = n^2 + Bn + C$.

7 **INVESTIGATION 2**

    a   Find the second differences for each of the following sequences by writing down the first six terms.

        i $T(n) = 2n^2 + 3n + 4$ **ii** $T(n) = 2n^2 + 4n + 3$

    b   What do you notice about each second difference?

    c   What do you expect the second difference to be for $T(n) = 3n^2 + 3n + 4$?

    d   Investigate what the second difference will be when $T(n) = An^2 + Bn + C$.

A sequence is defined by:

    First term, $T(1) = a$

    Term-to-term rule is 'Add b to the previous term', which gives:

        $T(2) = b + T(1)$

    and so on.

Write down five numbers in sequences for which $T(1) = a$ and the term-to-term rule is 'Add b', which obey each of the following conditions:

a   Every other number is an integer, the rest are fractions.

b   Every fourth number is an integer, the others are fractions.

c   Every number is an even number.

d   Every other number is a multiple of 10, the rest are not.

e   Every fourth number is a multiple of 10, the rest are not.

Pattern spotting

Many situations generate patterns of numbers whose representations by diagram will be complicated to draw.

Example 1.7   Look at the following diagrams.

    1 line   2 lines   3 lines

    2 regions   4 regions   7 regions

Each circle has a number of lines drawn inside its circumference. The lines intersect one another to create many regions.

continued

Example 1.7
continued

The table below shows the maximum number of regions which can be made each time a new line is added.

Number of lines	1	2	3
Maximum number of regions	2	4	7

a Before drawing a diagram, can you predict, from the table, the maximum number of regions you will have for four lines?

You can see that the numbers develop, but can you see a pattern?

The differences increase by one each time, suggesting that for four lines, there will be 7 + 4 = 11 regions.

b Draw the diagram for four lines, creating as many regions as you can. Count the number of regions. Were you right?

There are 11 regions. The table now looks like this.

Number of lines	1	2	3	4
Maximum number of regions	2	4	7	11

c Now predict the maximum number of regions for five lines and six lines.

d Check your results for part **c** by adding a new line each time to the diagram in part **b**, and seeing how many regions there are.

e Try to write down the term-to-term rule for the sequence of maximum regions.

Exercise 1B

1 Look at the way straight lines can intersect one another.

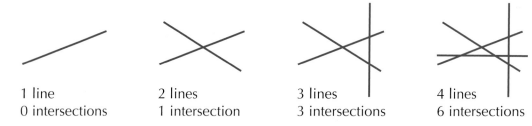

1 line	2 lines	3 lines	4 lines
0 intersections	1 intersection	3 intersections	6 intersections

The maximum number of intersections for each set of lines is shown in the table below.

Number of lines	1	2	3	4
Maximum number of intersections	0	1	3	6

a Before drawing a diagram, can you predict, from the table, the maximum number of intersections you will have for five lines?

b Draw the five lines so that they all intersect one another. Count the number of intersections. Were you right?

c Now predict the maximum number of intersections for six and seven lines.

d Check your results for part **c** by drawing a diagram in each case.

e Try to write down the term-to-term rule for the sequence of maximum intersections.

2 Look at the following diagrams.

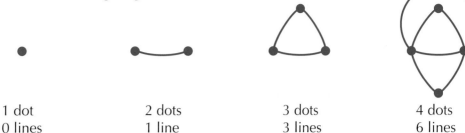

1 dot	2 dots	3 dots	4 dots
0 lines	1 line	3 lines	6 lines

Each dot is joined to as many other dots as possible without any lines crossing. The table below shows the maximum number of lines which can be joined each time a new dot is added.

Number of dots	1	2	3	4
Maximum number of lines	0	1	3	6

a Before drawing a diagram, can you predict, from the table, the maximum number of lines you will have for five dots?

b Copy the diagram for four dots, add a new dot and add as many new lines (without intersections) as you can. Count the number of lines. Were you right?

c Now predict the maximum number of lines for six and seven dots.

d Check your results for part **c** by adding a new dot each time to your diagram used in part **b**, and seeing how many lines can be drawn.

e Try to write down the term-to-term rule for the sequence of maximum number of lines.

3 Look at the following polygons. Each vertex is joined to every other vertex with a straight line, called a diagonal.

3 sides	4 sides	5 sides	6 sides	7 sides
0 diagonals	2 diagonals	5 diagonals	9 diagonals	14 diagonals

The table below shows the number of diagonals drawn inside each polygon.

Number of sides	3	4	5	6	7
Number of diagonals	0	2	5	9	14

a Before drawing a diagram, can you predict, from the table, the number of diagonals you will have for a polygon with eight sides?

b Draw an eight-sided polygon and put in all the diagonals. Count the number of diagonals. Were you right?

c Now predict the number of diagonals for polygons with nine and ten sides.

d Check your results for part **c** by drawing the polygons with their diagonals and seeing how many diagonals there are in each case.

e Try to write down the term-to-term rule for the sequence of diagonals.

4 If you play ten-pin bowling, you will know that the pins are set up in four rows, as shown in the diagram on the right.

If a much larger set was made, with twenty rows, it would not be called ten pin bowling because there would be more than ten pins. Without drawing the pins, find out what this game would be called.

Look at the three sets of circles.

Set 1   Set 2   Set 3

The table shows the number of grey and white circles in each set.

	Set 1	Set 2	Set 3
Grey circles	1	2	3
White circles	5	8	12

Investigate how many white circles there will be for n grey circles.

Functions

A **function** is a rule which changes one number, called the **input**, to another number, called the **output**. For example, $y = 2x + 1$ is a function. So, when $x = 2$, a new number $y = 5$ is produced. Another way of writing this function is:

$$x \rightarrow 2x + 1$$

Identity function

$x \rightarrow x$ is called the **identity function** because it maps any number onto itself. In other words, it leaves the inputs unaltered.

$$0 \rightarrow 0$$
$$1 \rightarrow 1$$
$$2 \rightarrow 2$$
$$3 \rightarrow 3$$
$$4 \rightarrow 4$$

Inverse function

Every linear function has an **inverse function** which reverses the direction of the operation. In other words, the output is brought back to the input.

Example 1.8 The inverse function of $x \rightarrow 4x$ is seen to be $x \rightarrow \frac{x}{4}$.

$$
\begin{array}{ccccc}
x & \rightarrow & 4x & & \\
0 & \rightarrow & 0 & \rightarrow & 0 \\
1 & \rightarrow & 4 & \rightarrow & 1 \\
2 & \rightarrow & 8 & \rightarrow & 2 \\
3 & \rightarrow & 12 & \rightarrow & 3 \\
& & x & \rightarrow & \frac{x}{4}
\end{array}
$$

Example 1.9 The inverse function of $x \rightarrow x + 3$ is seen to be $x \rightarrow x - 3$.

$$
\begin{array}{ccccc}
x & \rightarrow & x + 3 & & \\
0 & \rightarrow & 3 & \rightarrow & 0 \\
1 & \rightarrow & 4 & \rightarrow & 1 \\
2 & \rightarrow & 5 & \rightarrow & 2 \\
3 & \rightarrow & 6 & \rightarrow & 3 \\
& & x & \rightarrow & x - 3
\end{array}
$$

When a function is built up from two or more operations, you will need to consider the original operations and work backwards through these to find the inverse.

Example 1.10 Find the inverse function of $x \rightarrow 4x + 3$.

The sequence of operations for this function is:

Input $\longrightarrow$ $\boxed{\times 4}$ $\longrightarrow$ $\boxed{+ 3}$ $\longrightarrow$ Output

Reversing this sequence gives:

Input $\longleftarrow$ $\boxed{\div 4}$ $\longleftarrow$ $\boxed{- 3}$ $\longleftarrow$ Output

Then give the output the value x:

$$\frac{x - 3}{4} \leftarrow x - 3 \leftarrow x$$

So, the inverse function is:

$$x \rightarrow \frac{x - 3}{4}$$

Self-inverse function The inverse functions of some functions are the functions themselves. These are called **self-inverse functions**.

Example 1.11 The inverse function of $x \rightarrow 8 - x$ can be seen to be itself, as $x \rightarrow 8 - x$.

$$
\begin{array}{ccccc}
x & \rightarrow & 8 - x & & \\
0 & \rightarrow & 8 & \rightarrow & 0 \\
1 & \rightarrow & 7 & \rightarrow & 1 \\
2 & \rightarrow & 6 & \rightarrow & 2 \\
3 & \rightarrow & 5 & \rightarrow & 3 \\
4 & \rightarrow & 4 & \rightarrow & 4 \\
5 & \rightarrow & 3 & \rightarrow & 5 \\
& & x & \rightarrow & 8 - x
\end{array}
$$

1 Write down the inverse function of each of the following functions.

    a $x \to 2x$ **b** $x \to 5x$ **c** $x \to x + 6$

    d $x \to x + 1$ **e** $x \to x - 3$ **f** $x \to \dfrac{x}{5}$

2 Write down the inverse function of each of the following functions.

    a $x \to 2x + 3$ **b** $x \to 3x + 1$ **c** $x \to 4x - 3$

    d $x \to 5x - 2$ **e** $x \to 4x + 7$ **f** $x \to 6x - 5$

3 Write down two different self-inverse functions and show that they are self-inverse functions.

4 Write down the inverse function of each of the following functions.

    a $x \to 2(x + 3)$ **b** $x \to 3(x - 4)$ **c** $x \to \dfrac{(x + 3)}{4}$

    d $x \to \dfrac{(x - 2)}{5}$ **e** $x \to \frac{1}{2}x + 3$ **f** $x \to \frac{1}{2}x - 7$

5 The function $x \to 2x$ can also be expressed as $y = 2x$. Show this to be true by considering the input set {1, 2, 3, 4, 5}.

    a   What is the output set from {1, 2, 3, 4, 5} with the function $x \to 2x$?

    b   Find the values of y when x has values {1, 2, 3, 4, 5}, where $y = 2x$.

    c   Are the two sets of values found in parts **a** and **b** the same? If so, then you have shown that $y = 2x$ is just another way of showing the function $x \to 2x$.

6 Draw a graph of the function $x \to 2x$ by using $y = 2x$. On the same pair of axes, draw the graph of the inverse function of $x \to 2x$.

7 On the same pair of axes, draw the graphs representing the function $x \to 4x$ and its inverse function.

8 On the same pair of axes, draw the graphs representing the function $x \to 5x$ and its inverse function.

9 Look at the two lines on each graph you have drawn for Questions **6**, **7** and **8**. Do you notice anything special about each pair of lines?

Graphs

The distance–time graph on the right illustrates three people in a race.

The graph shows how quickly each person ran, who was ahead at various times, who won and by how many seconds.

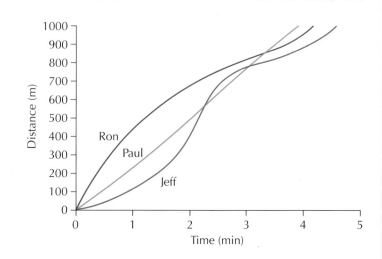

Paul

Notice that Paul's graph is a straight line. This means that he ran at the same speed throughout the race. Paul won the race, finishing about 20 seconds in front of Ron.

Ron

The shape of Ron's graph indicates that he started quickly and then slowed down. He was in the lead for the first 850 metres, before Paul overtook him.

Jeff

Jeff started slowly, but then picked up speed to overtake Paul for a minute before running out of steam and slowing down to come in last, about 30 seconds behind Ron.

Note that the steeper the graph, the faster the person is running.

Exercise 1D

1 Look at the distance–time graph, which illustrates how two rockets flew during a test flight. Rocket D flew higher than Rocket E.

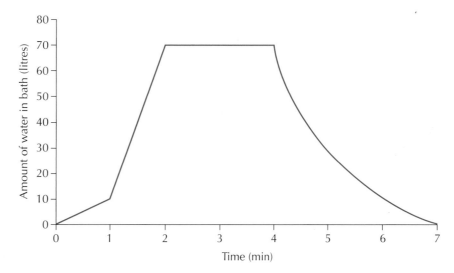

a Estimate the height reached by Rocket D.

b Estimate how much higher than Rocket E Rocket D went.

c How long after the launch were both rockets at the same height?

d For how long was each rocket higher than 150 metres?

e Can you tell which rocket travelled further? Explain your answer.

2 Look at the graph below, which illustrates the amount of water in a bath after it has started to be filled.

a Explain what might have happened 1 minute after the start.

b When was the plug pulled out for the bath to start emptying?

c Why do you think the graph shows a curved line while the bath was emptying?

d How long did the bath take to empty?

3 Water drips steadily into the container shown on the right. The graph shows how the depth of water varies with time.

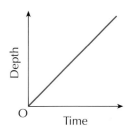

Sketch similar graphs for bottles with the following shapes.

a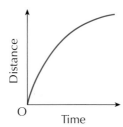

b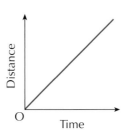

c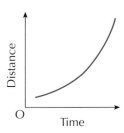

d

4 Suggest which graph below best fits each situation given.

a

b

c

A The distance travelled by a train moving at a constant speed.

B The distance travelled by a motorbike accelerating to overtake.

C The distance travelled by an old car, which starts well, but gradually slows down.

5 Suggest which graph below best fits each situation given.

a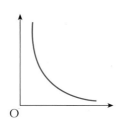

b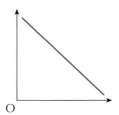

c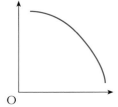

A The amount of fuel left in the tank of my car as I travel from Sheffield to Cornwall.

B The amount of infection in a body as it responds to medicine will first reduce gradually and then more quickly until it has all gone.

C The rate of cooling of a hot drink starts quickly and then slows down.

6 Sketch graphs to illustrate each of the following situations.

a   The number of euros that can be purchased with £x.

b   The temperature during the 24 hours of 21st July.

c   The temperature during the 24 hours of 12th February.

d   The number of empty car-park spaces in a supermarket on a Saturday between 8am and 8pm.

e   The amount of daylight each day of the year from 21st June to next 20th June.

The UK population has been increasing over the last 200 years. The following table shows the population every 20 years.

Year	Population (millions)	Year	Population (millions)
1801	12	1901	38
1821	15.5	1921	44
1841	20	1941	47
1861	24.5	1961	53
1881	31	1981	56

a   Draw a graph to show how the population has increased since 1801.

b   From the graph, estimate what the population was in 2001.

c   Try to find out what the actual population was in 2001.

Limits of sequences

Some sequences go on forever, as you have seen. These are called **infinite sequences**. Other sequences finish after so many numbers or terms. These are called **finite sequences**. Follow through Example 1.12, which shows an infinite sequence.

Example 1.12

Using the term-to-term rule 'Divide by 5 and add 4', find the first 10 terms of this sequence, which starts at 1.

This rule generates the following sequence:

1, 4.2, 4.84, 4.968, 4.9936, 4.998 72, 4.999 744, 4.999 948 8, 4.999 989 76, 4.999 997 952

Notice that the sequence gets closer and closer to 5, which is called the **limit** of the sequence.

Exercise 1E

1   Using the term-to-term rule 'Divide by 2 and add 3' to build a sequence and starting at 1:

   a   Find the first 12 terms generated by this sequence. Use a calculator or a spreadsheet.

   b   To what value does this sequence get closer and closer?

   c   Use the same term-to-term rule with different starting numbers. What do you notice?

2   Repeat Question 1, but change the 'add 3' in the term-to-term rule to 'add 4'.

3   Repeat Question 1, but change the 'add 3' in the term-to-term rule to 'add 5'.

4 a Look at your answers to Questions **1** to **3**. See whether you can estimate to what value the sequence will get closer and closer when you change the 'add 3' in Question **1** to 'add 6'.

b Work out the sequence to see whether you were correct in part **a**.

5 Repeat Question **1** but change the 'divide by 2' to 'divide by 3'.

6 Repeat Question **5** but change the 'add 3' to 'add 4'.

7 Repeat Question **5** but change the 'add 3' to 'add 5'.

8 a Look at your answers to Questions **5** to **7**. See whether you can estimate to what value the sequence will get closer and closer when you change the 'add 3' in Question **5** to 'add 6'.

b Work out the sequence to see whether you were correct in part **a**.

Extension Work

Continue the above investigation to see whether you can predict the limiting number that each sequence reaches from the term-to-term rule 'Divide by A and add B'.

What you need to know for level 6

- How to generate a sequence using the rule which gives the nth term of the sequence
- How to find sequences from diagrams displaying patterns or other information
- How to find information from distance–time graphs

What you need to know for level 7

- How to find the nth term of a linear sequence
- Be able to recognise identity functions and inverse functions
- How to draw graphs relating to real-life situations

What you need to know for level 8

- How to find second differences in a sequence
- How to recognise a quadratic sequence

National Curriculum SATs questions

LEVEL 6

1 *1998 Paper 1*

This is a series of patterns with grey and white tiles.

Pattern number
1

Pattern number
2

Pattern number
3

The series of patterns continues by adding each time.

a Copy and complete this table.

Pattern number	Number of grey tiles	Number of white tiles
5		
16		

b Copy and complete this table by writing expressions.

Pattern number	Expression for the number of grey tiles	Expression for the number of white tiles
n		

c Write an expression to show the total number of tiles in pattern number n. Simplify your expression.

d A different series of patterns is made with tiles.

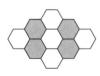

Pattern number
1

Pattern number
2

Pattern number
3

The series of patterns continues by adding each time.

For this series of patterns, write an expression to show the total number of tiles in pattern number n.

Show your working and simplify your expression.

2 *1999 Paper 1*

Each term of a number sequence is made by adding 1 to the numerator and 2 to the denominator of the previous term. Here is the beginning of the number sequence:

$$\frac{1}{3}, \frac{2}{5}, \frac{3}{7}, \frac{4}{9}, \frac{5}{11}, \cdots$$

a Write an expression for the nth term of the sequence.

b The first five terms of the sequence are shown on the graph.

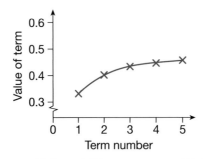

The sequence goes on and on for ever. Which of the four graphs below shows how the sequence continues?

i

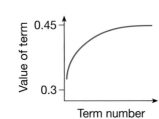

ii

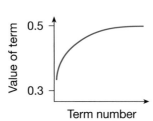

iii

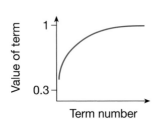

iv

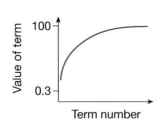

c The nth term of a different sequence is $\dfrac{n}{n^2 + 1}$.

The first term is $\frac{1}{2}$.

Write down the next three terms.

d This new sequence also goes on and on for ever. Which of these four graphs shows how the sequence continues?

i

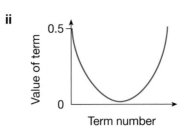

ii

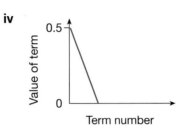

iii

iv

This chapter is going to show you

- how to multiply and divide fractions
- how to calculate with percentages in more complicated problems, such as compound interest
- how to solve problems using ratios
- what reciprocals are
- connection between enlargement of length, area and volume

What you should already know

- How to add and subtract simple fractions
- How to cancel simple fractions and ratios
- How to work out simple percentages of quantities

The four rules governing fractions

You met the addition and subtraction of fractions in Year 8. This section will show you how to solve all types of problem involving the addition, subtraction, multiplication and division of fractions.

Example 2.1 ▷ Work out the answer to each of these.

a $3\frac{1}{3} + 1\frac{2}{5}$ **b** $4\frac{3}{8} - 1\frac{2}{3}$

a When adding mixed numbers, you can convert them to improper (top-heavy) fractions and add them using a common denominator. If appropriate, cancel and/or convert the answer to a mixed number.

So, you have:

$$3\frac{1}{3} + 1\frac{2}{5} = \frac{10}{3} + \frac{7}{5}$$
$$= \frac{50}{15} + \frac{21}{15} = \frac{71}{15} = 4\frac{11}{15}$$

As this method involves large numbers, it is easy to make a mistake. A better method is to split up the problem:

$$3\frac{1}{3} + 1\frac{2}{5} = 3 + 1 + \frac{1}{3} + \frac{2}{5}$$

The whole-number part gives $3 + 1 = 4$, and the fraction part gives:

$$\frac{1}{3} + \frac{2}{5} = \frac{5}{15} + \frac{6}{15} = \frac{11}{15}$$

Hence, the total is:

$$4 + \frac{11}{15} = 4\frac{11}{15}$$

b Using the method of splitting up the calculation, you have:

$$4\frac{3}{8} - 1\frac{2}{3} = 4 + \frac{3}{8} - 1 - \frac{2}{3}$$
$$= 4 - 1 + \frac{3}{8} - \frac{2}{3}$$
$$= 3 + \frac{9}{24} - \frac{16}{24}$$
$$= 3 - \frac{7}{24} = 2\frac{17}{24}$$

So far, you have seen how to add and to subtract fractions. Now you will multiply and divide fractions. Surprisingly, this is easier.

Example 2.2 ▷ Jan's watering can is $\frac{3}{5}$ full. She waters her roses and uses half of this water. How full is her watering can now?

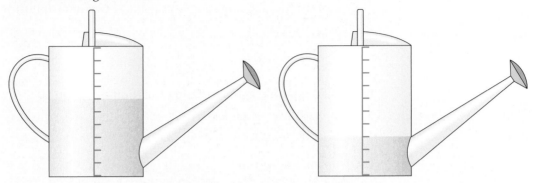

As you can see from the diagram, Jan's watering can is $\frac{3}{10}$ full after she has watered the roses. How can you calculate this result?

One half of $\frac{3}{5}$ is written as:

$$\frac{1}{2} \times \frac{3}{5} = \frac{1 \times 3}{2 \times 5} = \frac{3}{10}$$

This shows that when a fraction is multiplied by another fraction, the new numerator is found by multiplying together the two original numerators, and the new denominator by multiplying together the two original denominators.

Example 2.3 ▷ Work out each of these.

    a $\frac{3}{4} \times \frac{2}{9}$ **b** $2\frac{3}{7} \times 2\frac{4}{5}$

    a   Following Example 2.2, you can calculate mentally that the answer is $\frac{6}{36}$, which can be cancelled to $\frac{1}{6}$. However, this is an example of where it is easier to cancel before you complete the multiplication.

          When numerators and denominators have factors in common, you can cancel them. In this example, 3 and 9 will cancel, as do 2 and 4. The calculation is therefore given like this:

$$\frac{\overset{1}{\cancel{3}}}{\underset{2}{\cancel{4}}} \times \frac{\overset{1}{\cancel{2}}}{\underset{3}{\cancel{9}}} = \frac{1}{6}$$

          The remaining numbers are multiplied together to give the new numerator and the new denominator. When the fractions are cancelled properly, the final answer will not cancel.

    b   Convert the mixed numbers to improper (top-heavy) fractions and cancel when possible. Change the answer to a mixed number if appropriate.

          Hence, you have:

$$2\frac{3}{7} \times 2\frac{4}{5} = \frac{17}{\underset{1}{\cancel{7}}} \times \frac{\overset{2}{\cancel{14}}}{5}$$

$$= \frac{34}{5} = 6\frac{4}{5}$$

Example 2.4 ▷ Work out each of these.

a $\frac{3}{5} \div \frac{1}{4}$ b $\frac{15}{24} \div \frac{9}{16}$ c $2\frac{2}{7} \div 1\frac{11}{21}$

a When you are dividing by a fraction, always use the following rule:

Turn the dividing fraction upside down and multiply by it.

So, you have:

$$\frac{3}{5} \div \frac{1}{4} = \frac{3}{5} \times \frac{4}{1} = \frac{3 \times 4}{5 \times 1} = \frac{12}{5} = 2\frac{2}{5}$$

b When possible, cancel during the multiplication.

$$\frac{15}{24} \div \frac{9}{16} = \frac{\cancel{15}^5}{\cancel{24}_3} \times \frac{\cancel{16}^2}{\cancel{9}_3} = \frac{5 \times 2}{3 \times 3} = \frac{10}{9} = 1\frac{1}{9}$$

c Convert the mixed numbers to improper (top-heavy) fractions. Turn the dividing fraction upside down, put in a multiplication sign and cancel if possible. Then change the result to a mixed number if appropriate.

$$2\frac{2}{7} \div 1\frac{11}{21} = \frac{16}{7} \div \frac{32}{21}$$

$$= \frac{\cancel{16}^1}{\cancel{7}_1} \times \frac{\cancel{21}^3}{\cancel{32}_2} = \frac{3}{2} = 1\frac{1}{2}$$

Exercise 2A

1 Convert each of the following pairs of fractions to a pair of equivalent fractions with a common denominator. Then work out the answer, cancelling down or writing as a mixed number if appropriate.

   a $1\frac{2}{3} + 1\frac{1}{4}$ b $2\frac{2}{5} + 2\frac{1}{6}$ c $2\frac{1}{3} + 1\frac{2}{5}$ d $2\frac{1}{3} + 1\frac{1}{2}$

   e $4\frac{1}{5} + 1\frac{3}{4}$ f $5\frac{1}{2} + 1\frac{5}{6}$ g $6\frac{5}{6} + 2\frac{1}{9}$ h $7\frac{1}{6} + 3\frac{7}{8}$

2 a $3\frac{1}{3} - 1\frac{1}{4}$ b $4\frac{2}{5} - 1\frac{1}{6}$ c $2\frac{2}{5} - 1\frac{1}{3}$ d $3\frac{1}{2} - 1\frac{1}{3}$

   e $3\frac{2}{5} - 1\frac{3}{4}$ f $5\frac{1}{2} - 1\frac{5}{6}$ g $7\frac{5}{6} - 2\frac{8}{9}$ h $6\frac{5}{6} - 3\frac{7}{8}$

3 Work out each of the following.

   a $\frac{3}{4} + \frac{9}{14}$ b $\frac{2}{9} + \frac{4}{21}$ c $\frac{11}{28} + \frac{9}{35}$

   d $\frac{5}{12} - \frac{2}{21}$ e $\frac{31}{48} - \frac{15}{32}$ f $\frac{19}{25} - \frac{7}{15}$

4 Work out each of the following. Cancel before multiplying when possible.

   a $\frac{1}{3} \times \frac{2}{5}$ b $\frac{3}{4} \times \frac{3}{4}$ c $\frac{2}{7} \times \frac{5}{8}$ d $\frac{3}{8} \times \frac{4}{9}$

   e $\frac{5}{8} \times \frac{12}{25}$ f $\frac{5}{6} \times \frac{3}{5}$ g $\frac{1}{2} \times \frac{6}{11}$ h $\frac{1}{4} \times \frac{8}{15}$

   i $\frac{3}{4} \times \frac{8}{9}$ j $\frac{3}{5} \times \frac{15}{22} \times \frac{11}{18}$

5 Work out each of the following. Write as improper (top-heavy) fractions and cancel before multiplying when possible.

   a $1\frac{3}{5} \times 2\frac{1}{8}$ b $2\frac{3}{4} \times 3\frac{1}{5}$ c $2\frac{1}{2} \times 1\frac{3}{5}$ d $1\frac{1}{4} \times 1\frac{4}{5}$

   e $2\frac{1}{5} \times \frac{10}{21}$ f $3\frac{1}{2} \times \frac{8}{35}$ g $\frac{1}{2} \times 3\frac{3}{5}$ h $2\frac{2}{7} \times 2\frac{4}{5}$

   i $1\frac{5}{6} \times 2\frac{2}{5}$ j $4\frac{1}{2} \times 2\frac{3}{5}$

6 Work out each of the following. Cancel at the multiplication stage when possible.

a $\frac{1}{2} \div \frac{1}{8}$ b $\frac{2}{3} \div \frac{3}{5}$ c $\frac{5}{6} \div \frac{2}{3}$ d $\frac{1}{3} \div \frac{6}{7}$

e $\frac{4}{5} \div \frac{3}{10}$ f $\frac{5}{8} \div \frac{15}{16}$ g $\frac{2}{7} \div \frac{7}{8}$ h $\frac{3}{4} \div \frac{9}{13}$

i $\frac{1}{2} \div \frac{3}{5}$ j $\frac{1}{4} \div \frac{3}{8}$

7 Work out each of the following. Write as improper (top-heavy) fractions and cancel at the multiplication stage when possible.

a $1\frac{1}{4} \div \frac{5}{8}$ b $3\frac{1}{2} \div 1\frac{3}{5}$ c $2\frac{1}{2} \div 1\frac{1}{4}$ d $1\frac{2}{3} \div 1\frac{3}{5}$

e $2\frac{5}{6} \div 1\frac{7}{12}$ f $1\frac{1}{2} \div 2\frac{3}{8}$ g $4\frac{1}{2} \div \frac{3}{5}$ h $4\frac{1}{2} \div \frac{8}{9}$

i $\frac{7}{8} \div 2\frac{3}{4}$ j $3\frac{1}{2} \div \frac{3}{4}$

8 A rectangle has sides of $\frac{3}{7}$ cm and $\frac{14}{27}$ cm. Calculate its area.

9 A rectangle has sides of $5\frac{1}{4}$ cm and $4\frac{5}{8}$ cm. Calculate its area.

10 How many $\frac{2}{3}$-metre lengths of cloth can be cut from a roll that is $3\frac{2}{9}$ metres long?

11 A rectangle has an area of $7\frac{4}{5}$ m². Its length is $3\frac{1}{4}$ m. What is its width?

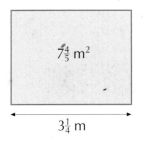

$7\frac{4}{5}$ m²

$3\frac{1}{4}$ m

Extension Work

This is a fractional magic square.

What is the magic number?

Find the missing values in the cells.

$\frac{2}{15}$		
$\frac{7}{15}$	$\frac{1}{3}$	$\frac{1}{5}$

Percentages and compound interest

If you put £100 in a bank and it earns 5% interest each year, which graph do you think represents the way the amount of money in the bank changes as time passes – assuming you don't spend any of it!

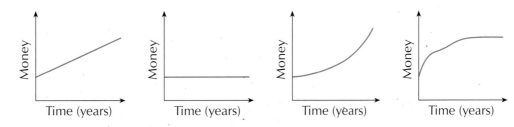

Example 2.5 ▷ Jenny puts £100 in a bank and it earns 5% interest per annum (Latin for 'each year'). How much will she have after 3 years?

Making calculations such as this are sometimes called **compound interest** problems. There are two ways to solve such problems.

Method 1 *Increase and add on*

Calculate the amount of interest earned after each year and add it to the previous year's total, as shown below.

After first year: 5% of £100 = £5, which gives Jenny £100 + £5 = £105.

After second year: 5% of £105 = £5.25, which gives Jenny £105 + £5.25 = £110.25.

After third year: 5% of £110.25 = £5.51, which gives Jenny £110.25 + £5.51 = £115.76.

The last amount of interest has been rounded to the nearest penny. As you can see, the increase gets bigger year by year.

Method 2 *Use a multiplier*

When dealing with percentage increase, the multiplier is found by adding the percentage increase expressed as a decimal to 1, which represents the original value. So, in this case, the multiplier is given by 1 + 0.05 = 1.05.

(When dealing with a percentage decrease, the multiplier is found by subtracting the decrease from 1, which gives a value for the multiplier of less than 1.)

So, you have:

After first year: £100 × 1.05 = £105

After second year: £105 × 1.05 = £110.25

After third year: £110.25 × 1.05 = £115.76

This can also be done using the power key on the calculator as £100 × $(1.05)^3$ = £115.7625 ≈ £115.76.

The second method is very easy if you just use a calculator to get the final answer. But there is no intermediate working, so be careful not to make any mistakes!

Example 2.6 ▷ A petri dish containing 200 000 bacteria is treated with a new drug. This reduces the number of bacteria by 16% each day.

a   How many bacteria remain after 7 days?

b   How long does it take to reduce the bacteria to below a safe level of 20 000?

a   The method of calculating the decrease and subtracting it day by day will take too long. It is quicker to use a multiplier. For a 16% decrease, the multiplier is 0.84.

Key into your calculator:

$$2 \; 0 \; 0 \; 0 \; 0 \; 0 \; \times \; (\; 0 \; . \; 8 \; 4 \;) \; x^y \; 7 \; =$$

You may not need the brackets and your power key may be different.

This gives an answer of 59 018.069 31, which can be rounded to 59 000 bacteria.

b Using trial and improvement to make this calculation, gives these rounded values:

168 000,   141 120,   118 541,   99 574,   83 642,   70 260,   59 018,

49 575,   41 643,   34 980,   29 383,   24 682,   20 733,   17 416.

So, it takes 14 days to get below 20 000.

Check by calculating $200\,000 \times 0.84^{13}$ and $200\,000 \times 0.84^{14}$.

Compound interest does not only concern money. It can be applied to, for example, growth in population and increases in the body weight of animals. It can also involve reduction by a fixed percentage, such as decrease in the value of a car, pollution losses and water losses.

Exercise 2B

1 Write down the multiplier which is equivalent to each of these.

a	12% increase	**b**	5% decrease	**c**	8% decrease
d	7% increase	**e**	4% decrease	**f**	2% increase
g	3.2% increase	**h**	$2\frac{1}{2}$% increase	**i**	15% decrease
j	6% increase	**k**	2.6% decrease	**l**	$\frac{1}{2}$% increase
m	24% decrease	**n**	7% decrease	**o**	$17\frac{1}{2}$% increase

You may want to check your answers, as they will help you with the rest of the questions.

2 How much would you have in the bank if you invest:

a £200 at 2% interest per annum for 4 years?

b £3000 at 3.2% interest per annum for 7 years?

c £120 at 6% interest per annum for 10 years?

d £5000 at 7% interest per annum for 20 years?

e £75 at $2\frac{1}{2}$% interest per annum for 3 years?

3 Investments (including stocks and shares) can decrease in value as well as increase. How much would your investments be worth in each of the following cases?

a You invested £3000 which lost 4% each year for 6 years.

b You invested £250 which lost 2.6% each year for 5 years.

c You invested £4000 which lost 24% each year for 4 years.

4 To decrease the rabbit population in Australia, the disease mixomatosis was introduced into rabbit colonies. In one colony, there were 45 000 rabbits. The disease decreased the population by 7% each month. How many rabbits were left in that colony after **a** 4 months   and   **b** a year?

5 Some Internet sales sites will decrease the price of a product by a certain percentage each day until someone buys it.

Freda is interested in buying a computer. She has £1500 to spend. An Internet site has the computer Freda wants but it is £2000. The price is to be decreased by 5% per day. How many days will Freda have to wait until she can afford the computer?

6 During a hot spell, a pond loses 8% of its water each day due to evaporation. It has 120 gallons in it at the start of the hot spell. How many days will it take before the pond's volume of water falls to 45 gallons?

Jane started drinking a bottle of cola a day, which cost her £1.50.

Her brother Jack put £1.50 into a jar each day and took the money (£45) to the bank each month.

The bank paid Jack $\frac{1}{2}$% compound interest each month.

a How much does Jane spend on cola in a year (365 days)?

b The first £45 that Jack pays in earns 11 months of interest. How much does the first £45 increase to over the 11 months?

c The second £45 that Jack pays in earns 10 months of interest. How much does the second £45 increase to over the 10 months?

d Now work out the value of each £45 that Jack pays in. For example, the third £45 is in the bank for 9 months and the final £45 is paid in on the last day of the year, so gets no interest.

e Add up the answers to parts **b**, **c** and **d** to find out how much Jack has in the bank at the end of the year.

A computer spreadsheet is useful for this activity.

Reverse percentages and percentage change

In Britain, most prices in shops include VAT. In the USA, a sales tax (similar to VAT) has to be added to the displayed price.

Which camera is cheaper if the exchange rate is $1.56 to one pound?

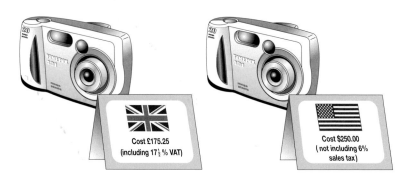

Cost £175.25
(including 17½% VAT)

Cost $250.00
(not including 6% sales tax)

Example 2.7 After a 10% pay rise, John now gets £5.50 an hour. How much per hour did he get before the pay rise?

Making calculations such as this are sometimes called **reverse percentage** problems. There are two ways to solve such problems.

Method 1 *Unitary method*

£5.50 represents 110%

£0.05 represents 1% (dividing both sides by 110)

£5.00 represents 100% (multiplying both sides by 100)

So, before his pay rise, John was paid £5.00 an hour.

Method 2 *Use a multiplier*

A 10% increase is represented by the multiplier 1.1.

Hence, divide £5.50 by the multiplier to find John's hourly rate of pay before his pay rise. This gives:

$$£5.50 \div 1.1 = £5.00$$

Example 2.8

The price of a hi-fi system increases from £189 to £199. What percentage of the original price is the increase?

The increase is £10 and the original price was £189. So, the percentage increase is:

$$\frac{10}{189} \times 100 = 5.3\%$$

Example 2.9

A shop's offer is shown on the right.

Explain why this is misleading.

A $17\frac{1}{2}\%$ increase on £510 is £599.25 but an £89 reduction on £599 is:

$$\frac{89}{599} \times 100 = 14.9\%$$

So, the reduction is only about 15%.

> We will pay your VAT of $17\frac{1}{2}\%$.
>
> **Typical example**
> A sofa costing £599 including VAT will cost you £510.
>
> This is a $17\frac{1}{2}\%$ reduction on the normal price!

Exercise 2C

1 The label on a packet of soap powder states it is 25% bigger! The packet now contains 1500 grams. How much did it weigh before?

2 After a 10% price increase, a trombone now costs £286. How much was it before the increase?

3 This table shows the cost of some goods after $17\frac{1}{2}\%$ VAT is added. Work out the cost of the goods before VAT is added.

Item	Cost (inc VAT)	Item	Cost (inc VAT)
Camera	£223.25	Dishwasher	£293.75
Heater	£70.50	Sofa	£528.75
Printer	£82.25	Computer	£2115.00

4 A suit is on sale at £96, which is 75% of its original price. What was the original price?

5 There was a 20% discount in a sale. A young woman bought a pair of boots for £40 in the sale. What was the original price of the boots?

6 In 2002, the Prime Minister's salary went up from £114 600 to £162 000. What percentage increase is that?

7 Adina asked for a 40% pay rise. In the end, her pay went up from £21 500 to £22 400 per annum. What percentage increase is that?

8 In the second year it was open, the attendance at the Magna exhibition went up by 30% to 1 230 000 visitors. How many visitors were there in the first year it was open?

9 I bought a CD in a sale and saved £2.25 off the normal price. This was a 15% reduction. What was the normal price of the CD?

10 The table shows the prices of a typical three-bedroom, semi-detached house in various parts of the country in 1990 and 2000. Calculate the percentage increase for each area.

Area	Price in 1990 (£)	Price in 2000 (£)
South-east England	160 000	198 400
Scotland	95 000	110 200
Yorkshire	68 000	78 200
East Anglia	124 000	168 640

Extension Work

Credit card companies and loan companies quote the Annual Percentage Rate or APR. This is the equivalent over a year to the interest which they charge monthly.

For example, if 2% is charged each month on a loan of £1000, the amount owed after 12 months will be £1000 × $(1.02)^{12}$ = £1268, which is equivalent to 26.8% APR (because £1000 increased by 26.8% gives £1268).

Work out the APR for companies which charge an interest rate of:

a 1.5% per month   **b** 0.9% per month

c 1% per month   **d** 5% per month

e Now work out the monthly interest rate for an APR of 30%. [**Hint** Try trial and improvement.]

A computer spreadsheet is useful for this activity.

Direct and inverse proportion

Example 2.10 Six tubes of toothpaste have a total mass of 972 grams. What is the mass of 11 tubes?

If six tubes have a mass of 972 grams, one tube has a mass of 972 ÷ 6 = 162 grams.

Hence, 11 tubes have a mass of 11 × 162 = 1782 grams = 1.782 kg.

Example 2.11 A guitarist plays for 40 minutes with 400 people in the audience. How long would it take him to play the same set if there were only 300 people in the audience?

It takes exactly the same time of 40 minutes! The number of people in the audience does not affect the length of the performance.

Example 2.12 Six girls take 4 days to paint a fence. How long will it take eight girls?

If it takes six girls 4 days to paint the fence, it would take one girl 6 × 4 = 24 days to paint the fence.

Hence, eight girls will take 24 ÷ 8 = 3 days to paint the fence.

Example 2.13 Four men take 5 days to lay a pipeline that is 300 metres long. What length of pipe could be laid by six men working for 8 days?

It takes 4 × 5 = 20 man-days to lay 300 metres of pipe.

Hence 1 man-day would lay 300 ÷ 20 = 15 metres of pipe.

So, 6 × 8 = 48 man-days would lay 48 × 15 = 720 metres of pipe.

Example 2.14 Six shirts hanging on a washing line take 2 hours to dry. How long would it take three shirts to dry?

It would take the same time! The number of shirts on the line does not make any difference.

Exercise 2D

Be careful! Some of these questions may trip you up.

You may use a calculator for this exercise.

1. In 5 hours a man earns £28. How much does he earn in 7 hours?

2. A girl walks 3 miles in 1 hour. How long would it take her to walk 5 miles?

3. Four men lay a pipeline in 5 days. How long would ten men take?

4 Travelling at 8 miles an hour, a boy takes 5 hours for a cycling trip. How long would he take at a speed of 12 miles per hour?

5 Seven chocolate bars cost £1.82. How much would 11 chocolate bars cost?

6 In 2 days my watch loses 4 minutes. How much does it lose in 1 week (7 days)?

7 It takes 6 minutes to hard-boil three eggs in a pan. How long would it take to hard-boil two eggs in the same pan?

8 I have three cats who eat a large bag of cat food every 4 days. If I get another cat how long will the bag of food last now?

9 In 20 minutes an aircraft travels 192 miles. How far would it travel in 25 minutes at the same speed?

10 Four buckets standing in a rain shower take 40 minutes to fill. How long would three buckets standing in the same rain shower take to fill?

11 Nine men build a wall in 20 days. How long will the job take 15 men?

12 A distance of 8 km is represented by a distance of 12.8 cm on a map.
   a How many centimetres would represent a distance of 14 km?
   b What distance is represented by 7 cm on the map?

13 My motorbike travels 120 miles on 10 litres of petrol.
   a How many miles will it travel on 12 litres?
   b How many litres will I need to travel 55 miles?

14 Four taps fill a bath in 36 minutes. How long would it take three taps to fill the same bath?

15 An electric light uses 5 units of electricity in 120 minutes. If 9 units of electricity have been used, how long has it been switched on?

16 It takes 12 seconds to dial the 12-digit number of a friend that lives 100 miles away.
   a How long will it take to dial the 12-digit number of a friend who lives 50 miles away?
   b How long will it take to dial the 6-digit number of a friend who lives 10 miles away?

17 At peak times, a phone card gives 120 minutes of calls. At off-peak times, the cost is one-third of the cost at peak times. How many minutes of calls will the phone card give at off-peak times?

18 A box of emergency rations can feed 12 men for 6 days. For how long would the box of rations feed eight men?

19 A man takes 10 minutes to hang out a load of washing. How long would it take two men?

20 One woman went to mow a meadow. It took her 15 minutes to walk there. If two women went to mow a meadow how long would it take them to walk there?

21 Some tins of beans are packed into seven boxes each of which holds 12 tins. If I pack them into four boxes instead, how many tins will be in each box?

22 Two men can paint a room in 6 hours. How long would five men take?

23 A shelf is filled with 20 books each 3.5 cm thick. If the books are replaced by 28 books of equal thickness, how thick would they have to be to fill the shelf?

24 From the top of a hill, two girls can see 20 miles. How far would three girls be able to see from the top of the same hill?

25 A 2.5 gallon cylinder of gas will keep a patio heater burning at full power for 30 hours. How many hours will a 1.5 gallon cylinder of gas keep the heater burning at half power?

26 Three women building a patio, lay 30 m² in 4 days. How many days would it take two women to lay a patio that is 45 m²?

27 A family use four tubes of toothpaste in 9 weeks, brushing their teeth twice a day. They decide to give a 4-week trial to brushing their teeth three times a day. How many tubes of toothpaste will they use in that time?

28 A haulage company charges £240 to transport four pallets a distance of 300 miles. How far would they transport five pallets for a cost of £180?

29 Seven men can pack 2352 boxes of chocolate bars in a 4 hour shift. How long would it take five men to pack 3150 boxes of chocolate bars?

30 In one hour, eight teachers can mark 90 exam papers. How many exam papers can 15 teachers mark in one and a half hours?

Extension Work

You are told that:

$a \times b \times c = d$

a What would the answer be if a were doubled?

b What would the answer be if b were trebled?

c What would the answer be if c were halved?

d What would the answer be if, at the same time, a were doubled, b trebled and c halved?

e What would the answer be if, at the same time, a were doubled, b doubled and c doubled?

f What would the answer be if, at the same time, a were halved, b halved and c halved?

Ratio in area and volume

Investigation

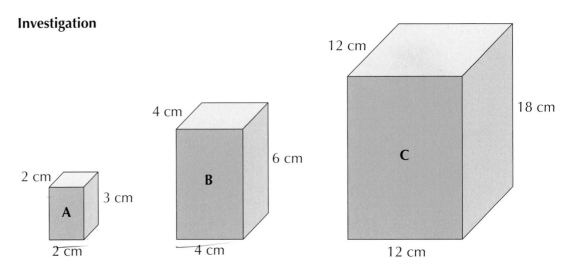

These three blocks are similar. This means that the ratio height : length : width is the same for all three blocks.

a   Work out the area of the front face of each block.

b   Work out the volume of each block.

Work out each of the following ratios and write it in the form $1 : n$.

c **i**   Length of block A to length of block B.
    ii   Area of the front face of block A to area of the front face of block B.
    iii Volume of block A to volume of block B.

d **i**   Length of block A to length of block C.
    ii   Area of the front face of block A to area of the front face of block C.
    iii Volume of block A to volume of block C.

e **i**   Length of block B to length of block C.
    ii   Area of the front face of block B to area of the front face of block C.
    iii Volume of block B to volume of block C.

Look at your answers to parts **c**, **d** and **e**. What do you notice?

Explain the connection between the ratio of the lengths, areas and volumes of similar shapes.

Exercise 2E

1 You will have found out that two similar shapes with their lengths in the ratio $1 : a$ have areas in the ratio $1 : a^2$.

The following shapes are similar. The drawings are not to scale. For each shape, you are given the width. You are also given the area of shape P.

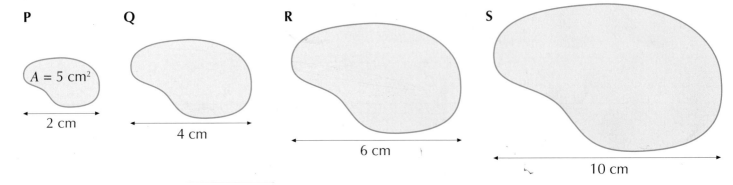

P

$A = 5 \text{ cm}^2$

2 cm

Q

4 cm

R

6 cm

S

10 cm

Copy and complete the following. (The first has been done for you.)

a **i** The ratio of lengths of shapes P and Q is 1 : 2.
   ii The ratio of areas of shapes P and Q is 1 : 4.
   iii The area of shape Q is 4 × area of shape P. So, area of Q = 4 × 5 = 20 cm².

b **i** The ratio of lengths of shapes P and R is 1 : ....
   ii The ratio of areas of shapes P and R is 1 : ....
   iii The area of shape R is ... × area of shape P. So, area of R = ... × 5 = ... cm².

c **i** The ratio of lengths of shapes P and S is 1 : ....
   ii The ratio of areas of shapes P and S is 1 : ....
   iii The area of shape S is ... × area of shape P. So, area of S = ... × 5 = ... cm².

2 You will have found out that two similar shapes with their lengths in the ratio 1 : a have volumes in the ratio 1 : a^3.

The following shapes are similar. The drawings are not to scale. For each shape you are given the width. You are also given the volume of shape J.

J
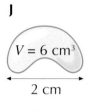
$V = 6$ cm³
2 cm

K
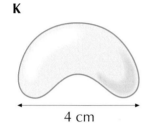
4 cm

L
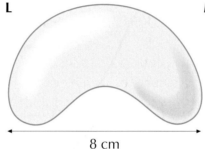
8 cm

M
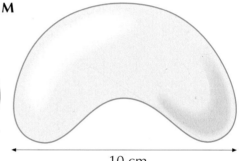
10 cm

Copy and complete the following. (The first has been done for you.)

a **i** The ratio of lengths of shapes J and K is 1 : 2.
   ii The ratio of volumes of shapes J and K is 1 : 8.
   iii The volume of shape K is 8 × volume of shape J.
     So, volume of K = 8 × 6 = 48 cm³.

b **i** The ratio of lengths of shapes J and L is 1 : ....
   ii The ratio of volumes of shapes J and L is 1 : ....
   iii The volume of shape L is ... × volume of shape J.
     So, volume of L = ... × 6 = ... cm³.

c **i** The ratio of lengths of shapes J and M is 1 : ....
   ii The ratio of volumes of shapes J and M is 1 : ....
   iii The volume of shape M is ... × volume of shape J.
     So, volume of M = ... × 6 = ... cm³.

3 The following pair of shapes, A and B, are similar. The drawings are not to scale. Work out the area of shape B.

A   B

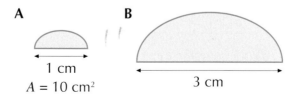

1 cm   3 cm
A = 10 cm²

4 Two similar shapes, P and Q, are shown below. The drawings are not to scale. Work out the area of shape P.

P   Q

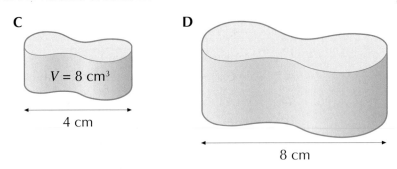

$A = 64$ cm²

11 cm

44 cm

5 The following pair of solids, C and D, are similar. The drawings are not to scale. Work out the volume of solid D.

C   D

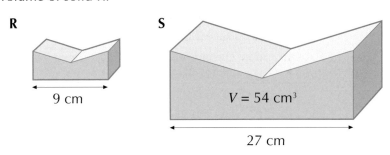

$V = 8$ cm³

4 cm

8 cm

6 Two similar solids, R and S, are shown below. The drawings are not to scale. Work out the volume of solid R.

R   S

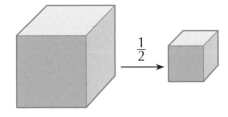

9 cm

$V = 54$ cm³

27 cm

7 The sides of a cube are reduced by a half.

$\frac{1}{2}$

    a By what fraction is the area of a face reduced?

    b By what fraction is the volume of the cube reduced?

8 A one-centimetre cube is placed alongside a metre cube.

    a What is the ratio of the lengths of the two cubes?

    b What is the ratio of the areas of a face of the two cubes?

    c What is the ratio of the volumes of the two cubes?

Three cylinders have the dimensions shown.

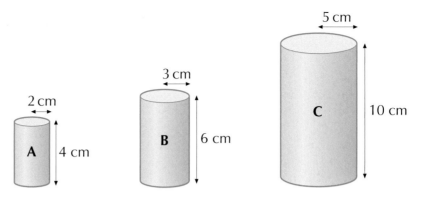

a Explain how you know that the cylinders are similar.

b For cylinders A, B and C work out each of the following.
 i The area of the circular end.
 ii The volume of the cylinder. (Formula for the volume is πr^2h.)

c Work out each of the following ratios.
 i End area of A : End area of B
 ii End area of A : End area of C
 iii Volume of A : Volume of B
 iv Volume of A : Volume of C

d Another similar cylinder, D, has a radius of 15 cm. Write down each of the following ratios.
 i End area of C : End area of D
 ii Volume of C : Volume of D

Numbers between 0 and 1

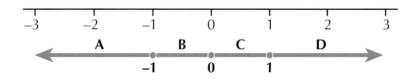

The special numbers –1, 0 and 1 divide the number line shown above into four sets of numbers: A, B, C and D.

A contains all the numbers less than –1. B contains all the numbers between –1 and 0. C contains all the numbers between 0 and 1 and D contains all the numbers greater than 1.

Example 2.15 ▷

  a What happens when a number from set A is multiplied by a number from set D?

  b What happens when a number from set B is divided by 1?

  a Choose any number from set A, say −2. Choose any number from set D, say + 3. Multiply them together:

$$-2 \times +3 = -6$$

The answer belongs to set A.

Try other combinations of numbers from set A and set D. For example:

$$-4 \times +4 = -16 \quad -1.5 \times 5 = -7.5 \quad -5 \times 1.5 = -7.5$$

They all belong to set A. So, a number from set A multiplied by a number from set D always gives a number in set A.

  b Pick numbers from set B and divide each one by 1. For example:

$$-0.4 \div 1 = -0.4 \quad -\tfrac{2}{3} \div 1 = -\tfrac{2}{3} \quad -0.03 \div 1 = -0.03$$

The answers are the same as the values from set B. So, they all give numbers in set B.

Exercise 2F

1 Copy and complete this table, which shows the result of multiplying the first number by the second number. The result from Example 2.15, part **a**, has been filled in along with some other results.

Second number

×	Set A	−1	Set B	0	Set C	1	Set D
Set A			C or D			Set A	
−1						−1	
Set B							
0	0						
Set C	A or B						
1						1	
Set D	Set A						

(First number — rows)

2 Copy and complete this table, which shows the result of dividing the first number by the second number. The result from Example 2.15, part **b**, has been filled in along with some other results. One thing you cannot do in maths is to divide by zero. So, this column has been deleted.

Second number

÷	Set A	−1	Set B	0	Set C	1	Set D
Set A	C or D						
−1						−1	
Set B			C or D		A or B		
0	0						
Set C							
1							
Set D							

(First number — rows)

3 Use your tables to answer each of the following. Choose one answer.

   a When any positive number is divided by a number between 0 and 1, the answer is:
- **i** The same
- **ii** Always bigger
- **iii** Always smaller
- **iv** Sometimes bigger, sometimes smaller

   b When any positive number is divided by a number bigger than 1, the answer is:
- **i** The same
- **ii** Always bigger
- **iii** Always smaller
- **iv** Sometimes bigger, sometimes smaller

   c When any positive number is multiplied by a number between 0 and 1, the answer is:
- **i** The same
- **ii** Always bigger
- **iii** Always smaller
- **iv** Sometimes bigger, sometimes smaller

   d When any positive number is multiplied by a number bigger than 1, the answer is:
- **i** The same
- **ii** Always bigger
- **iii** Always smaller
- **iv** Sometimes bigger, sometimes smaller

4 In each case, give an example to show that the statement is not true. (Such an example is called a **counter-example**.)

   a When you divide any number by –1, the answer is always negative.

   b When you multiply any number by a number less than –1, the answer is always bigger.

   c Dividing any number by a number between –1 and 1 (except 0) always gives a bigger number.

   d Multiplying any number by a number between –1 and 1 (except 0) always gives a smaller number.

Extension Work

Repeat Example 2.15 but this time add and subtract the numbers from each set. Can you reach any definite conclusions?

Reciprocal of a number

The reciprocal of a number is the number divided into 1. For example, the reciprocal of 2 is $1 \div 2 = 0.5$.

On a calculator, the reciprocal key is usually marked in one of the ways shown below.

x^{-1} $1/x$ $^{1}/x$

Example 2.16 Find the reciprocals of **a** 25 and **b** 0.625.

Using the reciprocal key on your calculator, or dividing the number into 1, you will get:

   a $1 \div 25 = 0.04$

   b $1 \div 0.625 = 1.6$

1 a Find, as a decimal, the reciprocal of each and every integer from 1 to 20.

b Which of the reciprocals are terminating decimals?

2 Find the reciprocal of each of the following numbers. Round your answers if necessary.

a	30	**b**	0.005	**c**	80	**d**	0.001 25
e	2000	**f**	0.002	**g**	100	**h**	10^6

3 Investigation Using a calculator and its fraction key, find the reciprocals of some fractions.

For example, $\frac{2}{3}$ has a reciprocal of $1 \div \frac{2}{3} = 1\frac{1}{2} = \frac{3}{2}$.

You will need to convert any mixed numbers to improper fractions.

Repeat this until you can write down a rule for quickly finding the reciprocal of a fraction.

4 Investigation The grid shows five pairs of lines.

a What is the geometrical relationship between each pair of lines?

b Copy and fill in the following table. Some values have been filled in.

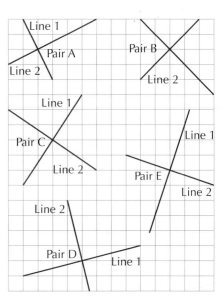

Pair	Gradient line 1	Gradient line 2
A	$\frac{1}{2}$	
B		
C		$-\frac{2}{3}$
D		
E	3	

c Look at the values of the gradients of each pair of lines. What is the relationship between them?

Copy and complete the following statement.

When a pair of lines are …… their gradients are the …… …… of each other.

5 Calculate the sum of each of the following numbers with its reciprocal.

a 1   **b** −1

Is it always true that the sum of a number and its reciprocal is the positive value of the sum of the negative number and its reciprocal? Investigate.

6 Is there a reciprocal of zero ?

The powers of two are 2, 2^2, 2^3, 2^4, …, which are equal to 2, 4, 8, 16, ….

Use a calculator to find the negative powers of two, namely: 2^{-1}, 2^{-2}, 2^{-3}, ….

Use your calculator to investigate the relationship between the reciprocals of positive powers of two and those of negative powers of two.

Rounding and estimation

Example 2.17 ▷ Round each of the following numbers to one significant figure.

    a   582   **b**   0.0893   **c**   0.732   **d**   0.291

When rounding to one significant figure, you need to find the nearest number which has just one digit followed or preceded by zeros. This gives:

    a $582 \approx 600$ (1 sf)   **b** $0.0893 \approx 0.09$ (1 sf)

    c $0.732 \approx 0.7$ (1 sf)   **d** $0.291 \approx 0.3$ (1 sf)

Example 2.18 ▷ By rounding the numbers to one significant figure, estimate the value of each of the following.

    a $(3124 \times 0.476) \div 0.283$ **b** $0.067 \times (0.82 - 0.57)$

    a   Round each number to one significant figure. Then proceed with the calculation using the rules which you have already learnt.

$$(3124 \times 0.476) \div 0.283 \approx (3000 \times 0.5) \div 0.3$$
$$= 1500 \div 0.3$$
$$= 15\,000 \div 3 = 5000$$

    b   Proceed as in part **a**.

$$0.067 \times (0.82 - 0.57) \approx 0.07 \times (0.8 - 0.6)$$
$$= 0.07 \times 0.2 = 0.014$$

Exercise 2H

1 Round each of the following numbers to one significant figure.

a 598	**b** 0.312	**c** 0.06734	**d** 109
e 0.327	**f** 0.092	**g** 345	**h** 0.378
i 0.65	**j** 0.609	**k** 888	**l** 0.98

2 Work out each of the following.

a 200×400	**b** 300×5000	**c** 60×70	**d** 80×2000
e 90×90	**f** 0.6×0.3	**g** 0.09×0.7	**h** 0.05×0.8
i 2000×0.05	**j** $200 \times 0.\dot{7}$	**k** 0.08×3000	**l** 0.6×700

3 Work out each of the following.

a $300 \div 50$	**b** $600 \div 0.2$	**c** $2000 \div 400$	**d** $24000 \div 60$
e $800 \div 20$	**f** $1500 \div 30$	**g** $200 \div 0.4$	**h** $300 \div 0.5$
i $20 \div 0.05$	**j** $4 \div 0.08$	**k** $60 \div 0.15$	**l** $0.09 \div 0.3$

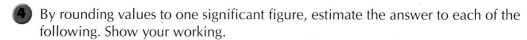

4 By rounding values to one significant figure, estimate the answer to each of the following. Show your working.

a	0.73×621	**b**	$278 \div 0.47$
c	$3127 \div 0.58$	**d**	0.062×0.21
e	$(19 \times 0.049) \div 0.38$	**f**	$(0.037 + 0.058) \times (0.067 + 0.083)$
g	$(211 \times 0.112) \times (775 \div 0.018)$	**h**	$0.475 \times (33.66 \div 0.41)$
i	$4.8^2 \times 7.8 \div 0.19^2$	**j**	$(19.7 \times 0.38) \div (1.98 + 0.46)$

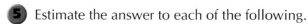

5 Estimate the answer to each of the following.

a	$\dfrac{231 \times 0.615}{0.032}$	**b**	$\dfrac{298 + 376}{0.072}$	**c**	$\dfrac{185^2}{0.38^2}$
d	$\dfrac{0.831 \times 0.478}{387}$	**e**	$\dfrac{715 \times 0.723}{341 \times 0.058}$	**f**	$\dfrac{632}{0.41} + \dfrac{219}{0.46}$

Extension Work

You can round to any number of significant figures. For example, rounding to three significant figures is very common in trigonometry problems, which you will meet later.

Take, for example, 253.78, which has five significant figures.

$$253.78 \approx 253.8 \text{ (4 sf)} \approx 254 \text{ (3 sf)} \approx 250 \text{ (2 sf)} \approx 300 \text{ (1 sf)}$$

Now, take as an example 0.098 54, which has four significant figures.

$$0.098\,54 \approx 0.0985 \text{ (3 sf)} \approx 0.099 \text{ (2 sf)} \approx 0.1 \text{ (1 sf)}$$

Round each of the following to the accuracy shown.

a	347 (2 sf)	**b**	4217 (3 sf)	**c**	4217 (2 sf)
d	0.6187 (3 sf)	**e**	0.6187 (2 sf)	**f**	302 (1 sf)
g	4698 (2 sf)	**h**	4698 (2 sf)	**i**	0.0785 (2 sf)
j	978.32 (4 sf)	**k**	978.32 (3 sf)	**l**	978.32 (2 sf)

What you need to know for level 6

- Which number to consider as 100%, or a whole, in problems involving comparisons
- How to evaluate one number as a fraction or percentage of another
- How to add and subtract fractions by writing them with a common denominator
- How to use the equivalences between fractions, percentages and decimals
- How to calculate using ratios

What you need to know for level 7

- How to round to one significant figure, and to multiply, and divide mentally
- The effects of multiplying and dividing by numbers between 0 and 1
- How to solve problems with numbers of any size using a calculator efficiently and appropriately

What you need to know for level 8

- How to use percentages to solve problems involving repeated proportional changes, such as compound interest
- How to use percentages to calculate the original quantity given the result of a proportional change

National Curriculum SATs questions

LEVEL 6

1 *1999 Paper 2*

A report on the number of police officers in 1995 said:

> There were 119 000 police officers. Almost 15% of them were women.

a The percentage was rounded to the nearest whole number, 15. What is the smallest value the percentage could have been, to one decimal place? Choose the correct answer from below.

14.1%   14.2%   14.3%   14.4%   14.5%   14.6%   14.7%   14.8%   14.9%

b What is the smallest number of women police officers that there might have been in 1995? (Use your answer to part **a** to help you calculate this answer.) Show your working.

c A different report gives exact figures.

Number of women police officers	
1988	12 540
1995	17 468

Calculate the percentage increase in the number of women police officers from 1988 to 1995. Show your working.

d The table below shows the percentage of police officers in 1995 and 1996 who were women.

1995	14.7%
1996	14.6%

Use the information in the table to decide which one of the statements below is true. Choose the true statement.

In 1996 there were more women police officers than in 1995.·

In 1996 there were fewer women police officers than in 1995.

There is not enough information to tell whether there were more or fewer women police officers.

Explain your answer.

2 *1997 Paper 2*

The table shows some information about students in a school.

There are 408 students in the school.

	Left-handed	Right-handed
Girls	32	180
Boys	28	168

a What percentage of the students are boys? Show your working.

b What is the ratio of left-handed students to right-handed students? Write your ratio in the form 1 : … . Show your working.

c One student is chosen at random from the whole school. What is the probability that the student chosen is a girl who is right-handed?

LEVEL 7

3 *2002 Paper 2*

    a One calculation below gives the answer to the question:

        What is 70 increased by 9%?

    Choose the correct one.

      (70×0.9)   (70×1.9)   (70×0.09)   (70×1.09)

    Choose one of the other calculations. Write a question about percentages that this calculation represents.

        Calculation chosen: ……

        Question it represents: ……

    Now do the same for one of the remaining two calculations:

        Calculation chosen: ……

        Question it represents: ……

    b Fill in the missing decimal number.

        To decrease by 14%, multiply by ……

4 *1998 Paper 1*

This is what a student wrote:

    For all numbers t and w,

$$\frac{1}{t} + \frac{1}{w} = \frac{2}{t + w}$$

Show that the student was wrong.

LEVEL 8

5 *1998 Paper 2*

Look at the table.

    a In England, from 1961 to 1994, the birth rate fell by 26.1%. What was the birth rate in England in 1994? Show your working.

    b In Wales, the birth rate also fell. Calculate the percentage fall from 1961 to 1994. Show your working.

	Birth rate per 1000 population	
	1961	1994
England	17.6	
Wales	17.0	12.2

c From 1961 to 1994, the birth rates in Scotland and Northern Ireland fell by the same amount.

The percentage fall in Scotland was greater than the percentage fall in Northern Ireland.

Copy the statements below and put a tick by the statement which is true.

In 1961, the birth rate in Scotland was higher than the birth rate in Northern Ireland. ......

In 1961, the birth rate in Scotland was the same as the birth rate in Northern Ireland. ......

In 1961, the birth rate in Scotland was lower than the birth rate in Northern Ireland. ......

From the information given, you cannot tell whether Scotland or Northern Ireland had the higher birth rate in 1961. ......

6 *2001 Paper 2*

A shop had a sale. All prices were reduced by 15%.

A pair of shoes cost £38.25 in the sale. What price were the shoes before the sale? Show your working.

7 *2003 Paper 2*

Find the values of t and r.

$$\frac{2}{3} = \frac{t}{6}$$ $t = ...$

$$\frac{2}{3} = \frac{5}{r}$$ $r = ...$

8 *2002 Paper 1*

I fill a glass with orange juice and lemonade in the ratio 1 : 4.

I drink $\frac{1}{4}$ of the contents of the glass, then I fill the glass using orange juice. Now what is the ratio of orange juice to lemonade in the glass?

Show your working, and write the ratio in its simplest form.

9 *2002 Paper 2*

A 10% increase followed by another 10% increase is not the same as a total increase of 20%.

What is the total percentage increase? Show your working.

Simultaneous equations

Simultaneous equations are equations for which we want the same solution. Therefore, we solve them together.

The simultaneous equations you will meet are always in pairs and are always linear.

For example, $x + y = 8$ has many solutions:

$x = 2, y = 6$ $\quad$ $x = 3, y = 5$ $\quad$ $x = 4, y = 4$ $\quad$ $x = 5, y = 3$ ...

Also, $2x + y = 13$ has many solutions:

$x = 2, y = 9$ $\quad$ $x = 3, y = 7$ $\quad$ $x = 4, y = 5$ $\quad$ $x = 5, y = 3$ ...

but only *one* solution, $x = 5$ and $y = 3$, satisfies both equations at the same time.

One way to solve pairs of simultaneous equations is by the elimination method.

Elimination method Follow through the Examples 3.1 and 3.2 to see how this method works.

Example 3.1 $\quad$ Solve $\quad 5x + y = 23$
$\qquad\qquad 2x + y = 11$

First, number the equations:

$\quad 5x + y = 23$ $\quad$ (i)
$\quad 2x + y = 11$ $\quad$ (ii)

Since both equations have the same y-term, subtract equation (ii) from equation (i). This eliminates y to give:

$\quad 3x = 12$
$\quad\; x = 4$ $\quad$ (Divide both sides by 3.)

Now substitute $x = 4$ into one of the original equations (usually that with the smallest numbers).

So, substitute $x = 4$ into (ii): $\quad 2x + y = 11$
which gives: $\qquad\qquad\qquad\quad 8 + y = 11$
$\qquad\qquad\qquad\qquad\qquad\quad y = 11 - 8$
$\qquad\qquad\qquad\qquad\qquad\quad y = 3$

Next, test the solution in equation (i). So, substitute $x = 4$ and $y = 3$ into $5x + y$, which gives:

$$20 + 3 = 23$$

This is correct, so we can confidently say that the solution is $x = 4$ and $y = 3$.

Example 3.2

Solve $4x + 3y = 34$
$2x - 3y = 8$

First number the equations:

$$4x + 3y = 34 \quad \text{(i)}$$
$$2x - 3y = 8 \quad \text{(ii)}$$

Since both equations have the same y-term but different signs, add equations (i) and (ii). This eliminates y to give:

$$6x = 42$$
$$x = 7 \quad \text{(Divide both sides by 6.)}$$

Now substitute into equation (i).

So, put $x = 7$ into (i): $\quad 4x + 3y = 34$
which gives: $\qquad\qquad 28 + 3y = 34$
$$3y = 6$$
$$y = 2 \quad \text{(Divide both sides by 3.)}$$

Test the solution by putting $x = 7$ and $y = 2$ into the equation (ii), $2x - 3y$. This gives:

$$14 - 6 = 8$$

This is correct. So, the solution is $x = 7$ and $y = 2$.

In both Example 3.1 and Example 3.2, the y-term was eliminated. But with other pairs of equations, it could be easier to eliminate the x-term. See, for example, Questions 7, 8, and 10 in Exercise 3A.

Exercise 3A

Solve each pair of simultaneous equations.

1 $5x + y = 21$
$2x + y = 9$

2 $6x + 2y = 14$
$2x + 2y = 10$

3 $3x + y = 10$
$5x - y = 14$

4 $4x + 2y = 24$
$2x - 2y = 6$

5 $5x - 4y = 31$
$x - 4y = 3$

6 $4x + 2y = 26$
$7x - 2y = 29$

7 $x + 4y = 12$
$x + 3y = 10$

8 $2x + 4y = 20$
$2x + 3y = 16$

9 $5x - y = 10$
$3x + y = 14$

10 $2x + 5y = 19$
$2x + 3y = 13$

11 $5x - 3y = 11$
$2x + 3y = 17$

12 $6x - y = 26$
$3x - y = 11$

Extension Work

Solve each of the following problems by expressing it as a pair of simultaneous equations, for which you find the solution.

1 The two people in front of me in the post office bought stamps. One bought ten second-class and five first-class stamps at a total cost of £3.35. The other bought ten second-class and ten first-class stamps at a total cost of £4.80.

How much would I pay for

a one first-class stamp

b one second-class stamp?

2 In a fruit shop, one customer bought five bananas and eight oranges at a total cost of £2.85. Another customer bought five bananas and 12 oranges at a total cost of £3.65.

If I bought two bananas and three oranges, how much would it cost me?

Solving by substitution

Simultaneous equations can be solved another way. When one or other of the two variables can be easily made the subject of either of the two equations, it can be easier to substitute that variable in the other equation.

Example 3.3 Solve $3x + 2y = 18$
$2x - y = 5$

First number the equations:
$$3x + 2y = 18 \quad \text{(i)}$$
$$2x - y = 5 \quad \text{(ii)}$$

Take equation (ii) and add y to both sides, which gives:

$$2x - y = 5$$
$$2x = 5 + y$$

Subtracting 5 from both sides gives:

$$2x - 5 = y$$

By convention, this is written as:

$$y = 2x - 5$$

Substitute $y = 2x - 5$ into equation (i), which gives:

$$3x + 2(2x - 5) = 18$$

Expand the bracket to obtain:

$$3x + 4x - 10 = 18$$
$$7x - 10 = 18$$

Add 10 to both sides, which gives:

$$7x = 28$$
$$x = 4 \quad \text{(Divide both sides by 7.)}$$

Now substitute $x = 4$ into the equation with y as the subject, $y = 2x - 5$, giving:

$$y = 2 \times 4 - 5 = 3$$

Hence, the solution is $x = 4$ and $y = 3$.

Exercise 3B

Solve each of the following pairs of simultaneous equations by first changing the subject of one of the equations to give an equal term. Then, by addition or subtraction, eliminate the equal term.

1 $5x + 3y = 23$
$2x - y = 7$

2 $3x + y = 9$
$4x + 5y = 23$

3 $5x - 2y = 14$
$x - y = 1$

4 $4x + 3y = 37$
$2x + y = 17$

5 $2x + y = 9$
$6x + 2y = 22$

6 $10x - 3y = 19$
$x + 2y = 18$

7 $4x + 5y = 13$
$x + 3y = 5$

8 $3x + y = 14$
   $4x - 2y = 2$

9 $5x - 2y = 24$
   $3x + y = 21$

10 $5x - 2y = 36$
   $x + 6y = 20$

11 $x + 3y = 16$
   $4x + 7y = 39$

12 $3x - y = 7$
   $5x + 6y = 50$

Extension Work

Work out each of the following problems by expressing it as a pair of simultaneous equations, which are then solved.

1 At a local tea room, I couldn't help noticing that at one table, where the people had eaten six buns and had three teas, the total cost was £1.65.

   At another table, the people had eaten eleven buns and had seven teas at a total cost of £3.40.

   My guests and I had five buns and had six teas. What would it cost me?

2 A chef uses this formula to cook a roast:

   $T = a + bW$

   where T is the time it takes (minutes), W is the weight of the roast (kg), and both a and b are constants.

   The chef says it takes 2 hours 51 minutes to cook a 12 kg roast, and 1 hour 59 minutes to cook an 8 kg roast.

   How long will it take to cook a 5 kg roast?

Finding the nth term for a quadratic sequence

You found on page 3 that the nth term of a quadratic sequence is always given by:

$T(n) = An^2 + Bn + C$

Consider the sequence 6, 15, 28, 45, 66.

First, find its first and second differences.

First differences: 9   13   17   21
Second differences: 4   4   4

Now A = (Second difference) $\div$ 2 = 4 $\div$ 2 = 2.

So, the given sequence is of the form $T(n) = 2n^2 + Bn + C$.

When $n = 1$, $T(1) = 6$. So, you have: $6 = 2 + B + C$ $\qquad B + C = 4$

When $n = 2$, $T(2) = 15$. So, you have: $15 = 8 + 2B + C$ $\qquad 2B + C = 7$

Solve the two simultaneous equations: $\quad B + C = 4$ (i)

$$2B + C = 7 \text{ (ii)}$$

Subtract equation (i) from equation (ii) to obtain $B = 3$.

Substitute $B = 3$ into equation (i) to obtain $C = 1$.

Hence, $A = 2$, $B = 3$ and $C = 1$, giving:

$$T(n) = 2n^2 + 3n + 1$$

This gives the routine for finding the nth term of a quadratic sequence in the form $T(n) = An^2 + Bn + C$.

Step 1   Find the second difference, then $A =$ (Second difference) $\div$ 2.

Step 2   Find $T(1)$ and $T(2)$ by the substitution in $T(n) = An^2 + Bn + C$ of the value of A, and of $n = 1$ and 2.

Step 3   Solve the pair of simultaneous equations in B and C, which is given by Step 2.

Example 3.4 ▷   Find the nth term of the sequence 7, 21, 41, 67, 99.

Step 1   Look at the differences.

First differences: $\quad$ 14   20   26   32
Second differences: $\quad$ 6   6   6

The second differences are the same, so the sequence is quadratic. Hence, the nth term is in the form $T(n) = An^2 + Bn + C$, where $A =$ (Second difference) $\div$ 2, which gives $A = 6 \div 2 = 3$. That is, nth term is $T(n) = 3n^2 + Bn + C$.

Step 2   Find $T(1)$ and $T(2)$:

When $n = 1$, $T(1) = 7 = 3 + B + C$ $\qquad B + C = 4$

When $n = 2$, $T(2) = 21 = 12 + 2B + C$ $\qquad 2B + C = 9$

Step 3   Solve: $B + C = 4$ (i)

$$2B + C = 9 \text{ (ii)}$$

Subtract equation (i) from equation (ii) to give $B = 5$.

Substitute $B = 5$ into equation (i) to obtain $C = -1$.

Hence, $T(n) = 3n^2 + 5n - 1$.

1 Identify which of the following sequences are quadratic sequences. Give a reason for your choice in each case.

a	5, 8, 11, 14, 17	**b** 2, 5, 10, 17, 26	**c** 3, 4, 6, 9, 13
d	4, 10, 18, 28, 40	**e** 7, 16, 31, 52, 79	**f** 10, 100, 1000, 10000

2 **a**   Find $T(3)$ in the sequence given by $T(n) = n^2 + 5$.

$\quad$ **b**   Find $T(3)$ in the sequence given by $T(n) = n^2 + 5n$.

$\quad$ **c**   Find $T(3)$ in the sequence given by $T(n) = n^2 + 5n + 5$.

3 Find the first five terms in each of these sequences.

    a $T(n) = 2n^2 + 4n + 3$ **b** $T(n) = 3n^2 + 4n - 2$

4 Find the *n*th term for each of the following quadratic sequences.

    a   8, 18, 30, 44, 60   **b**   9, 19, 35, 57, 85   **c**   2, 13, 30, 53, 82

    d $\frac{1}{4}, \frac{2}{7}, \frac{3}{12}, \frac{4}{19}, \frac{5}{28}$ **e** $\frac{5}{9}, \frac{8}{16}, \frac{13}{25}, \frac{20}{36}, \frac{29}{39}$

Look at the three sets of circles.

 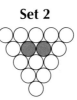 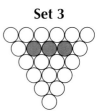

Set 1   Set 2   Set 3

The table shows the number of grey and white circles in each set.

	Set 1	Set 2	Set 3
Grey circles	1	2	3
White circles	9	13	18

Investigate how many white circles there will be for *n* grey circles.

Equations involving fractions

When you have to solve an equation which involves a fraction, you have to use the rules for working out ordinary fractions.

For example, to solve $\frac{x}{3} = 5$, you first multiply both sides by 3 in order to remove the denominator:

$$\frac{x}{3} \times 3 = 5 \times 3$$

which gives:

$$x = 15$$

Follow through Examples 3.5 to 3.7, which show you how to remove the fractional part of equations.

Example 3.5   Solve $\frac{4x + 5}{3} = 7$.

First, multiply both sides by 3 to obtain:

$$4x + 5 = 21$$

Subtract 5 from both sides, which gives:

$$4x = 16$$

Dividing both sides by 4 gives the solution:

$$x = 4$$

Example 3.6 ▶   Solve $\dfrac{x-1}{2} = \dfrac{2x+8}{6}$.

The product of the two denominators is 12. So, multiply both sides by 12 which, after cancelling, gives:

$\qquad 6(x - 1) = 2(2x + 8)$

Expand both sides to obtain:

$\qquad 6x - 6 = 4x + 16$

which simplifies to:

$\qquad 2x = 22$

$\qquad x = 11$

So, $x = 11$ is the solution.

Example 3.7 ▶   Solve $\frac{4}{5}(2x + 1) = \frac{2}{3}(x - 3)$.

Multiply both sides by the product of the denominators of the fractions, which is $5 \times 3 = 15$. This gives:

$\qquad 15 \times \frac{4}{5}(2x + 1) = 15 \times \frac{2}{3}(x - 3)$

Cancelling the fractions leaves:

$\qquad 3 \times 4(2x + 1) = 5 \times 2(x - 3)$

$\qquad 12(2x + 1) = 10(x - 3)$

Multiply out both brackets to obtain:

$\qquad 24x + 12 = 10x - 30$

which simplifies to:

$\qquad 14x = -42$

Dividing both sides by 14 gives the solution:

$\qquad x = -3$

Exercise 3D

1 Solve each of these equations.

  a $\dfrac{4x}{5} = 12$ **b** $\dfrac{2t}{5} = 6$ **c** $\dfrac{3m}{8} = 9$ **d** $\dfrac{2x}{3} = 8$ **e** $\dfrac{3w}{4} = 6$

2 Solve each of the following equations.

  a $\dfrac{(2x+1)}{5} = \dfrac{(x-4)}{2}$ **b** $\dfrac{(3x-1)}{3} = \dfrac{(2x+3)}{4}$ **c** $\dfrac{(2x-3)}{2} = \dfrac{(3x-2)}{5}$

3 Solve each of the following equations.

  a $\frac{3}{4}(x + 2) = \frac{1}{2}(4x + 1)$ **b** $\frac{1}{2}(2x + 5) = \frac{3}{4}(3x - 2)$

  c $\frac{3}{5}(2x + 3) = \frac{1}{2}(3x - 6)$ **d** $\frac{2}{3}(4x - 1) = \frac{3}{4}(2x - 4)$

4 Solve each of the following equations.

a $\dfrac{4}{(x+1)} = \dfrac{7}{(x+4)}$ **b** $\dfrac{5}{(x+3)} = \dfrac{4}{(x-1)}$ **c** $\dfrac{3}{(x+2)} = \dfrac{2}{(x-5)}$

d $\dfrac{7}{(x-3)} = \dfrac{5}{(x+4)}$ **e** $\dfrac{6}{(5x+1)} = \dfrac{2}{(2x-1)}$ **f** $\dfrac{2}{(4x+3)} = \dfrac{3}{(5x-1)}$

Extension Work

1 Solve each of the following equations.

a $4(2t+3) = 3(4t+1) - 5(3t-2)$ **b** $2(5h+4) = 6(2h+3) - 3(5h+1)$

c $5(3m+1) = 4(5m-2) - 4(2m-3)$ **d** $7(8g-5) = 5(6g+4) - 2(3g+4)$

e $3(4k-2) = 5(3k+1) - 2(4k-3)$ **f** $4(3x-1) = 3(5x-2) - 4(2x-7)$

2 Solve each of the following equations.

a $5(t+0.3) = 2(t+1.6) - 4(t-0.2)$ **b** $2(h+1.4) = 5(h+3.1) + 3(h+1.1)$

c $6(m+1.3) = 3(m-0.2) - 3(m-3.2)$ **d** $5(g-0.5) = 4(g+1.4) - 2(3g+0.4)$

e $4(4k-0.2) = 4(k+1.1) - 2(4k-3.1)$ **f** $3(2x-1.3) = 2(3x-2.1) - 3(x-0.7)$

Inequalities

$5x + 6 \geq 10$ is a linear inequality. It looks and behaves similarly to linear equations which you have already met, but instead of an equals sign, it contains one of the 4 inequality signs. It is important that you are familiar with them:

> is greater than

$\geq$ is greater than or equal to

< is less than

$\leq$ is less than or equal to

The same rules are used to solve linear inequalities as linear equations. However the solutions to linear inequalities can be expressed graphically on a number line as well as using standard inequality notation, as Examples 3.8 and 3.9 show.

Example 3.8 Solve $5x + 6 \geq 10$.

Subtract 6 from both sides to give: $5x \geq 4$

Divide both sides by 5 to obtain: $x \geq 0.8$

The solution expressed on a number line is shown below. To show that 0.8 is included in the solution, a filled in circle is used.

Example 3.9

Solve $\frac{1}{2}t - 1 < 4$.

Add 1 to both sides to give: $\qquad$ $\frac{1}{2}t < 5$

Multiply both sides by 2 to obtain: $\quad t < 10$

The solution expressed on a number line is shown below. An empty circle is used to show that the 10 is not included in the solution.

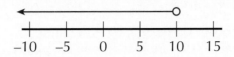

So:

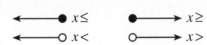

1 Solve the following inequalities and illustrate their solutions on number lines.

a	$x + 3 < 5$	**b**	$x - 2 \geq 7$	**c**	$t - 4 < 2$
d	$2t + 3 > 7$	**e**	$3t - 1 \leq 8$	**f**	$5x + 3 < 8$
g	$3x + 5 > 2$	**h**	$4t + 7 \leq -1$	**i**	$2x - 4 \geq 4$
j	$7t + 3 \geq 3$	**k**	$3(x + 4) \geq 6$	**l**	$2(x - 2) \leq 8$
m	$\frac{x}{4} > 3$	**n**	$\frac{1}{2}x + 1 < 3$	**p**	$4(2x - 3) \geq 12$

2 Write down the values of x that satisfy the conditions given.

a $x + 11 < 20$, where x is a positive integer.

b $x + 15 \leq 20$, where x is a positive, odd number.

c $2x - 3 < 14$, where x is a positive, even number.

d $5(3x + 4) < 100$, where x is a positive, prime number.

e $2x + 1 \leq 50$, where x is a positive, square number.

f $4x - 1 \leq 50$, where x is a positive, prime number.

g $5x + 3 < 60$, where x is a positive, multiple of three.

3 Solve the following linear inequalities.

a $\dfrac{x + 3}{2} \leq 4$ $\qquad\qquad$ **b** $\dfrac{x - 4}{3} > 7$

c $\dfrac{3x + 1}{5} < 2$ $\qquad\qquad$ **d** $\dfrac{2x - 5}{3} \geq 5$

4 Solve the following linear inequalities, illustrating their solutions on number lines.

a $2x + 4 < 17$ and $x > 3$ $\qquad$ **b** $4(x - 3) \leq 0$ and $x > -2$

c $5x - 4 > 18$ and $x \leq 8$ $\qquad$ **d** $2(5x + 7) \geq 15$ and $x < 1$

e $1 \leq 3x + 2 \leq 17$ $\qquad\qquad$ **f** $1 \leq 4x - 3 < 13$

Much like linear equations, linear inequalities can also be plotted on a graph. The result is a region that lies on one side of a straight line or the other, which is usually shaded.

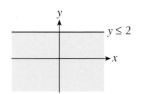

1   Show each of the following inequalities as a graph.

   a $y \geq 6$ **b** $x \leq 4$ **c** $y \leq 3x + 2$

2   The shaded area shown on the graph on the right shows a region that satisfies more than one inequality.

   Write down the three inequalities which describe the shaded area.

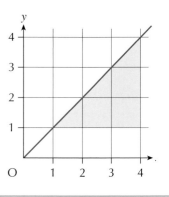

Graphs showing direct proportion

When a car is being filled with petrol, both the amount and the cost of the petrol are displayed on the pump. One litre of petrol costs about 80p but this does vary over the months and years.

The table below shows the costs of different quantities of petrol as displayed on the pump.

Amount of petrol (litres)	5	10	15	20	25	30
Cost (£)	4.00	8.00	12.00	16.00	20.00	24.00

The information can be graphed, as shown on the right. Because the cost is in direct proportion to the amount bought, the graph is a straight line.

Note that the equation of the graph is $C = 0.8P$, where C is the cost in pounds of the quantity bought and P is the quantity in litres. The gradient of the line, 0.8, is the cost of 1 litre of petrol.

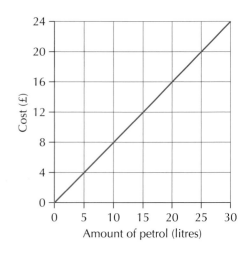

Example 3.10 ▷ Mr Evans wanted to convert all his French scores to standard percentage scores. He wanted to use the data shown on the right.

Student score (F)	0	28	56
Percentage (P)	0	50	100

He wanted there to be a direct proportion between each score and its percentage score.

a Create a graph which Mr Evans could use as a conversion graph from his French scores to percentage scores.

b What is the equation of this graph?

a Use the three points given above to draw a straight-line graph. Then use that graph to make a conversion graph.

b The gradient of the line is approximately 1.8, so the equation is $P = 1.8F$.

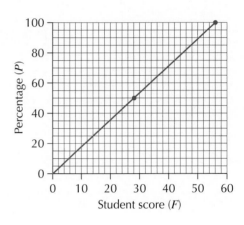

Exercise 3F

1 One morning in Scotland, Jenny recorded the temperature every hour from 8 am until noon. Her results are shown below.

Hours after 8 am	0	1	2	3	4
Temperature (°C)	4	5.5	7	8.5	10

a Plot the points on a graph and join them up with a suitable line.

b On this morning, are the temperatures given directly proportional to the number of hours after 8 am?

c Write down the equation of the line showing the relationship between the time, t, and temperature, C.

d If the relationship held all day, what would be the temperature at 4 pm, when $t = 8$?

2 Thousands of fans pour into a stadium ready to watch Joe King. A count is kept of the number of fans in the stadium after various time intervals.

Time after 1.30 pm	0	0.25	0.5	0.75
Number of fans	14 000	26 000	38 000	50 000

a Plot the points on a graph and join them up with a suitable line.

b For this hour, is the number of fans given directly proportional to the time after 1.30 pm?

c Write down the equation of the line showing the relationship between the time, t, and the number of fans, f.

d If the relationship held all evening, when did the first fan enter the stadium?

3 Given in the table below is the length of a stretched spring with each of a series of different weights hanging from it.

Weight (g)	0	200	400	600	800	1000
Length (cm)	0	12	14	16	18	20

    a Plot the points on a graph and join them up with a suitable line.

    b Is the extension directly proportional to the weight?

    c Write down the equation of the line showing the relationship between hanging weight, w, and length, L.

    d If the relationship continued to hold, what would be the hanging weight when the length of the spring is 27 cm?

4 Tea is served at a garden party between 3.00 pm and 5.30 pm. The number of cups of tea sold during the afternoon is shown in the table below.

Time after 3.00 pm	0	0.25	1	1.75	2	2.5
Cups of tea	0	13	52	91	104	130

    a Plot the points on a graph and join them up with a suitable line.

    b On this afternoon, is the number of cups of tea sold directly proportional to the time after 3.00 pm?

    c Write down the equation of the line showing the relationship between the time, t, and the number of cups of tea sold, S.

    d If the relationship held all day and the garden party continued, what is the value of S at 9.30 pm, when $t = 6.5$?

5 An experiment was done with a bouncing tennis ball. A tennis ball was dropped from different heights and the height of the first bounce was measured. The results are given in the table below.

Height of drop (cm)	25	50	75	100	125	150	175	200
Bounce (cm)	15	31	48	66	82	98	113	130

    a Plot the points on a graph and join them up with a suitable line.

    b Is the bounce directly proportional to the height of drop?

    c Write down the equation of the line showing the relationship between height of drop, h, and bounce, b.

    d If the relationship held, from what height would you need to drop the ball in order to have a bounce of 5 metres?

Extension Work

Solve this problem by drawing a graph.

Two women are walking on the same long, straight road towards each other. One sets off at 9.00 am at a speed of 4 km/h. The other also sets off at 9.00 am, 15 km away, at a speed of 5 km/h. At 9.10 am, a butterfly leaves the shoulder of the quicker woman and flies to the other woman at 20 km/h. It continues to fly from one woman to the other until they both meet, and take a photograph of it.

a At what time will the butterfly be photographed?

b How many times will the butterfly have landed on the woman walking at 4 km/h?

Solving simultaneous equations by graphs

Every equation can be graphed. Every pair of coordinates on the graph represent a possible solution for the equation. Hence, when the graphs of two equations are drawn between the same axes, where they intercept gives a solution which satisfies both equations.

Example 3.11 By drawing their graphs on the same grid, find the solution of these simultaneous equations:

$$3x + 5y = 25$$
$$5x - 3y = 2$$

First, number the equations:

$$3x + 5y = 25 \quad \text{(i)}$$
$$5x - 3y = 2 \quad \text{(ii)}$$

Equation (i) is drawn by plotting the points where the graph crosses both axes:

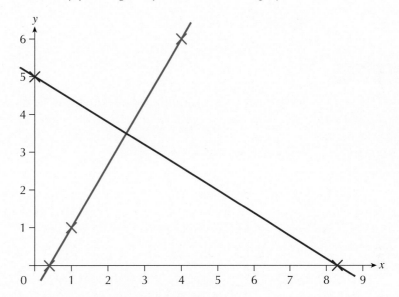

When $x = 0$, $y = 5$, giving the coordinates $(0, 5)$.
When $y = 0$, $x = 8.3$, giving the coordinates $(8.3, 0)$.

Equation (ii) is drawn by plotting three points for y and substituting:
When $y = 0$, $x = 0.4$, giving the coordinates $(0.4, 0)$.
When $y = 1$, $x = 1$, giving the coordinates $(1, 1)$.
When $y = 6$, $x = 4$, giving the coordinates $(4, 6)$.

The point where the graphs intercept is $(2.5, 3.5)$. So, the solution to the simultaneous equations is $x = 2.5$ and $y = 3.5$.

Exercise 3G Solve each pair of simultaneous equations by drawing their graphs. Give your solutions to one decimal place.

1 $x + y = 5$
$y = 5x - 4$

2 $x + y = 4$
$2y = 4x - 7$

3 $y = x - 1$
$y = 8 - x$

4 $x + y = 5$
$x = 8 - 3y$

5 $y = 6x - 5$
$x + y = 4$

6 $y = 3x - 5$
$2x + y = 6$

7 $4y = 12 + x$
$3x = 2y - 3$

8 $x + y = 4$
$5y - 3x = 3$

Extension Work

Solve each pair of simultaneous equations by drawing their graphs.

1 $y = x^2 - 1$ and $5x + 4y = 20$

2 $y = x^2 + x$ and $8x + 3y = 12$

What you need to know for level 6

- How to solve equations involving negative numbers
- Be able to construct simple equations to help solve problems
- How to solve certain non-linear equations by trial and improvement

What you need to know for level 7

- How to solve equations with the variable on both sides
- How to solve more difficult equations involving x^2 or x^3
- Be able to solve problems involving direct proportion

What you need to know for level 8

- How to solve simultaneous equations, including by graphs
- How to find the nth term of a quadratic sequence

National Curriculum SATs questions

LEVEL 6

1   *1999 Paper 2*

The length of one side of a rectangle is y. This equation shows the area of the rectangle:

$y(y + 2) = 67.89$

Find the value of y. Show your working.

You may find the table on the right helpful.

y	$y + 2$	$y(y + 2)$	
8	10	80	Too large

2   *2000 Paper 2*

Solve the following equations.

a $9 - 3x = 3$

b $3 + 2x + 7 = 2x + 7 + 3x$

c $5x - 2 = 2x + 5$

d $(x - 2)^2 = 0$

LEVEL 7

3   *2000 Paper 2*

A class collected information about the number of children in each of their families.

The information was displayed in a frequency chart, but you cannot see all the information.

Call the number of families that have two children n.

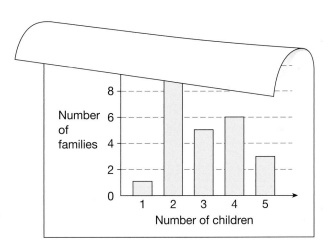

a   Show that the total number of children in all the families is $55 + 2n$.

b   Write an expression for the total number of families.

c   The mean number of children per familiy is 3. What is the value of n? Show your working.

LEVEL 8

4   *1999 Paper 1*

Solve this pair of simultaneous equations.

$y = 2x + 1$

$3y = 4x + 1$

CHAPTER 4

Shape, Space and Measures **1**

This chapter is going to show you

- how to use Pythagoras' theorem
- how to find the locus of a point using more complex rules
- how to recognise congruent triangles
- some important circle theorems
- how regular polygons tessellate
- the difference between a practical demonstration and a proof

What you should already know

- How to find the square and the square root of a number
- How to find the locus of a point
- How to construct the perpendicular bisector of a line segment and the bisector of an angle
- How to recognise congruent shapes
- The definition of a circle and the names of its parts
- How to calculate the interior and exterior angles of a polygon

Pythagoras' theorem

Thousands of years ago, the builders of the pyramids in Egypt used a rope with 12 equally spaced knots, which, when stretched out as shown on the right, formed a right-angled triangle.

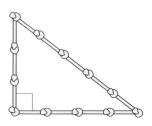

This helped the builders make sure that any right-angles required in the construction of the Pyramids were accurate.

In a right-angled triangle, the longest side opposite the right angle is called the **hypotenuse**.

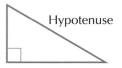

Hypotenuse

Activity

Make accurate copies of the three right-angled triangles below.

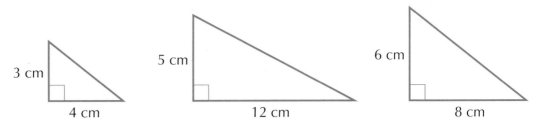

Next, measure the length of the hypotenuse of each one. Then copy and complete the table below.

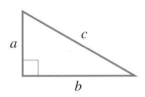

a	b	c	a^2	b^2	c^2
3	4				
5	12				
6	8				

Can you see a pattern in the last three columns? If you can, you have just rediscovered **Pythagoras' theorem.**

Pythagoras was a Greek philosopher and mathematician, who was born in about 581 BC on the island of Samos, just off the coast of Turkey. The following famous theorem about right-angled triangles is attributed to him.

> In any right-angled triangle, the square of the hypotenuse is equal to the sum of the squares of the other two sides.

Pythagoras' theorem is usually written as:

$$c^2 = a^2 + b^2$$

The following two examples will show you how to use Pythagoras' theorem.

Example 4.1 ▷

Finding the length of the hypotenuse

Calculate the length x in the triangle shown on the right.

Using Pythagoras' theorem:

$$x^2 = 6^2 + 5^2$$
$$= 36 + 25$$
$$= 61$$

So, $x = \sqrt{61} = 7.8$ cm (1 dp).

You should be able to work this out on a scientific calculator. Try the following sequence of keystrokes:

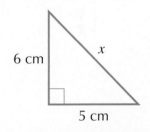

This may not work on some makes of calculator, and you may need to ask your teacher to help you.

Example 4.2 ▷ **Finding the length of a shorter side**

Calculate the length x in the triangle shown on the right.

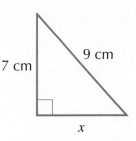

Using Pythagoras' theorem:
$$x^2 + 7^2 = 9^2$$
$$x^2 = 9^2 - 7^2$$
$$= 81 - 49$$
$$= 32$$
So, $x = \sqrt{32} = 5.7$ cm (1 dp).

Try the following sequence of keystrokes:

1 Calculate the length of the hypotenuse in each of the following right-angled triangles. Give your answers to one decimal place.

a

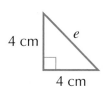

b

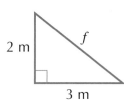

c

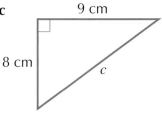

d

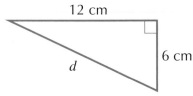

e

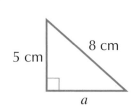

f

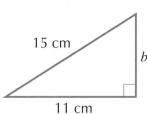

g

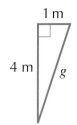

h

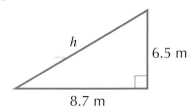

2 Calculate the length of the unknown side in each of the following right-angled triangles. Give your answers to one decimal place.

a

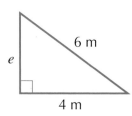

b

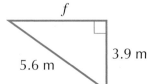

c

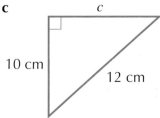

d

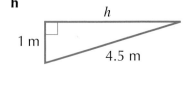

e

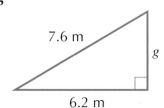

f

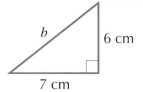

g

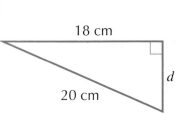

h

3 Calculate the lengths of x, y and z in the diagram on the right.

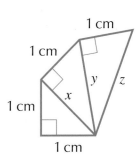

4 Calculate the length of the diagonal AC in the rectangle ABCD. Give your answer to one decimal place.

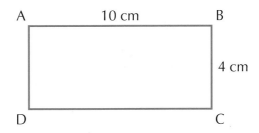

5 Calculate the length of the diagonal of a square with side length 5 cm. Give your answer to one decimal place.

Extension Work

The table below shows the lengths, in centimetres, of the three sides of six triangles.

Construct each one accurately, using a ruler and a pair of compasses. Label it as in the triangle on the right.

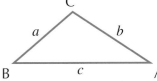

a	b	c	a^2	b^2	c^2	a^2+b^2	Is $a^2 + b^2 = c^2$? Is $a^2 + b^2 > c^2$? Is $a^2 + b^2 < c^2$? Write =, > or <	Is $\angle C$ right-angled, acute or obtuse?
3	4	5						
4	5	7						
5	6	7						
5	12	13						
4	8	10						
7	8	9						

Copy and complete the table. Then, write down a rule using the results in the last two columns.

Test your rule by drawing triangles with different lengths for a, b and c.

Solving problems using Pythagoras' theorem

Pythagoras' theorem can be used to solve various practical problems.

When solving such a problem:

- Draw a diagram for the problem, clearly showing the right angle.
- Decide whether the hypotenuse or one of the shorter sides needs to be found.
- Label the unknown side x.
- Use Pythagoras' theorem to calculate x.
- Round your answer to a suitable degree of accuracy.

Example 4.3 ▷ A ship sails 4 km due east. It then sails for a further 5 km due south. Calculate the distance the ship would have travelled had it sailed a direct route.

First, draw a diagram to show the distances sailed by the ship. Then label the direct distance, x.

Now use Pythagoras' theorem:
$$x^2 = 4^2 + 5^2$$
$$= 16 + 25$$
$$= 41$$
So, $x = \sqrt{41} = 6.4$ km (1 dp).

Exercise 4B

In this exercise, give your answers to a suitable degree of accuracy.

1 An aircraft flies 80 km due north. It then flies 72 km due west. Calculate how far the aircraft would have travelled had it taken the direct route.

2 A flagpole is 10 m high. It is held in position by two ropes which are fixed to the ground, 4 m away from the foot of the flagpole. Calculate the length of each rope.

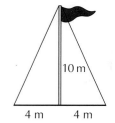

3 An 8 m ladder is placed against a wall so that the foot of the ladder is 2 m away from the bottom of the wall. Calculate how far the ladder reaches up the wall.

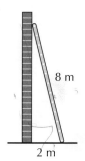

4 The diagram shows the side wall of a shed. Calculate the length of the sloping roof.

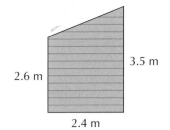

3.5 m

2.6 m

2.4 m

5 The diagram shows a walkway leading from the dock on to a ferry. Calculate the vertical height of the walkway above the dock.

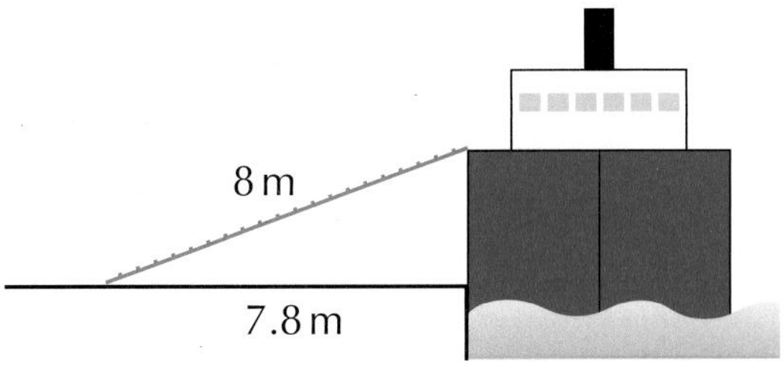

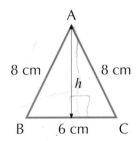

8 m

7.8 m

6 Two sides of a right-angled triangle are 20 cm and 30 cm. Calculate the length of the third side in each of the following cases.

    a It is the hypotenuse.

    b It is not the hypotenuse.

7 ABC is an isosceles triangle.

    a Calculate the perpendicular height, h.

    b Hence calculate the area of the triangle.

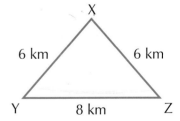

A

8 cm   8 cm

h

B   6 cm   C

8 The diagram shows three towns X, Y and Z connected by straight roads. Calculate the shortest distance from X to the road connecting Y and Z.

X

6 km   6 km

Y   8 km   Z

9 The triangle PQR is drawn on a coordinate grid, as shown on the right.

    a The length of PQ is 3 units. Write down the length of QR.

    b Calculate the length of PR.

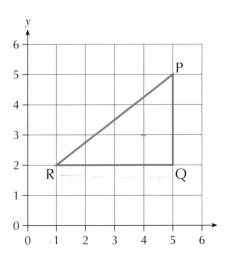

10 Calculate the length between each of the following pairs of coordinate points.

    a   A(2, 3) and B(4, 7)   **b**   C(1, 5) and D(4, 3)

    c   E(–1, 0) and F(2, –3)   **d**   G(– 5, 1) and H(4, –3)

Pythagorean triples

Each set of the three numbers in the table on the right obey Pythagoras' theorem, $c^2 = a^2 + b^2$, where a, b and c are whole numbers. Each set of numbers is called a **Pythagorean triple**, named after Pythagoras, who first discovered a formula for finding them.

a	b	c
3	4	5
5	12	13
7	24	25

    a   Continue the table to find other Pythagorean triples. You may wish to use a spreadsheet to help you.

    b   Can you find the formula which Pythagoras discovered, giving b and c when the value of a is known?

    c   Do multiples of any Pythagorean triple still give another Pythagorean triple?

Loci

A **locus** (plural 'loci') is the movement of a point according to a given set of conditions or a rule.

In Year 8, you met two important constructions, which can now be stated to be loci.

Example 4.4

- The locus of a point which is always equidistant from each of two fixed points, A and B, is the perpendicular bisector of the line joining the two points.

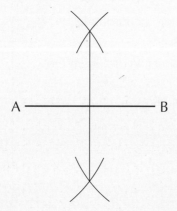

- The locus of a point which is equidistant from two fixed lines AB and BC, which meet at B, is the bisector of the angle ABC.

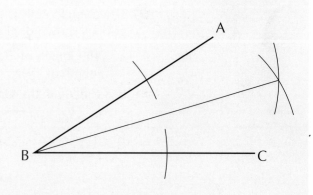

A locus can sometimes be a region.

Example 4.5

- A point which moves so that it is always 5 cm from a fixed point X has a locus which is a circle of radius 5 cm, with its centre at X.

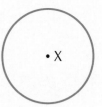

- The locus of a set of points which are 5 cm or less from a fixed point X is a region inside a circle of radius 5 cm, with its centre at X.

  Note that the region is usually shaded.

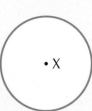

- The locus of a set of points which are less than 5 cm from a fixed point X is a region inside a circle of radius 5 cm, with its centre at X.

  Note that the boundary usually is drawn as a dashed line to show that the points which are exactly 5 cm from X are *not* to be included.

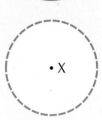

Exercise 4C

1 Using a ruler and compasses, construct the perpendicular bisector of each of the following lines.

a

A —————————— B
6 cm

b

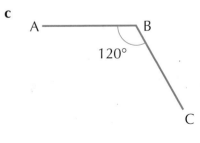

4.5 cm

2 Using a ruler and compasses, construct the bisector of each of the following angles.

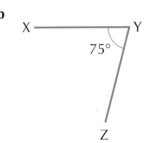

b

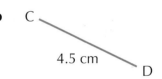

c

A ————————— B
120°

C

3 X is a fixed point. Draw diagrams to show the following.

a The locus of a point which is always 3 cm from X.

b The locus of a point which is always 3 cm or less from X.

c The locus of a point which is always less than 3 cm from X.

4 A and B are two points, 6 cm apart. Draw a diagram to show the region which is 4 cm or less from A and 3 cm or less from B.

5 Make a copy of Treasure Island, as shown on the right. The treasure is buried at a point X on the island.

X is equidistant from A and D and is also equidistant from B and C. Mark the position of the treasure on your map.

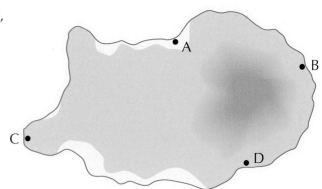

6 The diagram shows two perpendicular fences, PQ and QR. Bob wants to plant a tree so that it is equidistant from both fences and equidistant from P and R.

On a copy of the diagram, mark, with a cross, the position where Bob plants the tree.

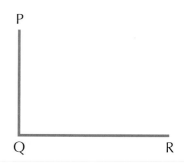

7 A radar station at X has a range of 100 km, and a radar station at Y has a range of 80 km. The direct distance from X to Y is 140 km.

Using a scale of 1 cm to 20 km, make a scale drawing to show the region where an aircraft can be picked up by both radar stations.

8 A and B are two barns which are 120 m apart. A farmer wants to fence off an area of land that is nearer to barn A than barn B and is within 80 m of barn B. Using a scale of 1 cm to 20 m, make a scale drawing to show the area of land enclosed by the fence.

120 m

9 P is a fixed point and a point Q moves in space so that the length of PQ is always 10 cm. Describe the locus of Q.

10 A fly moves around a strip light such that it is always 5 cm from the light. Describe the locus of the fly.

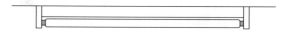

1   X is a point on the circumference of a circle. Draw the locus of X as the circle rolls along the line AB.

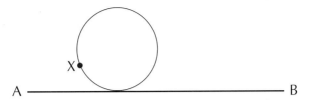

To help you draw the locus, use a coin and a ruler. Put a mark on the coin and as it rolls along the edge of the ruler, make marks on your paper for different positions of the coin, as on the diagram below. Join the marks with a curve to show the locus of X.

2   The diagram on the right shows a 6 m ladder leaning against the wall of a house. The ground is slippery and the ladder slides down the wall until it lies flat on the ground.

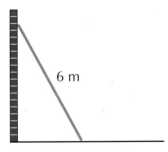

6 m

Make a scale drawing to show the locus of the middle point of the ladder as the ladder slides down the wall. Use a scale of 1 cm to 1m.

3   If you have access to ICT facilities, find how to draw the locus for more complex rules.

4   A builder wants to make a straight path from House A to the road, and another straight path from House B to the same point on the road.

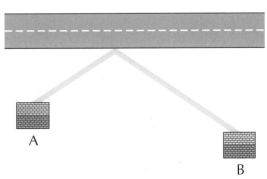

A

B

Draw a sketch to show where the paths should go in order to make the lengths of the paths as short as possible.

Congruent triangles

You already know how to construct triangles from given dimensions, as summarised below.

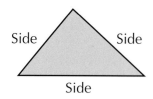

Three sides (SSS)

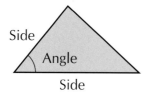

Two sides and the included angle (SAS)

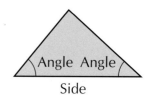

Two angles and the included side (ASA)

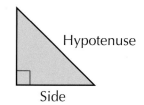

Right angle, hypotenuse and side (RHS)

You can use these conditions to show that two triangles are congruent, as Example 4.6 shows.

Example 4.6 ▶

Show that △ABC is congruent to △XYZ.

The diagram shows the following:

∠B = ∠X

∠C = ∠Y

BC = XY

So, △ABC is congruent to △XYZ (ASA).

This can be written as:

△ABC ≡ △XYZ

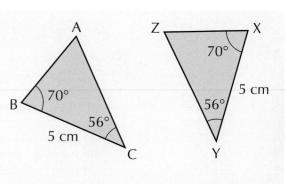

Exercise 4D

1 Show that each of the following pairs of triangles are congruent. Give reasons for each answer and state which condition of congruency you are using: SSS, SAS, ASA or RHS.

a

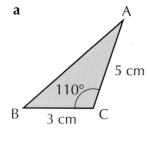

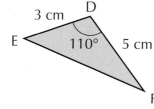

b

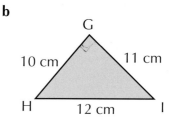

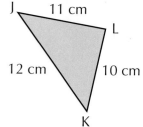

c

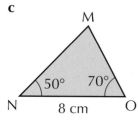

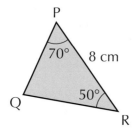

d

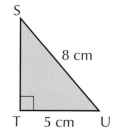

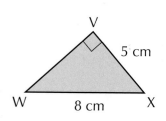

2 Explain why △ABC is congruent to △XYZ.

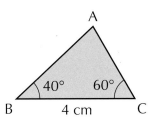

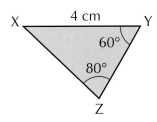

3 a Explain why △PQR is not necessarily congruent to △XYZ.

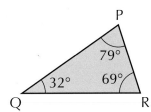

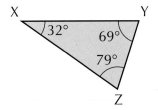

b Check your answer by trying to draw one of the triangles.

4 ABC is an isosceles triangle with AB = AC.
The perpendicular from A meets BC at D.

Show that △ABD is congruent to △ACD.

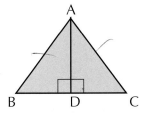

5 Draw a rectangle ABCD. Draw in the diagonals AC and BD to intersect at X. State the different sets of congruent triangles in your diagram.

Extension Work

1 Show that the opposite angles in a parallelogram are equal by using congruent triangles.

2 Draw a kite and label its vertices ABCD with AB = AD. Now draw the diagonals and label their intersection E.

    a Show that △ABC is congruent to △ADC.

    b State all other pairs of congruent triangles.

3 Construct as many different triangles as possible by choosing any three measurements from the following: 4 cm, 5 cm, 40° and 30°.

4 Show what happens when you try to construct a triangle for which the given angle is not included between the two given sides (SSA). There are three cases to consider.

Circle theorems

The following terms for parts of a circle were met in Year 8.

A circle is a set of points equidistant from a **centre**, O.

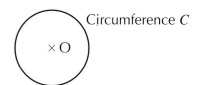

Circumference   The distance around a circle.

Radius   The distance from the centre of a circle to its circumference.

Diameter   The distance from one side of a circle to the other, passing through the centre.

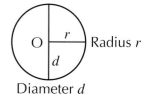

Chord   A line which cuts a circle into two parts.

Tangent   A line which touches a circle at a single point on its circumference.

Exercise 4E introduces two important circle theorems.

1 **The angle between a tangent and a radius**
- Draw a circle, centre O, with a radius of 3 cm.
- Draw a tangent to the circle with the point of contact at A.
- Draw the radius OA.
- Measure the angle between the tangent and the radius.
- Write down what you notice.
- Repeat for circles with different radii.

You have just completed a practical demonstration to show an important circle theorem:

A radius is perpendicular to a tangent at the point of contact.

Draw a diagram in your book to explain this theorem.

2 **The perpendicular bisector of a chord**
- Draw a circle, centre O, with a radius of 3 cm.
- Draw a chord anywhere inside the circle.
- Construct the perpendicular bisector of the chord.
- Write down what you notice.
- Repeat for circles with different radii.

You have just completed a practical demonstration to show another important circle theorem:

The perpendicular bisector of a chord passes through the centre of a circle.

Draw a diagram in your book to explain this theorem.

3 Calculate the size of the lettered angle in each of the following diagrams.

a

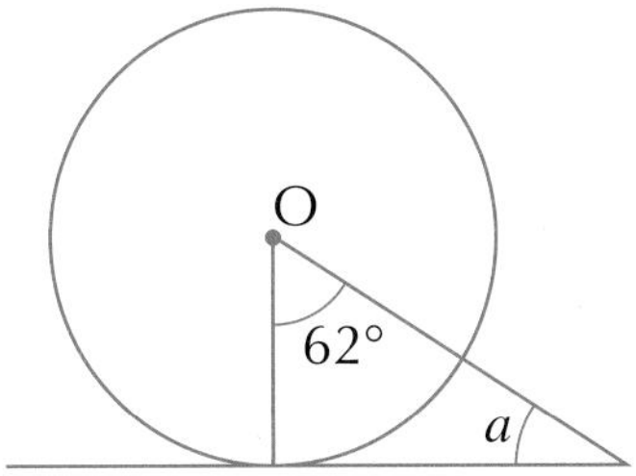

b

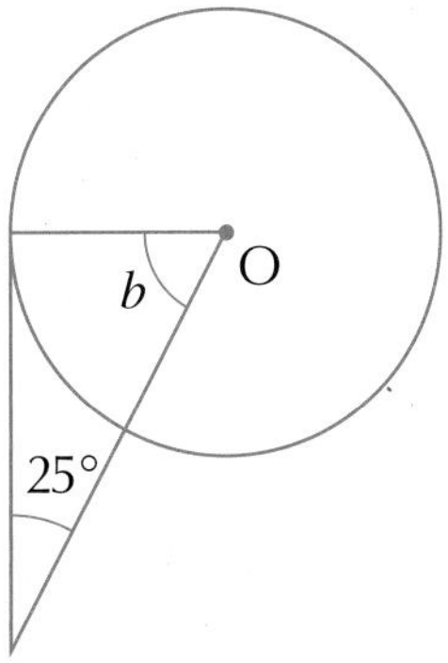

c

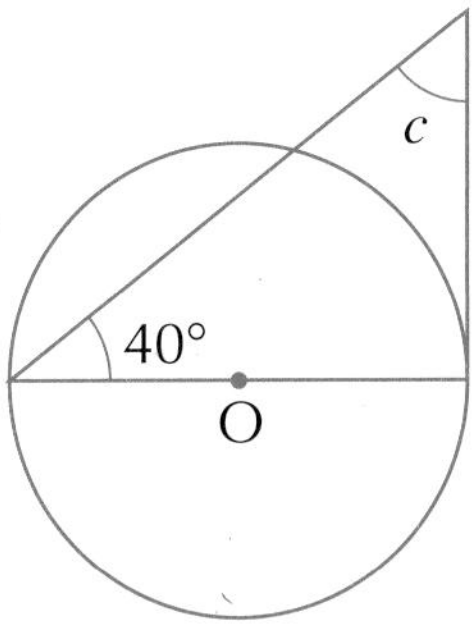

d

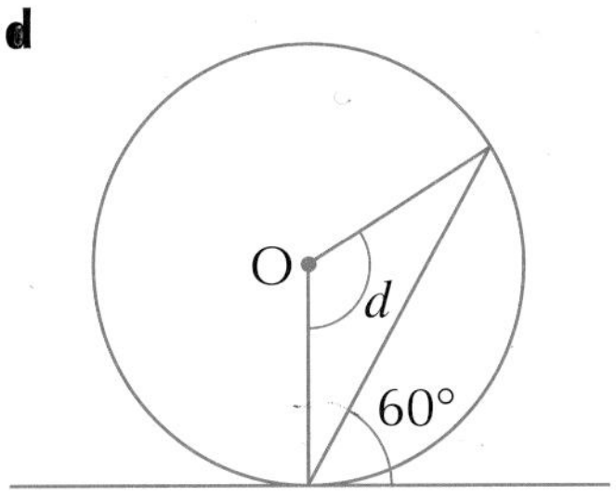

e

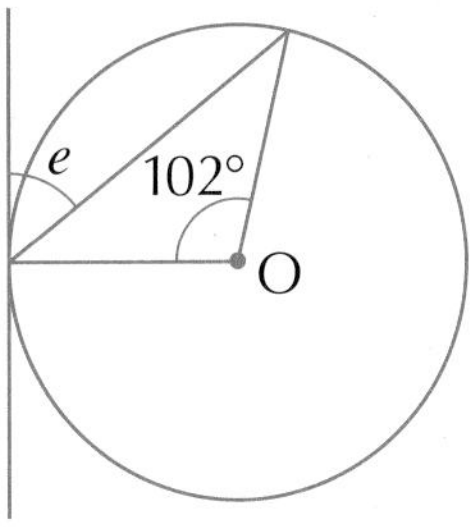

f

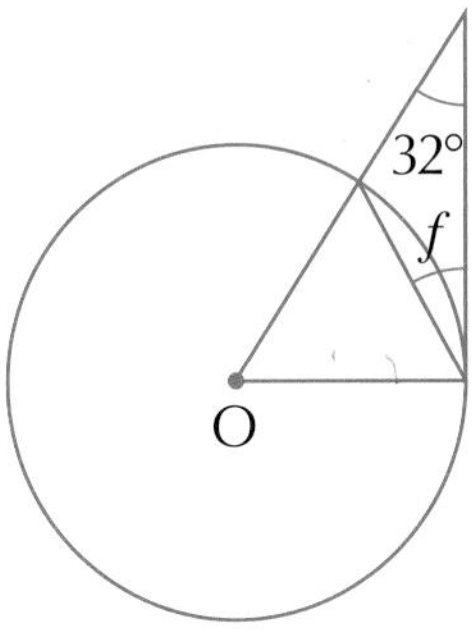

g

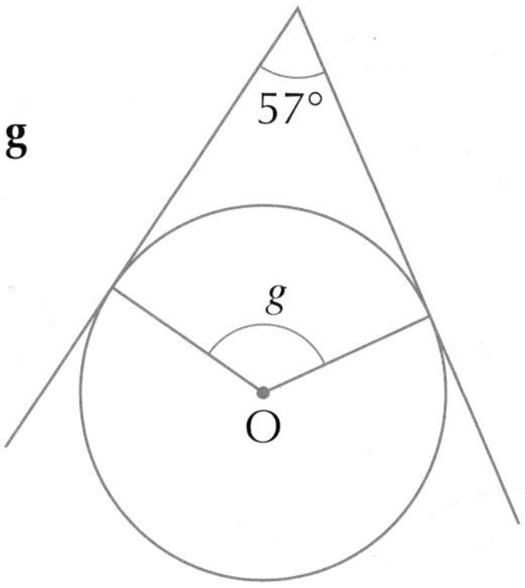

h

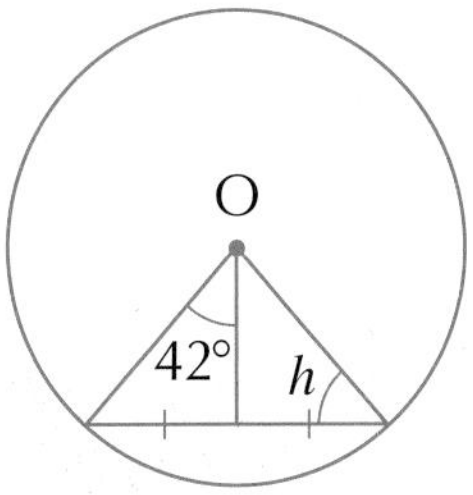

i

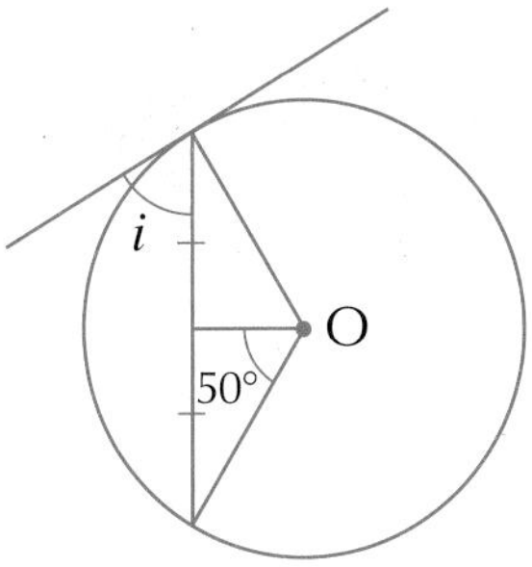

4 Use Pythagoras' theorem to calculate the length x in each of the following diagrams. Give your answers to one decimal place.

a

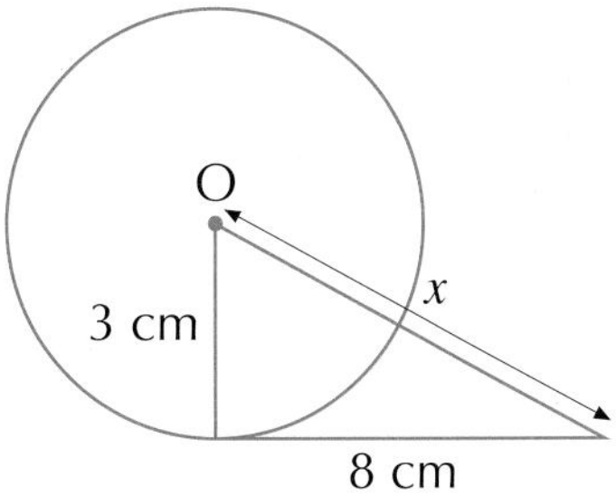

b

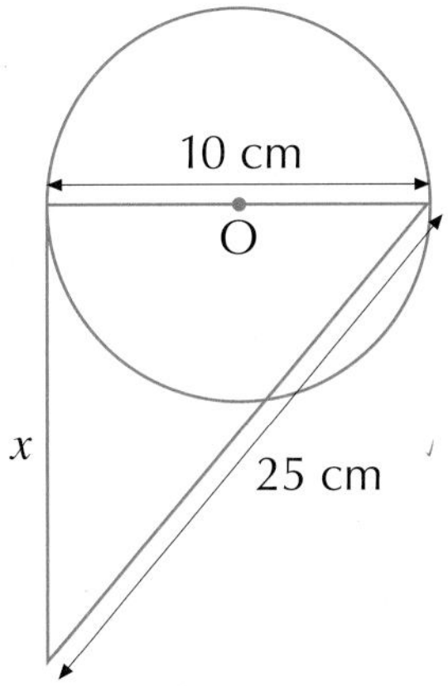

c

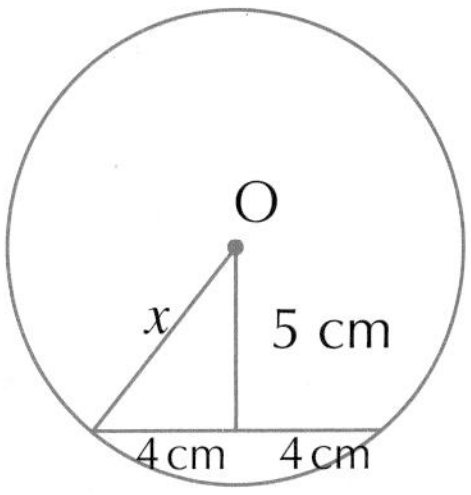

d

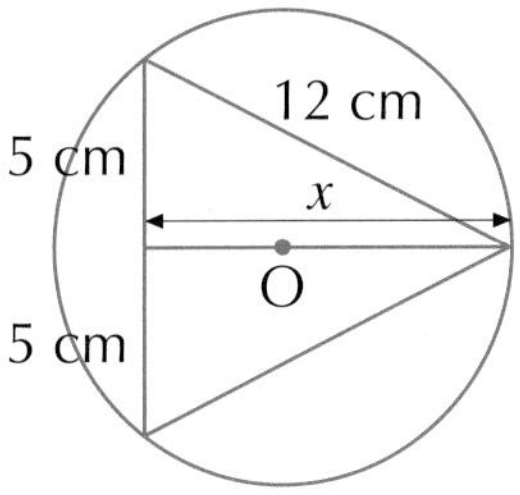

5 The lines AB and CD below are tangents to a circle. The circle touches the tangents at the points E and F. On a copy of the diagram, construct the circle, using a ruler and compasses.

Hint Construct two lines to find the centre of the circle.

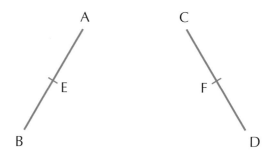

6 XY and XZ are two chords of the same circle. On a copy of the diagram, construct the circle, using a ruler and compasses.

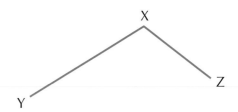

Extension Work

1 **The angle in a semicircle**

- Draw a circle, centre O, with a radius of 3 cm.
- Draw a diameter and label it AB.
- Mark a point P anywhere on the circumference.
- Complete the triangle APB in the semicircle.
- Measure ∠APB.
- Write down what you notice.
- Repeat for different points on the circumference.

You have just completed a practical demonstration to show yet another important circle theorem:

The angle formed in a semicircle equals 90°.

Draw a diagram in your book to explain this theorem.

Use this theorem to calculate the size of the lettered angles in each of the following diagrams.

a 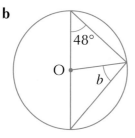 **b** 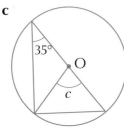 **c** **d** 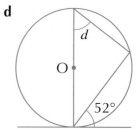 **e**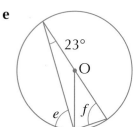

2 The diagram on the right shows two circles intersecting at B. O is the centre of the small circle and AO is the diameter of the large circle with its centre at P.

Prove that AB is a tangent to the small circle.

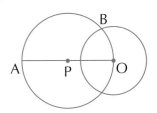

3 AP and BP are tangents to a circle with centre O. By using congruent triangles, prove that AP = BP.

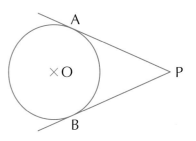

Tessellations and regular polygons

A **tessellation** is a repeating pattern made on a plane (flat) surface with identical shapes which fit together exactly, leaving no gaps.

This section will show you how some of the regular polygons tessellate.

Remember To show how a shape tessellates, draw up to about ten repeating shapes.

Example 4.7 ▷   The diagrams below show how equilateral triangles and squares tessellate.

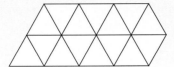 

Exercise 4F

1 On an isometric grid, show how a regular hexagon tessellates.

2 Trace this regular pentagon onto card and cut it out to make a template.

  a Use your template to show that a regular pentagon does not tessellate.

  b Explain why a regular pentagon does not tessellate.

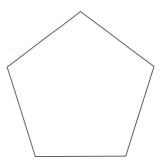

3 Trace this regular octagon onto card and cut it out to make a template.

    a Use your template to show that a regular octagon does not tessellate.

    b Explain why a regular octagon does not tessellate.

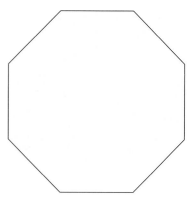

4 **a** Copy and complete the table below for regular polygons.

Regular polygon	Size of each interior angle	Does this polygon tessellate?
Equilateral triangle		
Square		
Regular pentagon		
Regular hexagon		
Regular octagon		

    b Use the table to explain why only some of the regular polygons tessellate.

    c Do you think that a regular nonagon tessellates? Explain your reasoning.

Extension Work

Polygons can be combined together to form a **semi-tessellation**. Two examples are shown below.

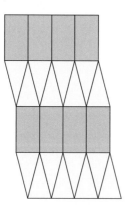

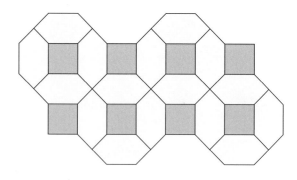

Rectangles and isosceles triangles   **Squares and hexagons**

Invent your own semi-tessellations and make a poster to display in your classroom.

Practical Pythagoras

This activity is a practical demonstration to show Pythagoras' theorem. You will need a sheet of thin card and a pair of scissors.

- In your book, draw the right-angled triangle X, as on the right.
- On the card, draw eight more triangles identical to X. Cut them out and place them to one side.
- On your original triangle, X, draw squares on each of the three sides of the triangle. Label them A, B and C, as below.

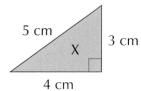

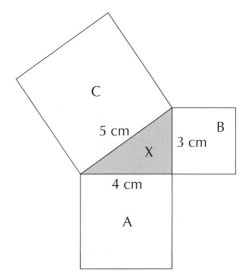

- On the card, draw another diagram identical to this. Cut out the squares A, B and C.
- Arrange the cut-outs of the eight triangles and three squares as in the two diagrams below.

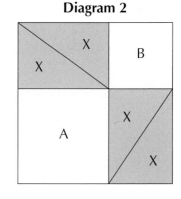

- What can you say about the total area of Diagram 1 and of Diagram 2?
- Now remove the four triangles from each diagram.
- What can you say about the areas of squares A, B and C?
- Show how this demonstrates Pythagoras' theorem.

The activity on page 75 showed a practical demonstration of Pythagoras' theorem. You can also prove Pythagoras' theorem by using algebra.

Copy the proof below into your book and make sure you can follow each step.

To prove Pythagoras' theorem

A right-angled triangle has sides a, b and c.

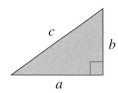

Draw the following diagram using four of these triangles.

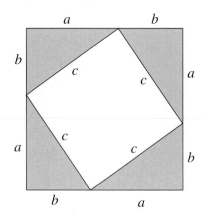

The area of each triangle = $\frac{1}{2}ab$.

So, the area of the four triangles = $2ab$.

The area of the large square = $(a + b)^2$.

The area of the large square can also be given as $c^2 + 2ab$.

Therefore: $(a + b)^2 = c^2 + 2ab$

$a^2 + 2ab + b^2 = c^2 + 2ab$

which gives $a^2 + b^2 = c^2$.

This is Pythagoras' theorem.

What you need to know for level 6

○ How to find and use interior and exterior angles of polygons

What you need to know for level 7

○ How to use and apply Pythagoras' theorem
○ How to find the locus of a set of points
○ How to recognise congruent triangles

What you need to know for level 8

○ The difference between a practical demonstration and a proof

National Curriculum SATs questions

LEVEL 6

1 *2000 Paper 2*

    a Any quadrilateral can be split into
two triangles.

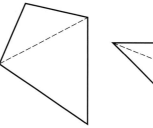

        Explain how you know that the angles inside a quadrilateral add
up to 360°.

    b What do the angles inside a pentagon add up to?

    c What do the angles inside a heptagon (seven-sided shape)
add up to?

        Show your working.

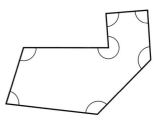

LEVEL 7

2 *2001 Paper 2*

    a Calculate the length of the unknown side
of this right-angled triangle.

        Show your working.

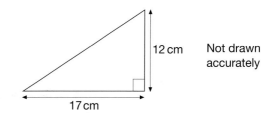

12 cm   Not drawn
accurately

17 cm

    b Calculate the length of the unknown side
of this right-angled triangle.

        Show your working.

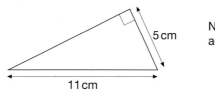

5 cm   Not drawn
accurately

11 cm

3 *2001 Paper 2*

The diagram shows five triangles. All lengths are in centimetres.

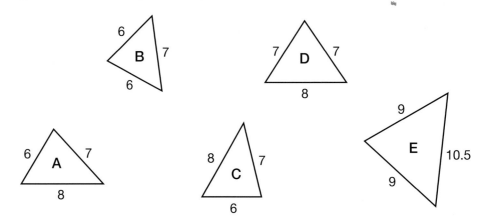

Write the letters of two triangles that are congruent to each other.

Explain how you know they are congruent.

4 *1997 Paper 2*

Some pupils want to plant a tree in the school's garden.

The tree must be at least 12 m from the school buildings. It must also be at least 10 m from the centre of the round pond.

Show accurately on a copy or a tracing of the plan, the region in which the tree can be planted. Shade this region.

Fence

5 *2003 Paper 2*

Two right-angled triangles are joined together to make a larger triangle ACD.

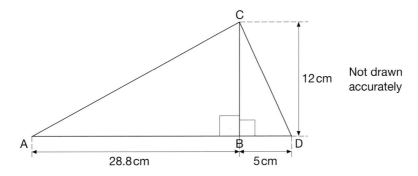

12cm   Not drawn
accurately

28.8cm   5cm

a Show that the perimeter of triangle ACD is 78 cm.

b Show that triangle ACD is also a right-angled triangle.

6 *2003 Paper 1*

The diagram shows three points, A, B and C, on a circle, centre O. AC is the diameter of the circle.

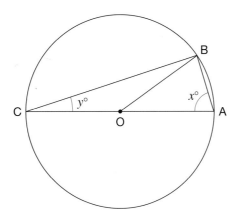

a Angle BAO is $x°$ and angle BCO is $y°$. Explain why angle ABO must be $x°$ and CBO must be $y°$.

b Use algebra to show that angle ABC must be 90°.

CHAPTER 5 Handling Data 1

This chapter is going to show you

- how to plan a statistical investigation
- how to interpret correlation from two scatter graphs
- how to draw and use lines of best fit on a scatter graph
- how to interpret time series graphs
- how to draw a cumulative frequency graph and use it to estimate median and interquartile range
- how to estimate a mean from a large set of data

What you should already know

- How to calculate statistics
- How to collect data using a suitable method
- How to draw and interpret graphs for discrete data
- How to compare two sets of data using mode, median, mean or range

Statistical investigations

Investigating a problem will involve several steps. Three examples will be studied from different subjects alongside an overall plan.

	Step	Example 1 PE	Example 2 Science	Example 3 Geography
1	Decide which general topic to study	How to improve student performance in sport	Effect of engine size on a car's acceleration	Life expectancy versus cost of housing
2	Specify in more detail	A throwing event	A particular make of car	Compare house prices in Yorkshire with those in South-east England
3	Consider questions which you could investigate	How much further do students throw using a run up? Is a Year 9 student able to throw as far as a Year 11 student of the same height?	Does a bigger engine always mean that a car can accelerate faster?	Do people who live in expensive housing tend to live longer?

Step	Example 1 PE	Example 2 Science	Example 3 Geography
4 State your hypotheses (Your guesses at what could happen)	Distance thrown will improve using a run up Year 11 students of the same height may be physically stronger and would therefore throw further	In general, more powerful engines produce the greater acceleration More powerful engines tend to be in heavier cars and therefore the acceleration will not be affected Larger engines in the same model of car will improve acceleration	People in expensive housing have greater incomes and also may have a longer life expectancy
5 Sources of information required	Survey of distance thrown with different lengths of run-up	Magazines and/or books with information on engine sizes and acceleration times for 0–60 mph	Library or the Internet for census data for each area
6 Relevant data	Choose students from different age groups with a range of heights Make sure that there is an equal number of boys and girls Choose students from the full range of ability	Make of car, engine size and acceleration **Note** The government requires car manufacturers to publish the time taken to accelerate from 0–60 mph	Average cost of housing for each area Data about life expectancy for each area
7 Possible problems	Avoid bias when choosing your sample or carrying out your survey	Petrol engines must be compared with other petrol engines not with diesel engines	
8 Data collection	Make sure that you can record all the factors which may affect the distance thrown: for example, age or height	Make sure that you can record all the information which you need, such as engine size and weight of car. Remember to quote sources of data	Extract relevant data from sources. Remember to quote sources of data
9 Decide on the level of accuracy required	Decide how accurate your data needs to be: for example, nearest 10 cm	Round any published engine sizes to the nearest 100 cm^3 (usually given as 'cc' in the car trade), which is 0.1 litre For example, a 1905 cc engine has a capacity of approximately 1.9 litres	
10 Determine sample size	Remember that collecting too much information may slow down the experiment		

Step	Example 1 PE	Example 2 Science	Example 3 Geography
11 Construct tables for large sets of raw data in order to make work manageable	Group distances thrown into intervals of 5 metres Use two-way tables to highlight differences between boys' and girls' data		Group population data in age groups of, for example, 10 year intervals
12 Decide which statistics are most suitable	When the distances thrown are close together, use the mean. When there are a few extreme values, use the median		Sample should be sufficiently large to be able to use the mean

Exercise 5A

Look at the three examples presented above and investigate either one of the problems given or a problem of your own choice. You should follow the steps given here, including your own ideas.

Extension Work

Think of a problem related to a piece of work, such as a foreign language essay or a history project. See whether you can use the step-by-step plan to carry out a statistical investigation.

For example, you may wish to compare the word length of an English and a French piece of writing, or you may wish to compare data about two wars.

Scatter graphs and correlation

The maximum temperature, rainfall and hours of sunshine were recorded each day in a town on the south coast of England.

Look at the two scatter graphs below, which were plotted from this data. Is it possible to work out the relationship between rainfall and hours of sunshine?

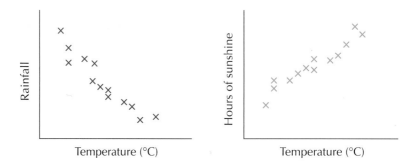

The graph on the left shows **negative correlation**. In this case, it means that the higher the temperature, the less rainfall there is.

The graph on the right shows **positive correlation**. In this case, it means that the higher the temperature, the more hours of sunshine there are.

Looking at both graphs together, what do they tell you about the effects of changes in temperature?

From the graph on the left, high rainfall means low temperature. From the graph on the right, low temperature means little sunshine. So, you can deduce that high rainfall means little sunshine. That is, rainfall and sunshine are negatively correlated. The graph opposite illustrates this.

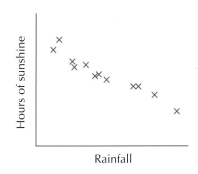

The graph on the right shows **no correlation** between the temperature and the number of fish caught daily off Rhyl – as you might expect.

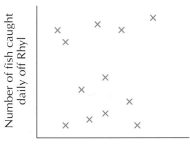

Here is a table which gives you the rules for combining two scatter graphs, which have a common axis, to obtain the resulting correlation.

	Positive correlation	No correlation	Negative correlation
Positive correlation	Positive	No correlation	Negative
No correlation	No correlation	*Cannot tell*	No correlation
Negative correlation	Negative	No correlation	Positive

As you may see from the table, the new graph can have its axes in either order, as this does not affect the correlation.

To remember these rules, think of the rules for multiplying together positive and negative numbers. See below.

Multiply (×)	+	0	–
+	+	0	–
0	0	*The exception*	0
–	–	0	+

1 In a competition there are three sections, P, Q and R. Copy and complete the table below for each correlation between Q and R.

	Correlation between P and Q	Correlation between P and R	Correlation between Q and R
a	Positive	Negative	
b	Negative	No correlation	
c	Negative	Negative	
d	No correlation	No correlation	
e	Positive	Positive	
f	No correlation	Negative	
g	Negative	Positive	
h	No correlation	Positive	
i	Positive	No correlation	

2 A post office compares the cost of postage with the weight of each parcel and also the cost of postage with the size of each parcel. The results are shown on the scatter graphs below.

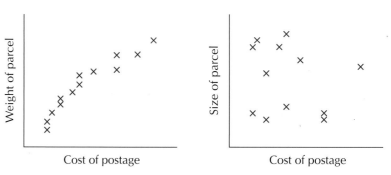

a Describe the type of correlation between the weight of parcels and the cost of postage.

b Describe the type of correlation between the size of parcels and the cost of postage.

c Describe the relationship between the weight of parcels and the size of parcels.

d Draw a scatter graph to show the correlation between the weight of parcels and the size of parcels. (Plot about ten points for your graph.)

3 A student compared the ages of a group of men with the length of their hair and also with their weights. His results are shown on the two scatter graphs.

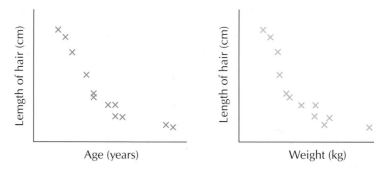

a Describe the type of correlation between the length of hair and age.

b Describe the type of correlation between the length of hair and weight.

c Describe the relationship between age and weight.

d Draw a scatter graph to show the correlation between age and weight. (Plot about ten points for your graph.)

Collect test marks for ten students in three different subjects: for example, mathematics, science and art. Draw the scatter graphs for mathematics/science, mathematics/art and science/art. Comment on your results. You may wish to use a table to show the test marks.

	Student 1	Student 2	Student 3	Student 4	Student 5	Student 6	Student 7	Student 8	Student 9	Student 10
Maths										
Science										
Art										

Scatter graphs and lines of best fit

Look at the two scatter graphs below. One shows a positive correlation and one shows a negative correlation, which you met in the previous lesson.

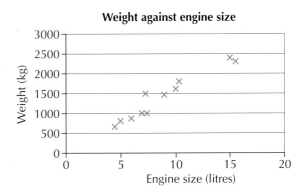

A **line of best fit** shows a trend on a scatter graph. Predictions, or estimates, can then be made using the line of best fit to show what might happen in certain circumstances.

To draw a line of best fit, first look at the correlation to decide which direction to draw the line. Then, using a ruler, draw a straight line between all the plotted points, passing as close as possible to all of them. Each line should have approximately equal numbers of points on each side.

All the lines of best fit which you will meet will be straight, ruled lines to show positive or negative correlation.

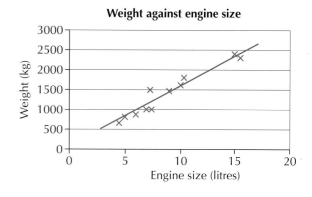

0–60 time against engine size

Weight against engine size

Example 5.1 The table shows the marks obtained by ten students in their maths and science tests.

a Draw a scatter graph to show the results.

b Draw a line of best fit

c Sarah scored 70 in her maths test but was absent for the science test. Use the line of best fit to estimate the result she would have obtained in science.

Student	1	2	3	4	5	6	7	8	9	10
Maths	32	75	53	76	25	62	85	48	39	50
Science	41	80	44	60	30	57	63	48	47	56

a

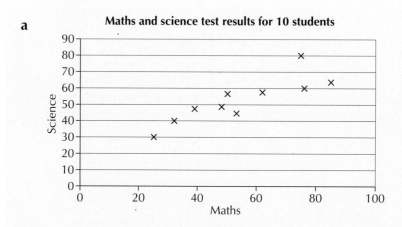

Maths and science test results for 10 students

b

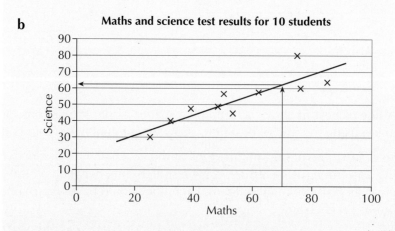

Maths and science test results for 10 students

c The estimate of Sarah's science mark is 62.

1 The table shows the scores of some students in a mental test and in a written test.

Student	Andy	Betty	Chris	Darren	Eve	Frank	Gina	Harry	Ingrid	Jack
Mental	12	16	21	25	20	11	17	14	13	19
Written	24	29	33	12	35	18	45	25	28	36

    a Plot the data on a scatter graph. Use the x-axis for the mental test from 0 to 30, and the y-axis for the written test from 0 to 50.

    b Draw a line of best fit.

    c One person did not do as well as expected on the written test. Who do you think it was? Give a reason.

2 The table shows the age of a group of home-owners and the distance that they live from their local shops.

Name	Kylie	Liam	Mick	Norris	Ollie	Philip	Qaysar	Richard	Steven	Trevor
Age (years)	18	22	28	34	40	42	50	56	65	72
Distance from shops (miles)	2.5	2	3	1.8	2.4	1.9	2.5	0.5	0.3	0.2

    a Plot the data on a scatter graph. Use the x-axis for the age (years) from 0 to 80, and the y-axis for the distance from the shops from 0 to 5 miles.

    b Draw a line of best fit.

    c State what you think your line of best fit tells you about this group of people.

3 A survey is carried out to compare students' ages with the amount of money that they spend each week.

Age (years)	10	10	11	11	12	12	12	14	14	15
Amount spent each week (£)	5	8	7	9.50	10	12	6	14	15	13

    a Plot the data on a scatter graph. Use the x-axis for age from 8 years to 20 years, and the y-axis for amount spent from £0 to £15.

    b Draw a line of best fit.

    c Use your line of best fit to estimate how much a 13-year-old would spend each week.

Extension Work

Look again at Questions **2** and **3**.

For Question **2**, explain why it might not be sensible to use your line of best fit to estimate the distance from the shops for a young child.

For Question **3**, explain why it would not be sensible to use your line of best fit to estimate the amount spent each week for a 20-year-old.

Time series graphs

A time series graph is any graph which has a time scale.

Look at the graphs below to see whether you can match each graph to one of the statements listed after graph 5.

Graph 1: Mean temperature difference from normal for UK in 2002

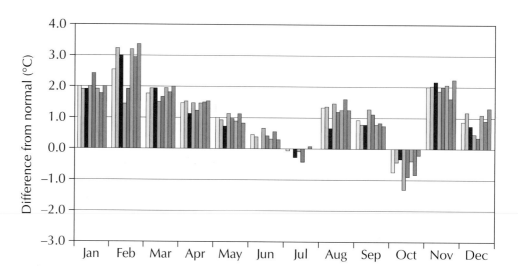

Graph 2: Average annual temperatures of Central England 1659–2001

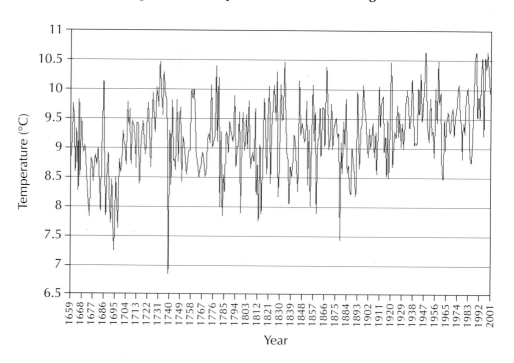

Graph 3: Monthly rainfall data for Perth, Australia

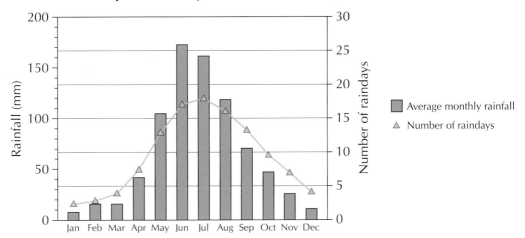

- ■ Average monthly rainfall
- △ Number of raindays

Graph 4: Monthly rainfall data for Brisbane, Australia

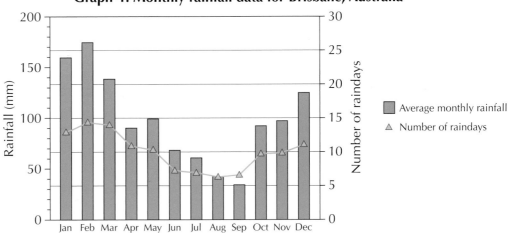

- ■ Average monthly rainfall
- △ Number of raindays

Graph 5: Monthly temperature data for Perth, Australia

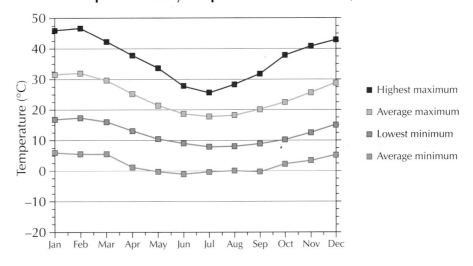

- ■ Highest maximum
- ■ Average maximum
- ■ Lowest minimum
- ■ Average minimum

Statement A: February is the hottest month here.

Statement B: October was colder than normal.

Statement C: September is a fairly dry month in Australia.

Statement D: This country is gradually getting warmer.

Statement E: The difference between the lowest and highest temperatures is least in July.

1 The time series graph shows the height to which a ball bounces against the time taken to reach that height.

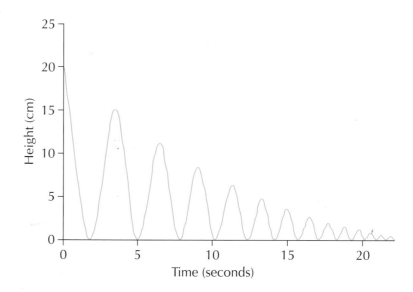

a Write a comment stating what happens to the length of time for which the ball is in the air after each bounce.

b This ball always bounces to a fixed fraction of its previous height. What fraction is this?

c After how many bounces does this ball bounce to less than half of the greatest height?

d In theory, how many bounces does the ball make before it comes to rest?

2 Look again at the graph showing the mean temperature changes in the UK for 2002.

a Use the graph to support an argument that global warming is taking place.

b Tammy says: 'The graph shows that global warming is taking place'. Give a reason why Tammy could be wrong.

3 Look again at the graphs showing the rainfall for Perth and Brisbane.

a Which month has the greatest rainfall in Perth?

b Which month has the least rainfall in Brisbane?

c Explain how you can tell that Perth and Brisbane are not in the same region.

d Which place, Perth or Brisbane, has more days of rainfall over the year? Show how you work it out.

Extension Work

Use an atlas, encyclopaedia or the Internet to find a graph on whose coordinates, shape and trend you would be able to comment.

Two-way tables

Jeff and Catherine go to the school car park and record data about the 80 cars parked there. Here is their record.

		Colour of cars				
		Red	**White**	**Blue**	**Black**	**Other**
Make of cars	**Peugeot**	8	1	4	1	4
	Ford	11	2	4	2	6
	Vauxhall	5	4	0	0	2
	Citroen	1	2	2	0	3
	Other	6	3	3	4	2

This is called a **two-way table.**

Example 5.2 Use the two-way table above to answer the questions about the cars in the car park.
  a   How many red Fords are there?
  b   How many Vauxhalls are not white?
  c   How many more blue Peugeots are there than white Citroens?

  a   There are 11 red Fords.
  b   There are 11 Vauxhalls but 4 are white, so 7 are not white.
  c   There are 4 blue Peugeots and 2 white Citroens, so there are 2 more blue Peugeots than white Citroens.

Example 5.3 An Internet company charges delivery for goods based on the type of delivery – normal delivery (taking 3 to 5 days) or next-day delivery – and also on the cost of the order. The table shows how it is calculated.

Cost of order	Normal delivery (3 to 5 days)	Next-day delivery
0–£10	£1.95	£4.95
£10.01–£30	£2.95	£4.95
£30.01–£50	£3.95	£6.95
£50.01–£75	£2.95	£4.95
Over £75	Free	£3.00

  a   Comment on the difference in delivery charges for normal and next-day delivery.
  b   Two items cost £5 and £29. How much would you save by ordering them together **i** using normal delivery and **ii** using next-day delivery?

  a   It always costs more using next-day delivery but for goods costing between £10.01 and £30, or between £50.01 and £75, it is only £2 more. It is £3 more for all other orders.
  b   Using normal delivery and ordering the items separately, it would cost £1.95 + £2.95 = £4.90, but ordering them together would cost £3.95. The saving would be £4.90 – £3.95 = 95p.

   Using next-day delivery and ordering the items separately, it would cost £4.95 + £4.95 = £9.90, but ordering them together would cost £6.95. The saving would be £9.90 – £6.95 = £2.95.

1 The cost of a set of old toys depends on whether the toys are still in the original boxes and also on the condition of the toys. The table shows the percentage value of a toy compared with its value if it is in perfect condition and boxed.

Condition	Boxed	Not boxed
Excellent	100%	60%
Very good	80%	50%
Good	60%	40%
Average	40%	25%
Poor	20%	10%

a Copy and complete the table.

Condition	Difference between boxed and not boxed
Excellent	100% − 60% = 40%
Very good	
Good	
Average	
Poor	

b Explain the effect of the set being boxed compared with the condition of the toys.

2 The table shows the percentage of boys and girls by age group who have a mobile phone.

a Comment on any differences between boys and girls.

b Comment on any other trends that you notice.

Age	Boys	Girls
10	18%	14%
11	21%	18%
12	42%	39%
13	53%	56%
14	56%	59%
15	62%	64%

3 A school analyses the information on the month of birth for 1000 students. The results are shown in the table.

Month	Jan	Feb	Mar	Apr	May	Jun	Jul	Aug	Sep	Oct	Nov	Dec
Boys	34	36	43	39	47	50	44	39	55	53	42	35
Girls	37	31	36	35	44	43	36	40	52	49	43	37

a On the same grid, plot both sets of values to give a time series graph for the boys and another for the girls.

b Use the graphs to examine the claim that more children are born in the summer than in the winter.

4 The heights of 70 Year 9 students are recorded. Here are the results given to the nearest centimetre.

Height (cm)	Boys	Girls
130–139	3	3
140–149	2	4
150–159	10	12
160–169	14	11
170–179	6	5

Use the results to examine the claim that boys are taller than girls in Year 9. You may use a frequency diagram to help you.

Extension Work

Look back at the two-way table on page 91. If a car is chosen at random, what is the probability that it is one of the following?

a Peugeot

b Red

c Red Peugeot

d Not blue

e Not a Ford

Cumulative frequency diagrams

In this section, you will learn how to draw cumulative frequency diagrams for large sets of grouped data. You will also find out how to use these to obtain estimates of the median and the interquartile range.

'Cumulative' means to build up or to accumulate.

Example 5.4 The table shows the waiting times of 100 people in a bus station.

Time waiting, T (min)	Number of passengers
$0 < T \leq 5$	14
$5 < T \leq 10$	35
$10 < T \leq 15$	26
$15 < T \leq 20$	18
$20 < T \leq 25$	7

a Draw a cumulative frequency diagram.

b Estimate the median and the interquartile range.

Example 5.4 ▷
continued

a First, you need to change the table from a **frequency** table into a **cumulative frequency** table. This is sometimes called a less than or less than or equal to cumulative frequency table.

There are 14 passengers with a waiting time of less than or equal to 5 minutes.

There are 14 + 35 = 49 passengers with a waiting time of less than or equal to 10 minutes.

Continue to build up until the table is complete for 100 passengers:

Time waiting, T (min)	Cumulative frequency
$T \leq 5$	14
$T \leq 10$	14 + 35 = 49
$T \leq 15$	49 + 26 = 75
$T \leq 20$	75 + 18 = 93
$T \leq 25$	93 + 7 = 100

Now plot this information onto a cumulative frequency graph, starting with (0, 0), (5, 14), (10, 49) and so on.

The points can be joined up with straight lines or a curve.

To estimate the median, read off from the graph at the mid-value of the cumulative frequency. In this case, read off at 50.

This gives the median as 10.2 minutes.

To estimate the interquartile range, first obtain the values of the lower quartile and the upper quartile.

To estimate the lower quartile, read off from the graph at the one-quarter value of the cumulative frequency, which is 25. This gives the lower quartile as 6.6 minutes.

To estimate the upper quartile, read off from the graph at the three-quarter value of the cumulative frequency, which is 75. This gives the upper quartile as 15 minutes.

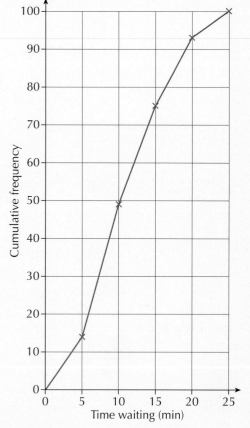

To work out the interquartile range:

Interquartile range = Upper quartile − Lower quartile
                 = 15 − 6.6
                 = 8.4 minutes.

For each table of data:

a   Copy and complete the cumulative frequency table.

b   Draw the cumulative frequency graph.

c   Use your graph to estimate the median and interquartile range.

1   The temperature over 100 days.

Temperature, T (°C)	Number of days	Temperature, T (°C)	Cumulative frequency
$0 < T \leq 5$	8	$T \leq 5$	
$5 < T \leq 10$	15	$T \leq 10$	
$10 < T \leq 15$	42	$T \leq 15$	
$15 < T \leq 20$	25	$T \leq 20$	
$20 < T \leq 25$	10	$T \leq 25$	

2   The time taken to walk to school by 40 students.

Time, t (min)	Number of students	Time, t (min)	Cumulative frequency
$0 < t \leq 5$	5	$t \leq 5$	
$5 < t \leq 10$	12	$t \leq 10$	
$10 < t \leq 15$	9	$t \leq 15$	
$15 < t \leq 20$	7	$t \leq 20$	
$20 < t \leq 25$	4	$t \leq 25$	
$25 < t \leq 30$	3	$t \leq 30$	

3   The mass of 80 sacks of potatoes

Mass, M (kg)	Number of sacks	Mass, M (kg)	Cumulative frequency
$23 < M \leq 24$	0	$M \leq 24$	
$24 < M \leq 25$	15	$M \leq 25$	
$25 < M \leq 26$	31	$M \leq 26$	
$26 < M \leq 27$	22	$M \leq 27$	
$27 < M \leq 28$	12	$M \leq 28$	

Estimation of a mean from grouped data

You are now going to learn how to estimate a **mean** from a table of **grouped data**.

When data is grouped, it is not possible to calculate an exact value for the mean, as you do not have the exact value of each piece of data.

Example 5.5

The times for 100 cyclists to complete a 200 metres time trial are grouped in the table.

Obtain an estimate for the mean time.

Time, t (seconds)	Frequency, f
$13 < T \le 14$	12
$14 < T \le 15$	21
$15 < T \le 16$	39
$16 < T \le 17$	20
$17 < T \le 18$	8

Because the data is grouped, you have to assume that in each class the data is centred on the mid-class value.

This means, for example, that in the first class $13 < T \le 14$, you assume that there are 12 cyclists with times around 13.5 seconds (the mid-value of the class).

Add an extra column to the table to give:

Time, t (seconds)	Frequency, f	Mid-value, x, of time (seconds)
$13 < T \le 14$	12	13.5
$14 < T \le 15$	21	14.5
$15 < T \le 16$	39	15.5
$16 < T \le 17$	20	16.5
$17 < T \le 18$	8	17.5

To calculate the mean time, you need to estimate the total time taken for each class.

For example, in the first class, you have 12 cyclists taking approximately 13.5 seconds. That is: $12 \times 13.5 = 162$ seconds.

Add a fourth column to show the total times for each class. Then add up these times to obtain:

Time, t (seconds)	Frequency, f	Mid-value, x, of time (seconds)	$f \times x$ (seconds)
$13 < T \le 14$	12	13.5	162
$14 < T \le 15$	21	14.5	304.5
$15 < T \le 16$	39	15.5	604.5
$16 < T \le 17$	20	16.5	330
$17 < T \le 18$	8	17.5	140
Total = 100			**Total = 1541**

Estimate of the total time taken by the 100 cyclists = 1541 seconds.

Estimate of the mean time = $\dfrac{1541}{100}$ = 15.41 seconds.

1 For each table of values given below:

    a   Rewrite the table with four columns, as shown in Example 5.5.

    b   Complete the table including the totals, as shown in Example 5.5.

    c   Obtain an estimate of the mean.

i

Mass, M (kg)	Frequency, f
$0 < M \leq 2$	8
$2 < M \leq 4$	11
$4 < M \leq 6$	10
$6 < M \leq 8$	5
$8 < M \leq 10$	6

ii

Length, L (cm)	Frequency, f
$20 < L \leq 24$	13
$24 < L \leq 28$	35
$28 < L \leq 32$	24
$32 < L \leq 36$	8

2 The temperature of a school swimming pool was recorded every day over a period of 100 days. The results are summarised in the table on the right.

Obtain an estimate of the mean temperature.

Temperature, T (°C)	Frequency, f
$0 < T \leq 10$	17
$10 < T \leq 20$	23
$20 < T \leq 30$	56
$30 < T \leq 40$	3
$40 < T \leq 50$	1

3 The times taken by 40 students to complete an obstacle course are given on the right.
Hint Be careful, these classes are different widths.

Time, t (min)	Frequency, f
$5 < t \leq 6$	8
$6 < t \leq 7$	10
$7 < t \leq 9$	11
$9 < t \leq 13$	5
$13 < t \leq 15$	6

Extension Work

For each of the questions above, find the class which contains the median.

What you need to know for level 6

- How to draw conclusions from scatter graphs
- Have a basic understanding of correlation

What you need to know for level 7

- How to draw a line of best fit on a scatter diagram by inspection

What you need to know for level 8

- How to interpret and construct cumulative frequency diagrams using the upper boundary of a class interval
- How to estimate the median and the interquartile range, and to use these to compare distributions and make inferences

National Curriculum SATs questions

LEVEL 6

1 *2002 Paper 2*

A newspaper wrote an article about public libraries in England and Wales. It published this diagram.

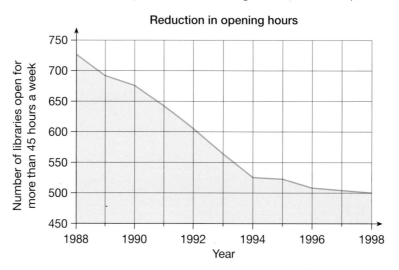

Reduction in opening hours

Use the diagram to decide whether each statement below is true or false, or whether you cannot be certain.

a The number of libraries open for more than 45 hours per week fell by more than half from 1988 to 1998.

[ ] True   [ ] False   [ ] Cannot be certain

Explain your answer.

b In 2004 there will be about 450 libraries open in England and Wales for more than 45 hours a week.

[ ] True   [ ] False   [ ] Cannot be certain

Explain your answer.

2   *1998 Paper 2*

A competition has three different games.

a   Jeff plays two games.

To win, Jeff needs a mean score of 60.

	Game A	Game B	Game C
Score	62	53	

How many points does he need to score in Game C? Show your working.

b   Imran and Nia play the three games.

Their scores have the same mean.

Imran's scores		40	
Nia's scores	35	40	45

The range of Imran's scores is twice
the range of Nia's scores. Copy the table above and fill in the missing scores.

The scatter diagrams show the scores of everyone who plays all three games.

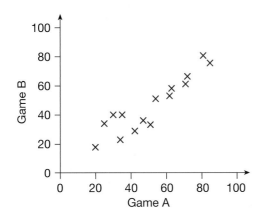 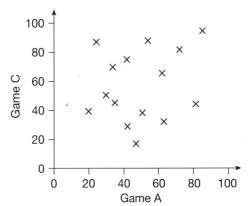

c   Look at the scatter diagrams.

Which statement most closely describes the relationship between the games?

Game A and Game B				
Perfect negative	Negative	No relationship	Positive	Perfect positive

Game A and Game C				
Perfect negative	Negative	No relationship	Positive	Perfect positive

d   What can you tell about the relationship between the scores on Game B and the scores on Game C?

Game B and Game C				
Perfect negative	Negative	No relationship	Positive	Perfect positive

LEVEL 7

3 *2003 Paper 1*

The scatter graph shows information about trees called poplars.

a What does the scatter graph show about the relationship between the diameter of the tree trunk and the height of the tree?

b The height of a different tree is 3 m. The diameter of its trunk is 5 cm. Use the graph to explain why this tree is not likely to be a poplar.

c Another tree is a poplar. The diameter of its trunk is 3.2 cm. Estimate the height of this tree.

d Below are some statements about drawing lines of best fit on scatter graphs. Copy each statement, and then tick it to show whether the statement is True or False.

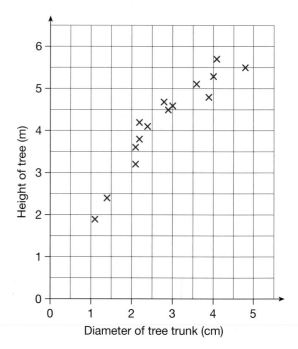

Lines of best fit must always …

go throught the origin.   True ☐   False ☐

have a positive gradient.   True ☐   False ☐

join the smallest and the largest values. True ☐   False ☐

pass through every point on the graph.   True ☐   False ☐

4 *2001 Paper 2*

The goldcrest is Britain's smallest species of bird.

On winter days, a goldcrest must eat enough food to keep it warm at night. During the day, the mass of the bird increases.

The scatter diagram shows the mass of goldcrests at different times during winter days. It also shows the line of best fit.

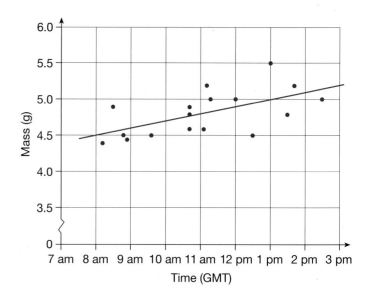

a Estimate the mass of a goldcrest at 11:30 am.

b Estimate how many grams, on average, the mass of a goldcrest increases during one hour.

c Which goldcrest represented on the scatter diagram is least likely to survive the night if it is cold?

Give your coordinates of the correct point on the scatter diagram. Then explain why you chose that point.

5 *1997 Paper 1*

The scatter diagram shows the total amounts of sunshine and rainfall for twelve seaside towns during one summer. Each town has been given a letter.

The dashed lines go through the mean amounts of sunshine and rainfall.

a Which town's rainfall was closest to the mean?

b On a copy of the scatter diagram, draw a line of best fit.

Use your line to find an estimate of the hours of sunshine for a seaside town that had 30 cm of rain.

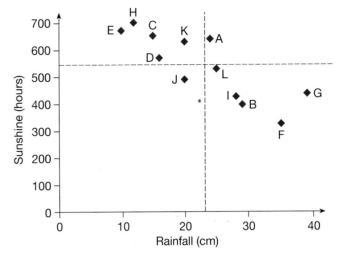

LEVEL 8

6 *2001 Paper 1*

The first 'Thomas the Tank Engine' stories were written in 1945. In the 1980s, the stories were rewritten.

The cumulative frequency graph shows the number of words per sentence for one of the stories.

There are 58 sentences in the old version.

There are 68 sentences in the new version.

a Estimate the median number of words per sentence in the old version and in the new version.

Show your method on the graph.

b What can you tell from the data about the number of words per sentence in the old version and in the new version?

c Estimate the percentage of sentences in the old version that had more than 12 words per sentence. Show your working.

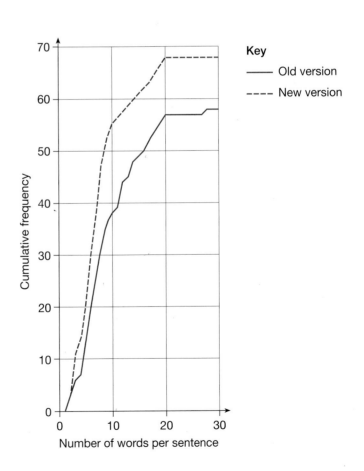

7 *1997 Paper 1*

Forty students worked on a farm one weekend. The cumulative frequency graph shows the distribution of the amount of money they earned. No one earned less than £15.

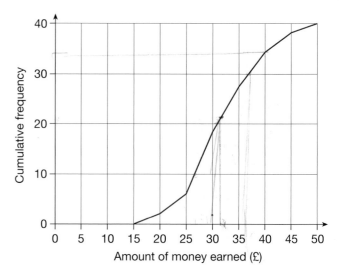

a Read the graph to estimate the median amount of money earned.

b Estimate the percentage of students who earned less than £40.

c Show on the graph how to work out the interquartile range of the amount of money earned. Write down the value of the interquartile range.

d Thirty of the students work on the farm another weekend later in the year. The tables below show the distribution of the amount of money earned by the students.

Money earned (£)	No. of students
≥ 25 and < 30	1
≥ 30 and < 35	2
≥ 35 and < 40	3
≥ 40 and < 45	4
≥ 45 and < 50	10
≥ 50 and < 55	7
≥ 55 and < 60	3

Money earned (£)	No. of students
< 25	0
< 30	1
< 35	3
< 40	6
< 45	10
< 50	20
< 55	27
< 60	30

Draw a cumulative frequency graph using the axes below.

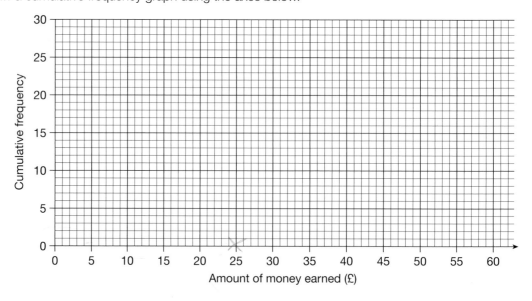

e Copy the following statements:

Put a ✔ by any statement below which is true.

Put a ✗ by any statement below which is false.

   A   Three of the students earned less than £35 each.

   B   The median amount earned is between £40 and £45.

   C   Most of the 30 students earned more than £50 each.

8 *2003 Paper 1*

Tom did a survey of the age distribution of people at a theme park. He asked 160 people. The cumulative frequency graph shows his results.

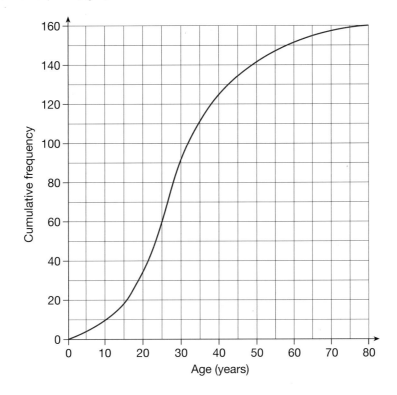

a   Use the graph to estimate the median age of people at the theme park.

b   Use the graph to estimate the interquartile range of the age of people at the theme park. Show your method on the graph.

c   Tom did a similar survey at a flower show. Results:

   The median age was 47 years.

   The interquartile range was 29 years.

Compare the age distribution of the people at the flower show with that of the people at the theme park.

Shape, Space and Measures **2**

This chapter is going to show you	**What you should already know**
<ul><li>how to solve problems using similar triangles</li><li>how to convert from one metric unit to another for area and volume</li><li>how to calculate the length of arcs and the area of sectors</li><li>how to calculate the volume of a cylinder</li><li>how to solve problems involving speed</li></ul>	<ul><li>How to use ratio</li><li>How to find alternate and corresponding angles in parallel lines</li><li>The metric units for area and volume</li><li>The formulae for the circumference and the area of a circle</li><li>How to calculate the volume of a prism</li></ul>

Similar triangles

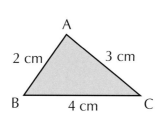
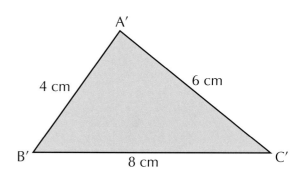

Triangle ABC has been mapped onto triangle A'B'C' by an enlargement of scale factor 2.

Under an enlargement, all of the angles are the same size, and the corresponding sides are in the same ratio.

So in this example, AB : A′B′ = AC : A′C′ = BC : B′C′ = 1 : 2.

This can also be written as $\frac{A'B'}{AB} = \frac{A'C'}{AC} = \frac{B'C'}{BC} = 2$.

The two triangles are said to be **similar.**

Two triangles are similar if their angles are the same size, or if their corresponding sides are in the same ratio. If one of these conditions is true, then so is the other.

Example 6.1

Show that the two triangles below are similar.

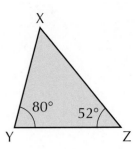

In triangle ABC, ∠C = 80° (the sum of the angles in a triangle = 180°). In triangle XYZ, ∠X = 48° (the sum of the angles in a triangle = 180°).

Since the angles in both triangles are the same, triangle ABC is similar to triangle XYZ.

Example 6.2

Triangle ABC is similar to triangle DEF. Calculate the length of the side DF.

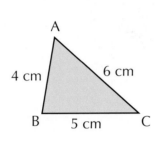

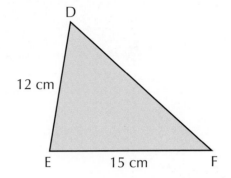

Let the side DF = x.

Since the triangles are similar, corresponding sides are in the same ratio.

So, $\dfrac{DE}{AB} = \dfrac{EF}{BC} = \dfrac{DF}{AC} = 3$.

Therefore, since $\dfrac{DF}{AC} = 3$, $\dfrac{x}{6} = 3$.

So, x = 18 cm.

Example 6.3

In the triangle below, EB is parallel to DC. Calculate the length of DC.

∠AEB = ∠ADC (corresponding angles in parallel lines) and ∠ABE = ∠ACD (corresponding angles in parallel lines).

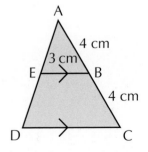

So, triangle AEB is similar to triangle ADC since the angles are the same size (∠A is common to both triangles).

Let the side DC = x.

Since triangle AEB is similar to triangle ADC, corresponding sides are in the same ratio.

So, $\dfrac{DC}{EB} = \dfrac{AC}{AB}$.

Therefore, $\dfrac{x}{3} = \dfrac{8}{4} = 2$.

So, $x = 2 \times 3 = 6$ cm.

1 State whether each of the pairs of triangles below are similar.

a

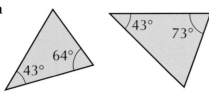

b

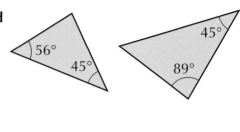

c

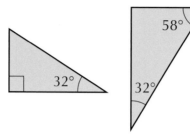

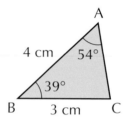

d

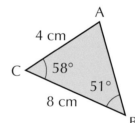

2 **a** Explain why triangle ABC is similar to triangle XYZ.

b Find the length of XY.

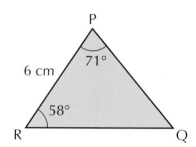

3 **a** Explain why triangle ABC is similar to triangle PQR.

b Find the length of the side QR.

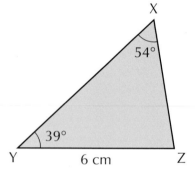

4 In the diagram on the right, ST is parallel to QR.

a Explain why triangle PST is similar to triangle PQR.

b Find the length of the side ST.

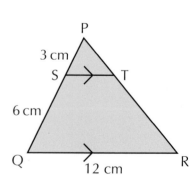

5 In the diagram on the right, AB is parallel to DE.

a Explain why triangle ABC is similar to triangle CDE.

b Find the length of the side DE.

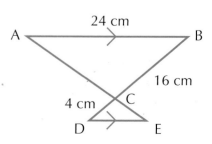

6 In the diagram on the right, LM is parallel to PQ. Given that OL = 15 cm, OQ = 10 cm and PQ = 8 cm, find the length of LM.

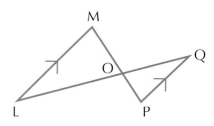

7 Use similar triangles to find the height of the tower in the diagram below.

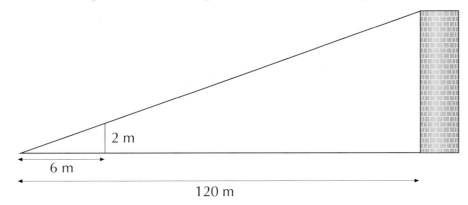

2 m

6 m

120 m

8 The rope on the pair of stepladders, shown on the right, stops the steps from opening too far. Use similar triangles to find the length of the rope.

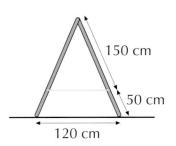

150 cm

50 cm

120 cm

1 In each of the following, write down the pair of similar triangles and find the length marked *x*.

a

A
5 cm
B   C
3 cm
10 cm
D   E
x

b

P
S
15 cm
10 cm
Q   *x*   T   12 cm   R

c

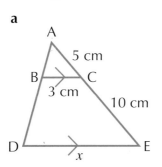

X
V
16 cm
12 cm
Y   15 cm   W   *x*   Z

d

J
x
K   L
3 cm
10 cm
M   9 cm   N

2 This question will show you how to divide a line in a given ratio.

Divide the line AB in the ratio 1:4

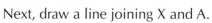

- Firstly, draw a line XB 5 cm in length in the ratio
  XY:YB = 1 cm : 4 cm.
- Next, draw a line joining X and A.
- Now, draw a line parallel to XA from the point Y to meet AB at C.
- Point C divides the line AB in the ratio 1 : 4

Use this method to divide four lines of any length in the following ratios:

a 1 : 3   **b** 1 : 5   **c** 2 : 3   **d** 3 : 5

Metric units for area and volume

The following are the metric units for area, volume and capacity which you need to know. Also given are the conversions between these units.

Area	Volume	Capacity
$10\,000\ \text{m}^2 = 1$ hectare (ha)	$1\,000\,000\ \text{cm}^3 = 1\ \text{m}^3$	$1\ \text{m}^3 = 1000$ litres (l)
$10\,000\ \text{cm}^2 = 1\ \text{m}^2$	$1000\ \text{mm}^3 = 1\ \text{cm}^3$	$1000\ \text{cm}^3 = 1$ litre
$1\,\text{m}^2 = 1\,000\,000\ \text{mm}^2$		$1\ \text{cm}^3 = 1$ millilitre (ml)
$100\ \text{mm}^2 = 1\ \text{cm}^2$		10 millilitres = 1 centilitre (cl)
		1000 millilitres = 100 centilitres = 1 litre

The unit symbol for litres is the letter l. To avoid confusion with the digit 1 (one), the full unit name may be used instead of the symbol.

Remember:

To change **large** units to **smaller** units, **always multiply** by the conversion factor.

To change **small** units to **larger** units, **always divide** by the conversion factor.

Example 6.4 ▷ Convert each of the following as indicated.

a 72 000 cm² to m²   **b** 0.3 cm³ to mm³   **c** 4500 cm³ to litres

a 72 000 cm² = 72 000 ÷ 10 000 = 7.2 m²

b 0.3 cm³ = 0.3 × 1000 = 300 mm³

c 4500 cm³ = 4500 ÷ 1000 = 4.5 litres

1 Express each of the following in cm².

    a   4 m²   **b**   7 m²   **c**   20 m²   **d**   3.5 m²   **e**   0.8 m²

2 Express each of the following in mm².

    a   2 cm²   **b**   5 cm²   **c**   8.5 cm²   **d**   36 cm²   **e**   0.4 cm²

3 Express each of the following in cm².

    a   800 mm²   **b**   2500 mm²   **c**   7830 mm²   **d**   540 mm²   **e**   60 mm²

4 Express each of the following in m².

    a   20 000 cm²   **b**   85 000 cm²   **c**   270 000 cm²   **d**   18 600 cm²
    e   3480 cm²

5 Express each of the following in mm³.

    a   3 cm³   **b**   10 cm³   **c**   6.8 cm³   **d**   0.3 cm³   **e**   0.48 cm³

6 Express each of the following in m³.

    a   5 000 000 cm³   **b**   7 500 000 cm³   **c**   12 000 000 cm³
    d   650 000 cm³   **e**   2000 cm³

7 Express each of the following in litres.

    a   8000 cm³   **b**   17 000 cm³   **c**   500 cm³   **d**   3 m³   **e**   7.2 m³

8 Express each of the following as indicated.

    a   85 ml in cl   **b**   1.2 litres in cl   **c**   8.4 cl in ml
    d   4500 ml in litres   **e**   2.4 litres in ml

9 How many square paving slabs, each of side 50 cm, are needed to cover a rectangular yard measuring 8 m by 5 m?

10 A football pitch measures 120 m by 90 m. Find the area of the pitch in

    a   m² and   **b**   hectares.

11 A fish tank is 1.5 m long, 40 cm wide and 25 cm high. How many litres of water will it hold if it is filled to the top?

12 The volume of the cough medicine bottle is 240 cm³. How many days will the cough medicine last?

13 How many lead cubes of side 2 cm can be cast from 4 litres of molten lead?

COUGH
MEDICINE

Two 5 ml spoonfuls to be
taken four times a day

1 A farmer has 100 m of fencing to enclose his sheep. He uses the wall for one side of the rectangular sheep-pen. If each sheep requires 5 m² of grass inside the pen, what is the greatest number of sheep that the pen can hold?

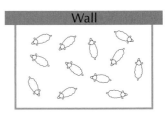
Wall

2
12 inches = 1 foot
3 feet = 1 yard

Use this information to find:

a the number of square inches in one square yard.

b the number of cubic inches in one cubic yard.

3 What is an acre? Use reference books or the Internet to find out.

Length of an arc and area of a sector

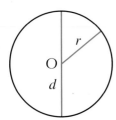

In Year 8, you found how to calculate the circumference and the area of a circle using the formulae:

$$C = \pi d = 2\pi r$$
$$A = \pi r^2$$

where $\pi = 3.142$, or use the $\boxed{\pi}$ key on your calculator.

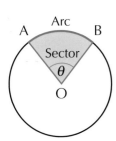

The arc, AB, is part of the circumference. The sector AOB is a slice of the circle enclosed by the arc AB, and the radii OA and OB.

∠AOB is the angle of the sector, and is usually denoted by the Greek letter θ (pronounced *theta*).

The length of the arc AB, as a fraction of the circumference, is $\dfrac{\theta}{360}$.

So, the length of the arc AB $= \dfrac{\theta}{360} \times \pi d$.

Similarly, the area of the sector AOB $= \dfrac{\theta}{360} \times \pi r^2$.

Example 6.5

Calculate:

a The length of the arc AB.

b The area of the sector AOB.

Give your answers correct to three significant figures.

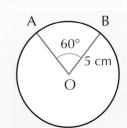

a Length of the arc AB $= \dfrac{60}{360} \times \pi \times 10 = 5.24$ cm (3 s.f.).

b Area of the sector AOB $= \dfrac{60}{360} \times \pi \times 5^2 = 13.1$ cm² (3 s.f.).

In this exercise, let π = 3.142 or use the π key on your calculator.

1 For each of the circles below, calculate:

a The length of the arc.

b The area of the sector.

Give your answers correct to three significant figures.

i
60°
10 cm

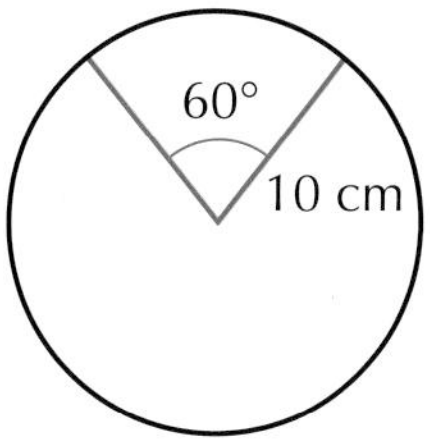

ii
45°
7 cm

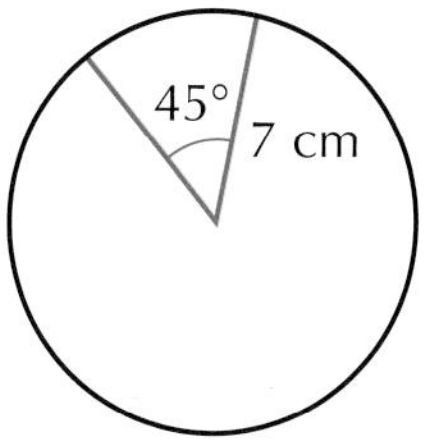

iii
12 cm
20°

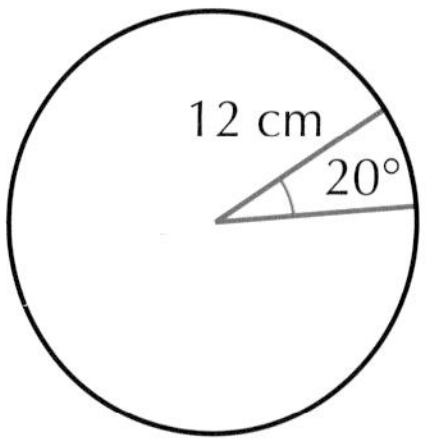

iv
4 m
75°

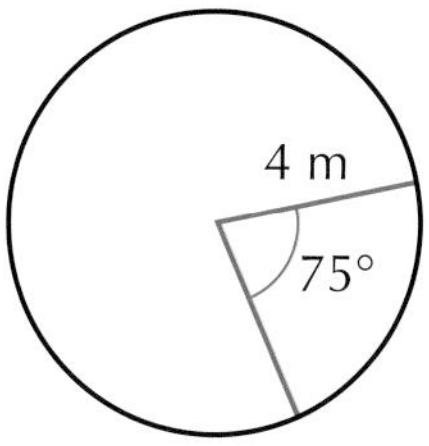

v
120°
2.5 m

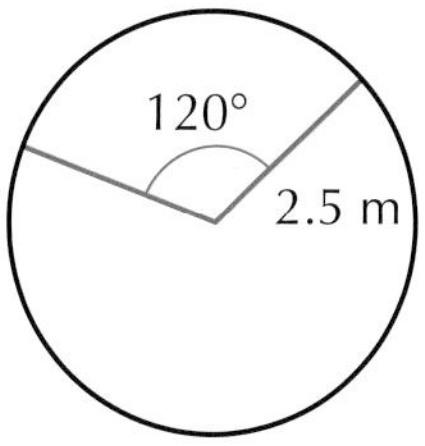

vi
7.2 m
150°

2 A flowerbed in a park is in the shape of a sector of a circle.

a Calculate the total perimeter of the flowerbed.

b Calculate the area of the flowerbed.

Give your answers correct to three significant figures.

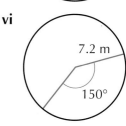
135°
5.4 m

3 Calculate the total perimeter of the 'Pacman' shape on the right. Give your answer to the nearest millimetre.

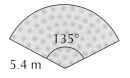
15 mm
60°

4 Calculate the area of the shaded segment on the right. Give your answer to the nearest square centimetre.

10 cm
10 cm

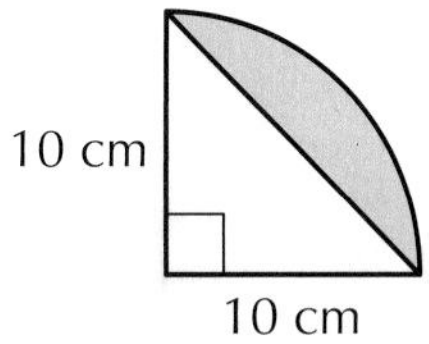

Extension Work

Calculate **i** the length of the arc and **ii** the area of the sector for each of the following circles.

Give your answers in terms of π.

a
60°
6 cm

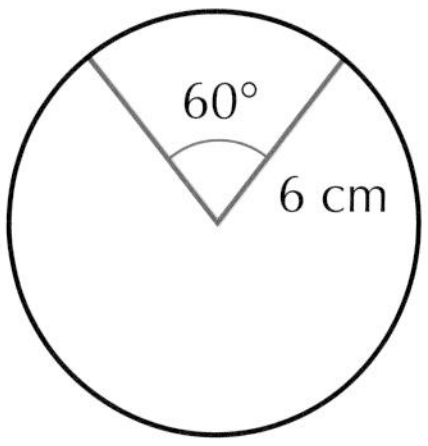

b
45°
16 cm

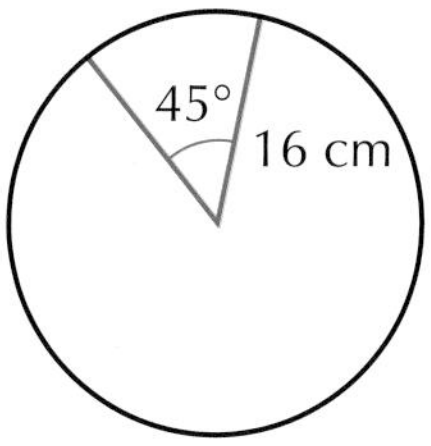

c
12 cm
30°

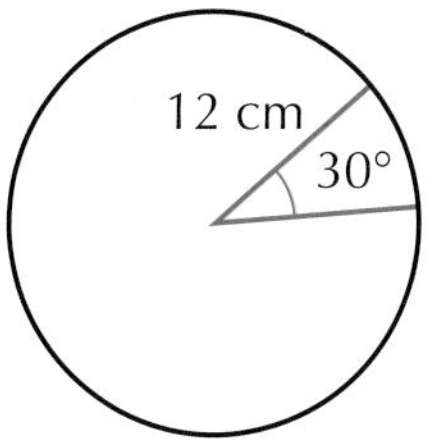

d
120°
9 cm

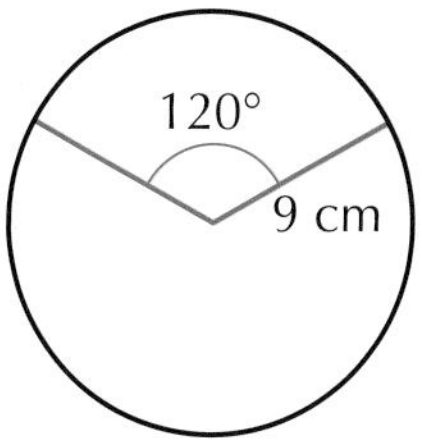

e
240°
3 cm

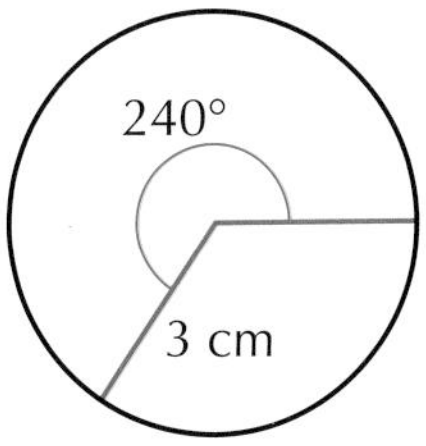

Volume of a cylinder

In Year 8 you found how to calculate the volume of a prism.

The volume V of a prism is found by multiplying the area A of its cross-section by its length l:

$V = Al$

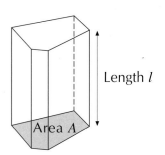

Length l

Area A

The cross-section of a cylinder is a circle with radius r.

The area of the cross-section is $A = \pi r^2$.

If the height of the cylinder is h, then the volume V for the cylinder is given by the formula:

$V = \pi r^2 \times h = \pi r^2 h$

Example 6.6

Calculate the volume of the cylinder, giving the answer correct to three significant figures.

$V = \pi \times 5^2 \times 8 = 628 \text{ cm}^3 \text{ (3 s.f.)}$

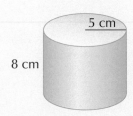

5 cm

8 cm

Exercise 6D

In this exercise take $\pi = 3.142$ or use the π key on your calculator.

1 Calculate the volume of each of the following cylinders. Give your answers correct to three significant figures.

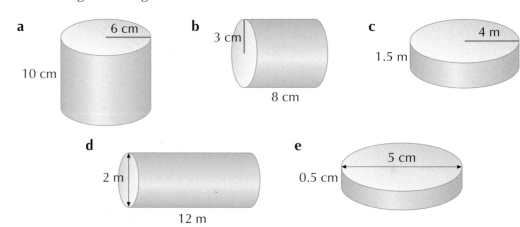

a 6 cm 10 cm

b 3 cm 8 cm

c 4 m 1.5 m

d 2 m 12 m

e 5 cm 0.5 cm

2 The diameter of a 2p coin is 2.6 cm and its thickness is 2 mm. Calculate the volume of the coin, giving your answer to the nearest cubic millimetre.

3 Three different shaped cake tins are shown below.

a

7 cm

24 cm

14 cm

b

25 cm

13 cm

8 cm

10 cm

c

20 cm

7.5 cm

Which cake tin has the greatest volume?

4 The diagram on the right shows a tea urn.

   a Calculate the volume of the urn, giving your answer in litres, correct to one decimal place.

   b A mug holds 25 cl of tea. How many mugs of tea can be served from the urn?

30 cm

50 cm

5 The diagram on the right shows a cylindrical paddling pool.

   a Calculate the volume of the pool, giving your answer in cubic metres, correct to three significant figures.

   b How many litres of water are in the pool when it is three quarters full? Give your answer to the nearest litre.

2 m

48 cm

6 The canister on the right has a capacity of 10 litres.

   a Write down the volume of the canister in cubic centimetres.

   b Calculate the area of the base of the canister.

   c Calculate the radius of the base of the canister, giving your answer correct to one decimal place.

40 cm

Capacity
10 l

Extension Work

In this exercise, take $\pi = 3.142$ or use the $\boxed{\pi}$ key on your calculator.

1 Surface area of a cylinder

When an open cylinder is cut and opened out, a rectangle is formed with the same length as the circumference of the base of the cylinder.

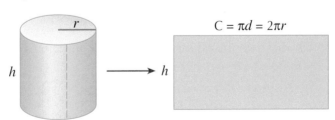

r

h

h

$C = \pi d = 2\pi r$

The curved surface area of the cylinder is the same as the area of the rectangle.

The area of the rectangle is $2\pi rh$.

The total surface area of the cylinder is the curved surface area plus the area of the circles at each end.

The formula for the total surface area of a cylinder is $A = 2\pi rh + 2\pi r^2$.

Use this formula to calculate the total surface area of the following cylinders. Give your answers correct to three significant figures.

a   b

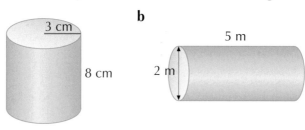

2   The volume of a can is to be 1000 cm³. The area of the metal used to make the can is to be kept to a minimum. What should the height and the radius of the can be?

A spreadsheet could be used to complete this question.

Rate of change

A **rate of change** is a way of comparing how one quantity changes with another. Examples of rates of change are:

Speed with units in miles per hour (mph), kilometres per hour (km/h) or metres per second (m/s).

Density with units in grams per cubic centimetre (g/cm³).

Fuel consumption with units in miles per gallon (mpg) or kilometres per litre (km/l).

Speed, distance and time

Speed is the distance travelled per unit of time. The relationships between speed, distance and time can be expressed by the following three formulae:

$$\text{Speed} = \frac{\text{Distance}}{\text{Time}} \qquad \text{Distance} = \text{Speed} \times \text{Time} \qquad \text{Time} = \frac{\text{Distance}}{\text{Speed}}$$

When we refer to speed, we usually mean **average speed**, as it is unusual to maintain the same exact speed in one journey.

The relationships between distance, D, time, T, and speed, S, can be remembered by using the triangle:

Covering up the quantity you want to find gives the three formulae you need:

$$S = \frac{D}{T} \qquad D = ST \qquad T = \frac{D}{S}$$

Example 6.7 ▷   A plane travels at an average speed of 500 mph. Find the distance travelled by the plane in $3\frac{1}{2}$ hours.

Using the formula $D = ST$, the distance travelled = $500 \times 3\frac{1}{2} = 1750$ miles.

Example 6.8 ▷ A coach travels 180 km on a motorway at an average speed of 80 km/h. Find the time taken for the journey.

Using the formula $T = \dfrac{D}{S}$, the time taken $= \dfrac{180}{80} = 2.25$ hours $= 2\frac{1}{4}$ hours or 2 hours 15 minutes.

Density

Density is the mass of a substance per unit of volume.

1 cm³ of gold has a mass of 19.3 g. We say that the density of gold is 19.3 g per cm³, written briefly as 19.3 g/cm³.

$$\text{Density} = \dfrac{\text{Mass}}{\text{Volume}}$$

The relationships between density, D, mass, M, and volume, V, can be remembered by using the triangle:

Covering up the quantity you want to find gives the three formulae you need:

$$D = \dfrac{M}{V} \qquad\qquad M = DV \qquad\qquad V = \dfrac{M}{D}$$

Example 6.9 ▷ The volume of a metal rod is 4 cm³ and its mass is 32 g. Find the density of the metal.

Using the formula $D = \dfrac{M}{V}$, the density of the metal is $\dfrac{32}{4} = 8$ g/cm³.

Example 6.10 ▷ Find the mass of a stone, which has a volume of 40 cm³ and a density of 2.25 g/cm³.

Using the formula $M = DV$, the mass of the stone $= 2.25 \times 40 = 90$ g.

Exercise 6E

1 An Intercity train has an average speed of 120 mph. Find the distance the train travels during the following times.

　　a　2 hours　　　　b　$1\frac{1}{2}$ hours　　　　c　15 minutes　　　　d　20 minutes

2 The road distance between Leeds and London is 210 miles. Find the average speed of a car for each of the following journey times between the two cities.

　　a　4 hours　　　　　　b　5 hours
　　c　$3\frac{1}{2}$ hours　　　　　d　3 hours 20 minutes

3 John's average cycling speed is 12 mph. Find the time it takes him to cycle the following distances.

　　a　36 miles　　　　b　30 miles　　　　c　40 miles　　　　d　21 miles

4 Copy and complete the following table.

	Distance travelled	Time taken	Average speed
a	150 miles	2 hours	
b	540 kilometres	$4\frac{1}{2}$ hours	
c		5 hours	25 mph
d		2 hours 15 minutes	100 km/h
e	250 metres		20 m/s
f	200 miles		60 mph

5 A gamekeeper fires his gun and the bullet travels at 120 m/s. Find the distance covered by the bullet in 1.8 seconds.

6 The distance between New York and San Francisco is 2550 miles. A plane takes off from New York at 7 am and lands at San Francisco at 11.15 am. Find the average speed of the plane.

7 Change each of the following speeds, given in kilometres per hour, to metres per second.

    a 36 km/h   **b** 90 km/h   **c** 120 km/h

8 If the density of a marble is 2.8 g/cm³, find the mass of a marble that has a volume of 56 cm³.

9 Find the volume of a liquid that has a mass of 6 kg and a density of 1.2 g/cm³. Give your answer in litres.

10 A 1 kg bag of sugar has a volume of 625 cm³. Find the density of the sugar in g/cm³.

SUGAR
1 kg

Extension Work

1 Frank travels 105 miles on a motorway. The first 30 miles of his journey are completed at an average speed of 60 mph. He then stops for 30 minutes at a service station before completing the final stage of his journey at an average speed of 50 mph.

Find the average speed for the whole of his journey.

2 A train travels at an average speed of 50 mph for 2 hours. It then slows down to complete the final 30 minutes of the journey at an average speed of 40 mph.

Find the average speed of the train for the whole journey.

3 Sue cycles to visit a friend who lives 30 km from her home. She cycles to her friend's house travelling at an average speed of 20 km/h and returns home travelling at an average speed of 15 km/h.

Find her average speed over the whole journey.

4 The density of kitchen foil is 2.5 g/cm³. A roll of kitchen foil is 10 m long, 30 cm wide and is 0.06 mm thick. Calculate the mass of the roll of foil.

5 A car uses petrol at a rate of 30 mpg.

a How far can the car travel on 3 gallons of petrol?

b How many gallons of petrol are required for a journey of 600 miles?

6 In Science, other measures for rates of change are used. Use reference books or the Internet to find the formulae and the units used for acceleration, pressure and power.

What you need to know for level 6

- How to use the formulae to calculate the circumference and the area of a circle
- The metric units for area, volume and capacity

What you need to know for level 7

- How to calculate the volume of a cylinder
- How to solve problems involving speed

What you need to know for level 8

- How to use similar triangles
- How to calculate the length of an arc and the area of a sector

National Curriculum SATs questions

LEVEL 6

1 *2001 Paper 2*

a A coach travels 300 miles at an average speed of 40 mph. For how many hours does the coach travel?

b An aeroplane flies 1860 miles in 4 hours. What is its average speed?

c A bus travels for $2\frac{1}{2}$ hours at an average speed of 24 mph. How far does the bus travel?

LEVEL 7

2 *2003 Paper 1*

The diagram shows the distance between my home, H, and the towns, A and B. It also shows information about journey times.

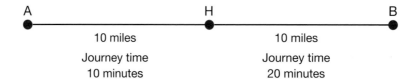

A   H   B

10 miles   10 miles

Journey time   Journey time
10 minutes   20 minutes

a What is the average speed of the journey from my home to town A?

b What is the average speed of the journey from my home to town B?

c I drive from town A to my home and then to town B. The journey time is 30 minutes. What is my average speed?

Show your working.

LEVEL 8

3 *2000 Paper 1*

a The triangles below are similar.

What is the value of p? Show your working.

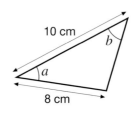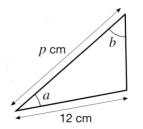

10 cm b p cm b Not drawn accurately

a a

8 cm   12 cm

b Triangles ABC and BDC are similar.

What is the length of CD?

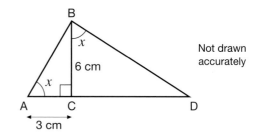

B

x

6 cm   Not drawn accurately

x

A   C   D

3 cm

c Look at the triangles on the right.

Are they similar? Show working to explain how you know.

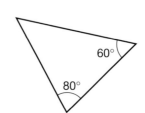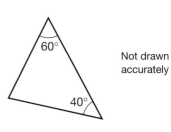

60°   60°   Not drawn accurately

80°   40°

4   *2001 Paper 2*

The diagram shows parts of two circles, sector A and sector B.

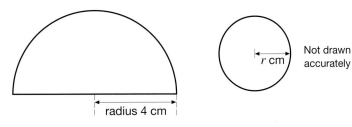

$\frac{1}{8}$ of a circle

A

radius 5 cm

$\frac{1}{5}$ of a circle

B

radius 4 cm

a   Which sector has the bigger area? Show working to explain your answer.

b   The perimeter of a sector is made from two straight lines and an arc. Which sector has the bigger perimeter?

Show working to explain your answer.

c   A semi-circle of radius 4 cm, has the same area as a complete circle of radius r cm.

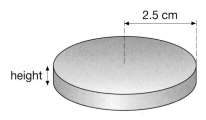

radius 4 cm

r cm

Not drawn accurately

What is the radius of the complete circle? Show your working.

5   *2003 Paper 2*

A cylinder has a radius of 2.5 cm. The volume of the cylinder, in cm³, is 4.5π.

What is the height of the cylinder? Show your working.

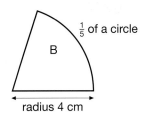

2.5 cm

height

This chapter is going to show you

- how to write numbers in standard form and how to calculate with them
- how to calculate with numbers given to different degrees of accuracy
- how to write recurring decimals as fractions

What you should already know

- How to multiply and divide by 10, 100, 0.1 and 0.01
- How to round numbers to various degrees of accuracy

Standard form

Standard form is a way of writing concisely very large and very small numbers such as those that occur in physics and astronomy. For example, 53 000 000 000 000 can be written as 5.3×10^{13}.

There are three things to remember about a number expressed in standard form. These are explained on the typical example given below.

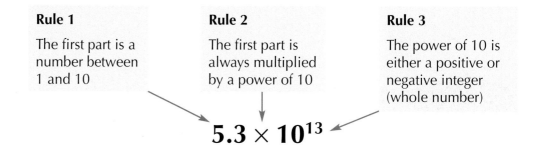

Rule 1

The first part is a number between 1 and 10

Rule 2

The first part is always multiplied by a power of 10

Rule 3

The power of 10 is either a positive or negative integer (whole number)

$$5.3 \times 10^{13}$$

In general, the standard form of a number is defined as:

$A \times 10^n$

where $1 \le A < 10$ and n is a positive or negative integer.

Examples of standard form are: radius of an electron, 2.82×10^{-15} m; mean radius of the earth, 6.4×10^6 m; speed of light, 2.998×10^8 m/s.

You have already met the way that calculators display numbers in standard form. For example, the number above may be displayed as:

5.3^{13}

Never write your answer in this way. You will **lose marks.**

Example 7.1   Express each of the following numbers in standard form.

   a   760 000   **b**   0.000 005 42   **c** 36×10^7 **d** 0.24×10^{-2}

   a   Count how many places the digits have to be moved to the right to get the number between 1 and 10:
   $$760\,000 = 7.6 \times 10^5$$

   b   Moving the digits to the left makes the power negative.
   $$0.000\,005\,42 = 5.42 \times 10^{-6}$$

   c 36×10^7 is not in standard form, as the first part is not a number between 1 and 10. So proceed as follows:
   $$36 \times 10^7 = 3.6 \times 10 \times 10^7 = 3.6 \times 10^8$$

   d   Proceed as in part **b**:
   $$0.24 \times 10^{-2} = 2.4 \times 10^{-1} \times 10^{-2} = 2.4 \times 10^{-3}$$

Example 7.2   Write each of the following standard form numbers as an ordinary number.

   a 3.45×10^6 **b** 8.9×10^{-2} **c** 7.632×10^4

   a   Move the digits to the left the same number of places as the power of 10:
   $$3.45 \times 10^6 = 3.45 \times 1\,000\,000 = 3\,450\,000$$

   b   A negative power of 10 means move the digits to the right:
   $$8.9 \times 10^{-2} = 8.9 \times 0.01 = 0.089$$

   c   Proceed as in part **a**:
   $$7.632 \times 10^4 = 7.632 \times 10\,000 = 76\,320$$

Exercise 7A

1   Write each of the following numbers in standard form. (All have positive powers of 10.)

   a   5 690   **b**   1 200 000   **c**   938 000   **d**   77 800
   e   396 500 000   **f**   561   **g**   73   **h**   4 300 000 000

2   Write each of the following numbers in standard form. (All have negative powers of 10.)

   a   0.0034   **b**   0.056   **c**   0.0000371   **d**   0.0000092
   e   0.76   **f**   0.0005   **g**   0.0000072   **h**   0.0004

3   Write each of the following numbers in standard form. (These have a mixture of positive and negative powers of 10.)

   a   8 900 000   **b**   0.0053   **c**   18 000   **d**   33 300 000
   e   0.0000067   **f**   8 923   **g**   0.735   **h**   0.00009

4 Write each of the following standard form numbers as an ordinary number.

    a 2.3×10^6 **b** 4.56×10^2 **c** 6.7×10^5 **d** 3.59×10^3

    e 9×10^6 **f** 2.01×10^6 **g** 3.478×10^4 **h** 8.73×10^7

5 Write each of the following standard form numbers as an ordinary number.

    a 6.7×10^{-5} **b** 3.85×10^{-2} **c** 7.8×10^{-4} **d** 5.39×10^{-3}

    e 8×10^{-6} **f** 1.67×10^{-1} **g** 3.21×10^{-3} **h** 6.6×10^{-7}

6 Write each of the following standard form numbers as an ordinary number.

    a 4.6×10^3 **b** 5.766×10^{-2} **c** 9.3×10^2 **d** 1.22×10^{-3}

    e 5×10^4 **f** 3.05×10^{-1} **g** 4.82×10^6 **h** 5.43×10^{-2}

7 Write each of the following numbers in standard form.

    a 43×10^5 **b** 56.8×10^2 **c** 0.78×10^4 **d** 0.58×10^3

    e 94×10^{-5} **f** 20.1×10^{-5} **g** 0.8×10^{-3} **h** 80×10^{-3}

    i 25×10^{-4} **j** 0.56×10^{-2} **k** 0.67×10^5 **l** 35.9×10^3

8 Work out the numbers shown by these calculator displays.

    a 8.8^{02} **b** 5.32^{04} **c** 3.14^{-03} **d** 9.03^{-01}

    e 1.82^{-03} **f** 7.95^{06} **g** 5.04^{08} **h** 6.842^{-04}

Extension Work

Calculate, or use the Internet, to find out the following and write the answers in standard form.

a Average distance of the sun from the earth in kilometres.

b Width of a red blood cell.

c How many seconds there are in 70 years.

d The mass of an electron.

e The mass of a cubic metre of uranium in grams at 4°C.

Multiplying with numbers in standard form

Example 7.3 ▷ Calculate each of the following. Give your answer in standard form. Do not use a calculator.

a $(3 \times 10^3) \times (2 \times 10^4)$ **b** $(4 \times 10^2) \times (5 \times 10^3)$ **c** $(2.5 \times 10^{-3}) \times (6 \times 10^5)$

a Rewrite the problem as $3 \times 2 \times 10^3 \times 10^4$. Then multiply the numbers and add the powers of 10:
$$3 \times 2 \times 10^3 \times 10^4 = 6 \times 10^7$$

b After multiplying 4 by 5, this is not in standard form, so it needs to be converted:
$$4 \times 5 \times 10^2 \times 10^3 = 20 \times 10^5$$
$$20 \times 10^5 = 2 \times 10 \times 10^5 = 2 \times 10^6$$

c After multiplying 2.5 by 6, this is also not in standard form, so proceed as in part **b**:
$$2.5 \times 6 \times 10^{-3} \times 10^5 = 15 \times 10^2$$
$$= 1.5 \times 10 \times 10^2$$
$$= 1.5 \times 10^3$$

Example 7.4 ▷ Light from the sun takes about 8 minutes to reach the earth. Light travels at 299 792 kilometres per second. How far is the sun from the earth? Give your answer in standard form.

First, convert 8 minutes to seconds:
$$8 \text{ minutes} = 8 \times 60 = 480 \text{ seconds}$$

Then multiply speed of light by number of seconds to get distance of the sun from the earth:
$$480 \times 299\,792 = 144\,000\,000 = 1.44 \times 10^8 \text{ km (rounded to 3 sf)}$$

Example 7.5 ▷ Use a calculator to work out each of the following. Give your answer in standard form to 3 sf.

a $(3.74 \times 10^4) \times (2.49 \times 10^3)$ **b** $(1.255 \times 10^{-3}) \times (5.875 \times 10^{-2})$

The key on a calculator with which to enter standard form is usually **EXP** or **EE**

Remember that a negative power will need either the negative key **−** or the sign change key **+/−**.

So, to enter 3.74×10^4 press these keys: **3** **.** **7** **4** **EXP** **4**

Note the $\times$ sign is *not* pressed. If this key is pressed the wrong value is entered.

a Enter the following:

3 **.** **7** **4** **EXP** **4** **×** **2** **.** **4** **9** **EXP** **3** **=**

The display will be 93126000 or 9.3126^7.

When rounded to 3 sf, the answer is 9.31×10^7.

b Enter the following:

$$\boxed{1}\ \boxed{.}\ \boxed{2}\ \boxed{5}\ \boxed{5}\ \boxed{\text{EXP}}\ \boxed{3}\ \boxed{+/-}\ \boxed{\times}\ \boxed{5}\ \boxed{.}\ \boxed{8}\ \boxed{7}\ \boxed{5}\ \boxed{\text{EXP}}\ \boxed{2}\ \boxed{+/-}\ \boxed{=}$$

The display will be:

0.000073731 or 7.3731^{-5}

When rounded to 3 sf, the answer is 7.37×10^{-5}.

Exercise 7B

1 Do not use a calculator for this question. Work out each of the following and give your answer in standard form.

a $(2 \times 10^3) \times (4 \times 10^2)$ **b** $(3 \times 10^2) \times (4 \times 10^5)$ **c** $(4 \times 10^3) \times (2 \times 10^4)$

d $(3 \times 10^{-2}) \times (3 \times 10^{-3})$ **e** $(4 \times 10^{-5}) \times (8 \times 10^{-3})$ **f** $(6 \times 10^3) \times (7 \times 10^{-6})$

g $(4.2 \times 10^{-4}) \times (5 \times 10^2)$ **h** $(6.5 \times 10^4) \times (4 \times 10^{-2})$ **i** $(7 \times 10^6) \times (8 \times 10^{-4})$

j $(2.5 \times 10^6) \times (9 \times 10^{-2})$ **k** $(2.8 \times 10^5) \times (4 \times 10^{-3})$ **l** $(6 \times 10^3)^2$

2 You may use a calculator for this question. Work out each of the following and give your answer in standard form. Do not round off your answers.

a $(4.3 \times 10^4) \times (2.2 \times 10^5)$ **b** $(6.4 \times 10^2) \times (1.8 \times 10^5)$

c $(2.8 \times 10^2) \times (4.6 \times 10^7)$ **d** $(1.9 \times 10^{-3}) \times (2.9 \times 10^{-2})$

e $(7.3 \times 10^{-2}) \times (6.4 \times 10^6)$ **f** $(9.3 \times 10^4) \times (1.8 \times 10^{-6})$

g $(3.25 \times 10^4) \times (9.2 \times 10^{-1})$ **h** $(2.85 \times 10^4) \times (4.6 \times 10^{-2})$

i $(3.6 \times 10^2)^3$

3 You may use a calculator for this question. Work out each of the following and give your answer in standard form. Round your answer to three significant figures.

a $(2.35 \times 10^5) \times (4.18 \times 10^5)$ **b** $(1.78 \times 10^5) \times (4.09 \times 10^2)$

c $(9.821 \times 10^2) \times (7.402 \times 10^6)$ **d** $(2.64 \times 10^{-2}) \times (8.905 \times 10^{-5})$

e $(4.922 \times 10^4) \times (8.23 \times 10^{-8})$ **f** $(7.92 \times 10^3) \times (7.38 \times 10^{-6})$

g $(4.27 \times 10^{-3}) \times (6.92 \times 10^8)$ **h** $(2.65 \times 10^{-5}) \times (5.87 \times 10^{-2})$

i $(7.83 \times 10^6)^2$ **j** $(2.534 \times 10^{-2})^3$

4 Zip discs are used to store large amounts of information. One megabyte (Mb) is 1 million bytes.

How many bytes are there in a pack of five 250 Mb zip discs? Answer in standard form.

5 There are approximately 120 000 hairs on a human head. Each hair is about 1×10^{-5} metres in diameter.

If all the hairs on a head were laid side by side, what would the total width be?

Extension Work

Use the Internet to find out about very large numbers. Look up 'googol' on a search engine.

Note The name of the well-known search engine is google, which is pronounced in the same way.

Can you find the meaning of 'googolplex'?

What is the largest number of any practical use?

Dividing with numbers in standard form

Example 7.6 ▶ Calculate each of the following. Give your answer in standard form. Do not use a calculator.

    a $(3 \times 10^6) \div (2 \times 10^2)$ **b** $(4 \times 10^{-6}) \div (5 \times 10^{-3})$ **c** $(1.2 \times 10^5) \div (4 \times 10^{-2})$

    a Rewrite the problem as $(3 \div 2) \times (10^6 \div 10^2)$. Note that the numbers and the powers have been separated but there is still a multiplication sign between them. This is because standard form numbers are always expressed in this way.

    Divide the numbers and subtract the powers of 10, which gives:

$$(3 \div 2) \times (10^6 \div 10^2) = 1.5 \times 10^4.$$

    b $(4 \div 5) \times (10^{-6} \div 10^{-3}) = 0.8 \times 10^{-3}$. After dividing 4 by 5, this is not in standard form, so it needs to be converted:

$$0.8 \times 10^{-3} = 8 \times 10^{-1} \times 10^{-3} = 2 \times 10^{-4}$$

    c After dividing 1.2 by 4, this is also not in standard form, so proceed as in part **b**:

$$(1.2 \div 4) \times (10^5 \div 10^{-2}) = 0.3 \times 10^7$$
$$= 3 \times 10^{-1} \times 10^7$$
$$= 3 \times 10^6$$

Example 7.7 ▶ A nanometre is a billionth of a metre, or about $\frac{1}{25\,400\,000}$ inch. Write $1 \div 25\,400\,000$ as a number in standard form to three significant figures.

Doing the calculation on a calculator, the display may say:

    3.937^{-8} or 0.00000003937

When rounded and put into standard form, the answer is 3.94×10^{-8}.

Exercise 7C

1 Do not use a calculator for this question. Work out each of the following and give your answer in standard form.

    a $(6 \times 10^6) \div (2 \times 10^2)$ **b** $(3 \times 10^6) \div (4 \times 10^3)$ **c** $(4 \times 10^3) \div (2 \times 10^4)$
    d $(9 \times 10^{-2}) \div (3 \times 10^{-7})$ **e** $(4 \times 10^8) \div (8 \times 10^2)$ **f** $(6 \times 10^3) \div (5 \times 10^{-6})$
    g $(4.5 \times 10^{-4}) \div (5 \times 10^2)$ **h** $(1.6 \times 10^6) \div (4 \times 10^{-3})$ **i** $(8 \times 10^9) \div (5 \times 10^4)$
    j $(2.5 \times 10^{-3}) \div (5 \times 10^{-6})$ **k** $(2.8 \times 10^5) \div (4 \times 10^{-3})$ **l** $\sqrt{(9 \times 10^6)}$

2 You may use a calculator for this question. Work out each of the following and give your answer in standard form. Do not round off your answers.

    a $(8.1 \times 10^9) \div (1.8 \times 10^5)$ **b** $(6.48 \times 10^5) \div (1.6 \times 10^3)$
    c $(3.78 \times 10^2) \div (1.35 \times 10^7)$ **d** $(9.86 \times 10^{-3}) \div (2.9 \times 10^{-5})$
    e $(5.12 \times 10^{-2}) \div (6.4 \times 10^6)$ **f** $(2.88 \times 10^4) \div (4.8 \times 10^{-6})$
    g $(6.44 \times 10^4) \div (9.2 \times 10^{-1})$ **h** $(3.68 \times 10^4) \div (4.6 \times 10^{-2})$
    i $\sqrt[3]{(8 \times 10^6)}$

3 You may use a calculator for this question. Work out the following and give your answer in standard form. Round your answer to three significant figures.

a $(2.3 \times 10^8) \div (4.1 \times 10^3)$
b $(6.7 \times 10^5) \div (4.9 \times 10^2)$
c $(9.8 \times 10^2) \div (7.4 \times 10^6)$
d $(2.6 \times 10^{-2}) \div (8.9 \times 10^{-5})$
e $(4.9 \times 10^4) \div (8.2 \times 10^{-8})$
f $(6.9 \times 10^3) \div (2.4 \times 10^{-6})$
g $(4.3 \times 10^{-3}) \div (6.9 \times 10^8)$
h $(2.6 \times 10^{-5}) \div (5.8 \times 10^{-2})$
i $\sqrt{(6.25 \times 10^6)}$
j $\sqrt[3]{(1.728 \times 10^9)}$

4 The circumference of the earth at the equator is 4×10^4 km. Calculate the radius of the earth. Give your answer in standard form.

5 A virus is 3×10^{-5} m wide. How many would fit across the head of a pin which is 1 mm wide?

Extension Work

Use the Internet to find out about very small numbers. Look up 'centi' on a search engine.

Can you find out the meaning of these prefixes: milli, micro, nano, pico, femto, atto, zepto and yocto?

Upper and lower bounds 1

Form 7Q are making invitations to their Christmas party. They cut pieces of card 10 cm wide on which to write the invitations. They make envelopes 10.5 cm wide in which to put them.

INVITATION

10 cm   10.5 cm

The invitations are accurate to the nearest centimetre and the envelopes are accurate to the nearest half centimetre. Will all of the invitations fit into all of the envelopes?

Example 7.8   Give the possible range of values for each of the following.

a   A football crowd which is 3400 to the nearest hundred.

b   A piece of wood which is 32 cm long to the nearest centimetre.

c   The mass of a marble which is 12 grams to two significant figures.

a   The smallest value is 3350 and the greatest is 3449.

b   The smallest value is 31.5 cm and the greatest is 32.4$\dot{9}$. But to make the range easier, the **upper bound** is given as 32.5 cm. Strictly speaking, the ranges should be expressed as:

$31.5 \leq$ Actual length < 32.5

Note The 'strict' inequality for the upper bound.

c   The actual values must be within three significant figure limits:

$11.5 \leq$ Mass < 12.5.

Example 7.9 ▷ A rectangle is measured as 15 cm by 10 cm. Both measurements are given to the nearest centimetre. What are the greatest and least possible values of the perimeter?

The length is $14.5 \leq$ Length < 15.5 and the width is $9.5 \leq$ Width < 10.5.

Least perimeter is given by:

$14.5 + 9.5 + 14.5 + 9.5 = 48$ cm

Greatest perimeter is given by:

$15.5 + 10.5 + 15.5 + 10.5 = 52$ cm

So, $48 \leq$ Perimeter < 52.

Note It is easier to calculate with upper bounds if recurring decimals are not used.

Exercise 7D

1 Find the upper and lower bounds between which each of the following quantities lie.

a   The number of toffees in a tin which is 30 to the nearest 10.

b   The amount of rice in a bag which is 20 grams to the nearest 10 grams.

c   The speed of a car which is 70 mph to the nearest 10 mph.

d   The speed of a car which is 70 mph to the nearest unit.

e   The length of a piece of string which is 20 cm to one significant figure.

f   The length of a piece of string which is 20 cm to two significant figures.

g   The mass of a cake which is 500 grams to the nearest 10 grams.

h   The mass of a donut which is 50 grams to the nearest gram.

i   The capacity of a jug which holds 1 litre to the nearest cubic centimetre.

j   The storage capacity of a hard drive which is 40 Gb to two significant figures.

2 A lawn is 4 metres by 3 metres, each measurement accurate to the nearest 10 cm.

a   What are the upper and lower bounds for the length of the lawn?

b   What are the upper and lower bounds for the width of the lawn?

c   What are the upper and lower bounds for the perimeter of the lawn?

3 A tile is 10 cm by 10 cm, measured to the nearest centimetre.

a   What are the smallest possible dimensions of the tile?

b   What are the largest possible dimensions of the tile?

c   If ten of the tiles are placed side by side will they be guaranteed to cover a length of 98 cm?

d   John wants to tile a wall which is 3 m long by 2 m high. Will he have enough tiles if he has 700 tiles?

4 Woodville United had crowds of 1200, 1300, 1600, 1000 and 1400 for the first five matches of the season. Each of these values was recorded to the nearest 100.

a   What was the least possible total for the five matches?

b   What was the greatest possible total for the five matches?

5 There are 200 sweets in a jar, measured to the nearest 10. They weigh 200 grams to the nearest 10 grams.

    a Between what bounds does the number of sweets lie?

    b Between what bounds does the mass of the sweets lie?

    c Why are the answers to parts **a** and **b** different?

6 A petri dish contains 24 000 bacteria, measured to the nearest thousand.

    a What is the least number of bacteria in the dish?

    b What is the most number of bacteria in ten similar dishes?

7 A bat colony has 230 bats, measured to the nearest 10.

    a What is the least number of bats there could be?

    b What is the greatest number of bats there could be?

8 Mr Ahmed wants to lay a path of slabs 20 m long. He buys 50 slabs which are 40 cm square to the nearest centimetre. Can he be sure he has enough slabs to cover 20 metres?

9 A mug holds 200 ml of a drink to the nearest 10 ml. A jug holds 1900 ml to the nearest 100 ml. Can you be sure that nine mugfuls can be poured into a jug without spilling?

10 An exam has five modules. The mark for each module is given to the nearest 5%. Melanie scores 45, 50, 65, 40 and 55 on the five modules. The final grade is based on the actual total of the marks. To get a pass a student needs a total of 250 marks (50%). Can Melanie be sure of passing?

Extension Work

    a A piece of wood is 1.2 m long to the nearest centimetre. A piece is cut off, which is 85 cm to the nearest cm. Assuming that there is no loss of length due to the cutting, explain why the largest possible length left is 36 cm and the smallest possible length left is 34 cm.

    b A rectangle has an area of 45 cm^2, measured to the nearest 5 cm^2. The width is 2 cm measured to the nearest cm. Explain why the largest possible length is 28.33 cm and the smallest possible length is 19 cm.

Upper and lower bounds 2

Form 7Q are making biscuits for their Christmas party. They take lumps of mixture, which weigh 25 grams to the nearest 5 grams, from a bowl of mixture containing 3 kg to the nearest 100 grams. Can they be sure to make enough biscuits to give each member of the form of 30, four biscuits each?

Example 7.10 A rectangle has a length of 20 cm and a width of 12 cm, both measured to the nearest cm. What are the upper and lower bounds of the area of the rectangle?

The upper and lower bounds of the length are 19.5 ≤ Length < 20.5.

The upper and lower bounds of the width are 11.5 ≤ Width < 12.5.

The lower bound of the area is:

$19.5 \times 11.5 = 224.25$ cm².

The upper bound of the area is:

$20.5 \times 12.5 = 256.25$ cm².

The upper and lower bounds of the area are 224.25 ≤ Area < 256.25 cm².

Example 7.11 A briefcase containing a laptop has a mass of 3.5 kg, measured to the nearest 100 grams. The laptop is taken out and the briefcase now has a mass of 0.5 kg, measured to the nearest 100 grams. What are the upper and lower bounds of the mass of the laptop?

The upper and lower bounds of the briefcase plus laptop are 3450 ≤ Mass < 3550.

The upper and lower bounds of the briefcase without laptop are 450 ≤ Mass < 550.

The greatest difference is:

$3550 - 450 = 3100 = 3.1$ kg.

The least difference is:

$3450 - 550 = 2900 = 2.9$ kg.

The upper and lower bounds of the laptop are 2.9 ≤ Mass < 3.1 kg.

Example 7.12 $a = 7.2$ to one decimal place; $b = 4.52$ to two decimal places. What are the upper and lower bounds of $a \div b$?

The upper and lower bounds of a are 7.15 ≤ a < 7.25.

The upper and lower bounds of b are 4.515 ≤ b < 4.525.

The greatest value from the division is:

$7.25 \div 4.515 = 1.606$ (3 dp)

The least value from the division is:

$7.15 \div 4.525 = 1.580$ (3 dp)

The upper and lower bounds for $\frac{a}{b}$ are 1.580 ≤ $\frac{a}{b}$ < 1.606.

Exercise 7E

1. Find the limits of the area of each of the following rectangles. All measurements are to the nearest centimetre.

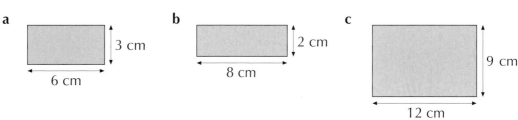

a   3 cm   6 cm

b   2 cm   8 cm

c   9 cm   12 cm

2 $a = 12$, $b = 18$ and $c = 24$. All the values are to the nearest whole number.

    a Write down the upper and lower bounds of a, b and c.

    b Work out the upper and lower bounds of each of these.

        i $a \times b$ **ii** $b \div a$ **iii** $(a + b) \times c$ **iv** c^2

3 Speed = Distance ÷ Time. A car travels for 40 miles, measured to the nearest mile, in a time of 30 minutes, measured to the nearest minute.

    a What is the greatest possible speed of the car?

    b What is the least possible speed of the car?

4 Distance = Speed × Time. A plane travels at 550 mph, to the nearest 10 mph, for 2 hours, measured to the nearest tenth of an hour.

    a What is the greatest possible distance travelled?

    b What is the least possible distance travelled?

5 There are 200 sweets in a jar, measured to the nearest 10. They weigh 600 grams to the nearest 10 grams.

    a What is the least possible mass of each sweet?

    b What is the greatest possible mass of each sweet?

6 A square has an area of 100 cm² measured to the nearest 10 cm². What are the upper and lower bounds of the side of the square?

7 $a = 3.2$, $b = 4.5$ and $c = 6.8$, all values being accurate to one decimal place. Work out the greatest and least possible values of:

    a $a \times b \times c$ **b** $\dfrac{(a + b)}{c}$ **c** $a + b - c$ **d** $(b - a)^2$

8 A rectangle has an area of 250 cm², measured to the nearest 10 cm². The length is 25 cm, measured to the nearest centimetre. What are the upper and lower bounds of the width of the rectangle?

9 On his bathroom scales, which measure to the nearest kilogram, Mr Wilson's case had a mass of 22 kg. On the way to the airport, he took out a coat. On the airport scales, which measure to the nearest tenth of a kilogram, the case weighed 19.8 kg. What are the upper and lower bounds for the weight of the coat?

10 Holes are drilled which have a radius of 4 cm measured to one significant figure. Cylindrical rods are made with a radius of 4.0 cm, measured to two significant figures. Will every rod fit in every hole?

Extension Work

1 A cube has a volume of 500 cm³, measured to the nearest 100 cm³. What are the upper and lower bounds for the surface area of the cube? Write your answer to 4 sf.

2 A sphere has a volume of 300 cm³, measured to the nearest 10 cm³. What are the upper and lower bounds for the surface area of the sphere? (Volume of a sphere = $\frac{4}{3}\pi r^3$; surface area = $4\pi r^2$). Write your answer to 4 sf.

Recurring decimals

$$\tfrac{3}{8} = 0.375 \qquad \tfrac{2}{3} = 0.666\,666\ldots \qquad \pi = 3.141\,59\ldots$$

The decimals shown above are, from left to right, a **terminating decimal**, a **recurring decimal** and a **decimal** which never terminates or recurs. (This is called an **irrational number**, which you may meet in your GCSE course.)

Every recurring decimal can be written as a fraction.

To show a recurring decimal, a small dot is placed over the first and last of the recurring digits. For example:

$$\tfrac{5}{18} = 0.2\dot{7} \qquad \tfrac{4}{11} = 0.\dot{3}\dot{6} \qquad \tfrac{2}{7} = 0.\dot{2}85\,71\dot{4}$$

Example 7.13 ▷ Write each of the following fractions as a recurring decimal.

    a $\tfrac{5}{9}$ **b** $\tfrac{4}{7}$ **c** $\tfrac{7}{11}$

Use a calculator to divide each numerator by its denominator.

    a $\tfrac{5}{9} = 5 \div 9 = 0.555\,555\ldots = 0.\dot{5}$

    b $\tfrac{4}{7} = 4 \div 7 = 0.571\,428\,5714\ldots = 0.\dot{5}71\,42\dot{8}$

    c $\tfrac{7}{11} = 7 \div 11 = 0.636\,363\ldots = 0.\dot{6}\dot{3}$

Example 7.14 ▷ Write each of the following recurring decimals as a fraction in its simplest form.

    a $0.\dot{4}\dot{8}$ **b** $0.\dot{3}4\dot{2}$ **c** $3.\dot{4}$

    a Because there are two recurring digits, the denominator is 99 (see table below).

Fraction	$\tfrac{1}{9}$	$\tfrac{1}{99}$	$\tfrac{1}{999}$
Decimal	0.111 111	0.010 101	0.001 001
Dot form	$0.\dot{1}$	$0.\dot{0}\dot{1}$	$0.\dot{0}0\dot{1}$

So, you have:

$$0.\dot{4}\dot{8} = \frac{48}{99} = \frac{16}{33} \quad \text{(Cancel by 3)}$$

    b Because there are three recurring digits, the denominator is 999. So you have:

$$0.\dot{3}4\dot{2} = \frac{342}{999} = \frac{38}{111} \quad \text{(Cancel by 9)}$$

    c Ignore the whole number. Hence, you have:

$$0.\dot{4} = \frac{4}{9}$$

This does not cancel, so $3.\dot{4} = 3\tfrac{4}{9}$.

Example 7.15 ▷ Write each of the following recurring decimals as a fraction in its simplest form.

    a $0.\dot{6}\dot{3}$ **b** $0.2\dot{3}\dot{8}$ **c** $2.0\dot{4}1\dot{2}$

In these examples (apart from **a**), the method used in Example 7.14 cannot be used because the recurring decimals do not occur immediately after the decimal point.

Example 7.15
continued

a Because there are two recurring digits, multiply the original number, x, by 100. This gives:

$$x = 0.63636363\ldots \quad (1)$$
$$100x = 63.636363\ldots \quad (2)$$

Subtract equation 1 from equation 2, to obtain:

$$99x = 63$$
$$x = \frac{63}{99} = \frac{7}{11}$$

b Because there are two recurring digits, multiply the original number, x, by 100. This gives:

$$x = 0.23838383\ldots \quad (1)$$
$$100x = 23.8383838\ldots \quad (2)$$

Subtract equation 1 from equation 2, to obtain:

$$99x = 23.6$$
$$x = \frac{23.6}{99} = \frac{236}{990} = \frac{118}{495}$$

c Because there are three recurring digits, multiply the original fraction, x, by 1000 (ignoring the whole number, 2). This gives:

$$x = 0.0412412412 \quad (1)$$
$$1000x = 41.2412412\ldots \quad (2)$$
$$999x = 41.2$$
$$x = \frac{41.2}{999} = \frac{412}{9990} = \frac{206}{4995}$$

Replace the 2, which gives $2\frac{206}{4995}$

Exercise 7F

1 Write each of the following fractions as a recurring decimal.

  a $\frac{4}{7}$ **b** $\frac{76}{101}$ **c** $\frac{23}{33}$ **d** $\frac{1}{3}$ **e** $\frac{2}{9}$

2 Write down the ninths as recurring decimals: for example, $\frac{1}{9} = 0.\dot{1}$. Describe any patterns you see.

3 Write down the elevenths as recurring decimals: for example, $\frac{1}{11} = 0.\dot{0}\dot{9}$, $\frac{2}{11} = 0.\dot{1}\dot{8}\ldots$. Describe any patterns you see.

4 Write down the sevenths as recurring decimals: for example, $\frac{1}{7} = 0.\dot{1}42\,85\dot{7}$, $\frac{2}{7} = 0.\dot{2}85\,71\dot{4}\ldots$. Describe any patterns you see.

5 Write each of the following recurring decimals as a fraction in its simplest form.

  a $0.\dot{4}\dot{5}$ **b** $0.\dot{3}2\dot{1}$ **c** $0.\dot{8}$ **d** $0.\dot{7}2\dot{9}$ **e** $0.\dot{1}\dot{2}$

  f $0.8\dot{1}$ **g** $0.\dot{1}10\dot{7}$ **h** $0.7\dot{8}$ **i** $0.\dot{8}0\dot{1}$ **j** $0.\dot{9}$

6 Write each of the following recurring decimals as a fraction. Write each fraction in its simplest form.

a 0.0$\dot{4}$ b 0.05$\dot{6}$ c 0.$\dot{5}$7$\dot{8}$ d 0.0$\dot{7}$0$\dot{4}$ e 0.03$\dot{4}\dot{5}$

7 Write each of the following recurring decimals as a mixed number.

a 2.3$\dot{9}\dot{2}$ b 1.0$\dot{5}$5$\dot{5}$ c 5.2$\dot{1}$0$\dot{8}$ d 2.40$\dot{8}\dot{2}$

Extension Work

The thirteenths are recurring decimals. They always have six recurring digits which fit into one of two cycles. These are shown below.

 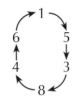

For example: $\frac{1}{13}$ = 0.$\dot{0}$76 92$\dot{3}$ and $\frac{2}{13}$ = 0.$\dot{1}$53 84$\dot{6}$

Without using a calculator, and by working out the first one or two digits, write down all the thirteenths as recurring decimals.

For example:

$$\frac{1}{13} = \frac{0.07\ldots}{13/1.000\,000}$$

So, the recurring decimal must be 0.$\dot{0}$76923.

Efficient use of a calculator

You have previously used the keys which control brackets, memory, sign change and fractions. This section will remind you how to use these keys and a few others which can be found on most scientific calculators.

Example 7.16 ▷ Use a calculator to evaluate each of the following.

a $[3.5^2 + (5.2 - 2.34)]^2$ b $\dfrac{36.7 \times 18.32}{3.7(5.6 - 2.91)}$ c $\dfrac{13}{15} - \dfrac{11}{18}$

a Key in as follows:

(3 . 5 x^2 + (5 . 2 − 2 . 3 4)) x^2 =

The answer is 228.3121.

b Key in as follows:

(3 6 . 7 × 1 8 . 3 2) ÷ (3 . 7 ×
(5 . 6 − 2 . 9 1)) =

The answer is 67.551 8939…, which can be rounded to 67.6.

Example 7.16 continued

c Key in as follows:

The answer is $\frac{23}{90}$

Example 7.17 Use the power key to evaluate **a** 5.9^4 and **b** $81^{\frac{3}{4}}$.

The power key may be marked x^y or y^x, or be an inverse or shift function.

a Key in the following:

The answer is 1211.7361.

b Key in the following:

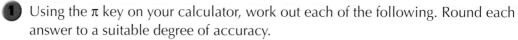

The answer is 27.

Exercise 7G

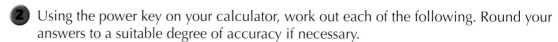

1 Using the π key on your calculator, work out each of the following. Round each answer to a suitable degree of accuracy.

    a $\pi \times 7^2$
    b $\sqrt{\pi} \div 8$
    c $2 \times \pi \times 10 \times 9 + \pi \times 9^2$

2 Using the power key on your calculator, work out each of the following. Round your answers to a suitable degree of accuracy if necessary.

    a 3.7^2
    b 8^5
    c 1.25^3
    d 0.074^5

3 Using the power key and the fraction key, calculate each of the following.

    a $9^{\frac{1}{2}}$
    b $64^{\frac{1}{2}}$
    c $121^{\frac{1}{2}}$
    d $2.25^{\frac{1}{2}}$

4 Using the power key and the fraction key, calculate each of the following.

    a $8^{\frac{1}{3}}$
    b $64^{\frac{1}{3}}$
    c $125^{\frac{1}{3}}$
    d $0.216^{\frac{1}{3}}$

5 Use your calculator to work out each of the following. Round your answers to a suitable degree of accuracy.

    a $\sqrt{16.5^2 - 4.7^2}$
    b $\dfrac{5.65 \times 56.8}{3.04(3.4 - 1.9)}$
    c $[4.6^2 + (3.2 - 1.73)]^2$

    d $3.8 - [2.9 - (12.3 \times 8.4)]$
    e $\dfrac{6\sqrt{5.2^2} + 4^2}{5}$

6 Use the fraction key to work out each of these.

    a $\frac{11}{18} + \frac{17}{22}$
    b $(\frac{7}{8} - \frac{5}{6}) \times (\frac{5}{7} - \frac{3}{5})$
    c $(\frac{2}{3} + \frac{5}{8}) \div (\frac{4}{9} - \frac{1}{6})$

Choose a number between 1 and 2, say 1.5. Key it into the calculator display.

Perform the following sequence of key presses: $+$ 1 $=$ $1/x$ $=$

Note: the $1/x$ key may be in the form x^{-1}. This is called the **reciprocal** key.

After the sequence has been performed, the display should show 0.4.

Repeat the above sequence of key presses. The display should now show 0.714 … .

Keep repeating the above sequence of key presses until the first three decimal places of the number in the display start to repeat.

What you need to know for level 6

- How to use the power and/or the cube and cube root keys on your calculator
- How to round numbers to any power of 10, and to two decimal places

What you need to know for level 7

- The effect of multiplying and dividing by numbers between 0 and 1
- How to round to one significant figure
- How to multiply and divide mentally by making appropriate estimates of the numbers involved
- How to multiply and divide decimal numbers by treating them as whole numbers and then pointing off the required number of decimal places

What you need to know for level 8

- How to solve problems with roots and powers
- How to interpret and write numbers in standard form
- How to calculate with numbers in standard form
- How to solve problems such as compound interest that involve repeated proportional change

National Curriculum SATs questions

LEVEL 6

1 *2002 Paper 2*

A company sells and processes films of two different sizes. The tables show how much the company charges.

I want to take 360 photos. I need to buy the film, pay for the film to be printed and pay for the postage.

a Is it cheaper to use all films of 24 photos or all films of 36 photos?

b How much cheaper is it?

Film size: 24 photos	
Cost of each film	£2.15
Postage	Free
Cost to print film	£0.99
Postage of each film	60p

Film size: 36 photos	
Cost of each film	£2.65
Postage	Free
Cost to print film	£2.89
Postage of each film	60p

LEVEL 7

2   *1999 Paper 2*

The compactness value, C, of a shape can be calculated using the formula:

$$C = \frac{4A}{\pi K^2}$$

The area of the shape is A.

The distance between two points in the shape that are furthest apart is K.

a   Calculate the compactness value for this square.

(The distance K is the length of a diagonal.) Show your working.

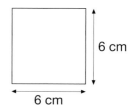

6 cm

6 cm

b   Calculate the compactness value for this rectangle. Show your working.

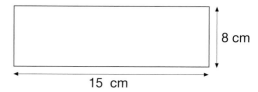

8 cm

15 cm

3   *1998 Paper 1*

Find the values of a and b when $p = 10$.

$$a = \frac{3p^2}{2}$$

$$b = \frac{2p^3(p-3)}{7p}$$

4   *1999 Paper 2*

The ship 'Queen Mary' used to sail across the Atlantic Ocean.

The ship's usual speed was 33 miles per hour.

On average, the ship used fuel at the rate of 1 gallon for every 13 feet sailed.

Calculate how many gallons of fuel the ship used in one hour of travelling at the usual speed. (There are 5280 feet in one mile.)

Show your working and write down the full calculator display.

Now write your answer correct to two significant figures.

5   *1999 Paper 2*

Look at the table:

	Earth	Mercury
Mass (kg)	5.98×10^{24}	3.59×10^{23}
Atmospheric pressure (N/m²)		2×10^{-8}

a   The atmospheric pressure on Earth is 5.05×10^{12} times as great as the atmospheric pressure on Mercury. Calculate the atmospheric pressure on Earth.

b   What is the ratio of the mass of Earth to the mass of Mercury? Write your answer in the form of $x : 1$.

c The approximate volume, V, of a planet with radius r is given by:

$$V = \frac{4}{3}\pi r^3$$

Assume the radius of Mercury is 2400 km.

Calculate the volume of Mercury. Give your answer to 1 significant figure in standard form.

6 *2001 Paper 1*

$\dfrac{1}{2500}$ is equal to 0.0004.

a Write 0.0004 in standard form.

b Write $\dfrac{1}{2500}$ in standard form.

c Work out

$$\frac{1}{2500} + \frac{1}{2500}$$

Show your working, and write your answer in standard form.

7 *2002 Paper 2*

The star nearest the Earth (other than the Sun) is Proxima Centauri. Proxima Centauri is 4.22 light-years away. (One light-year is 9.46×10^{12} kilometres.)

Suppose a spaceship could travel at 40 000 km per hour.

a Copy the following calculations. Then state what each one represents. The first one is done for you.

   i $4.22 \times 9.46 \times 10^{12}$ Number of km from Earth to Proxima Centuari

   ii $\dfrac{4.22 \times 9.46 \times 10^{12}}{40\,000}$ ......

   iii $\dfrac{4.22 \times 9.46 \times 10^{12}}{40\,000 \times 24 \times 365.25}$ ......

b Work out

$$\frac{4.22 \times 9.46 \times 10^{12}}{40\,000 \times 24 \times 365.25}$$

Give your answer to the nearest thousand.

CHAPTER **8**   Algebra **4**

This chapter is going to show you	What you should already know
○ how to interpret negative powers	○ How to find square roots and cube roots
○ how to interpret powers given as fractions, including square roots and cube roots	○ What a factor is
○ how to construct quadratic and cubic graphs	

Index notation with algebra – negative powers

You met two rules of algebra regarding indices in Year 8.

When multiplying powers of the same variable, *add the indices*:

$$x^A \times x^B = x^{A+B}$$

Example 8.1 ▷   Simplify each of these.

    a $g^4 \times g$ **b** $3t^2 \times 5t^4$

    a $g^4 \times g = g^{4+1} = g^5$

    b $3t^2 \times 5t^4 = (3 \times 5)t^{2+4} = 15t^6$

When dividing powers of the same variable, *subtract the indices*:

$$x^A \div x^B = x^{A-B}$$

Example 8.2 ▷   Simplify each of these.

    a $m^6 \div m^3$ **b** $6w^5 \div 2w$

    a $m^6 \div m^3 = m^{6-3} = m^3$

    b $6w^5 \div 2w = (6 \div 2)w^{5-1} = 3w^4$

As you have already seen, powers of numbers and variables can be negative, as in 4^{-1}, x^{-3} and 10^{-5}. This section will show you that negative powers obey the same rules as positive powers stated above. Follow through Examples 8.3 and 8.4 to see how the rules work for negative powers.

Example 8.3 ▷ Simplify each of the following.

  a $6x^4 \div 2x^{-1}$ **b** $2m^{-1} \times 4m^{-2}$

  a $6x^4 \div 2x^{-1} = (6 \div 2)x^{4--1} = 3x^5$

  b $2m^{-1} \times 4m^{-2} = (2 \times 4)m^{-1+-2} = 8m^{-3}$

Investigation ▷ Work through each of the following. Write your answer using **i** a negative power and **ii** in fraction form. The answers to the first two questions have been completed for you.

  a **i** $4 \div 4^2 = 4^{1-2} = 4^{-1}$ **ii** $4 \div 4^2 = 4 \div 16 = \dfrac{1}{4}$ That is: $4^{-1} = \dfrac{1}{4^1}$

  b **i** $4 \div 4^3 = 4^{1-3} = 4^{-2}$ **ii** $4 \div 4^3 = 4 \div 64 = \dfrac{1}{16} = \dfrac{1}{4^2}$ That is: $4^{-2} = \dfrac{1}{4^2}$

  c **i** $4 \div 4^4 =$ **ii**   That is:

  d **i** $4 \div 4^5 =$ **ii**   That is:

  Write down a generalisation from the investigation of x^{-n}.

Exercise 8A **1** Simplify each of the following.

  a $4x^2 \times x^3$ **b** $m^3 \times 7m$ **c** $n^5 \div n^3$ **d** $x^6 \div x$
  e $8m^5 \div 2m$ **f** $3x \times 2x^3$ **g** $5t^3 \times 3t$ **h** $10m^6 \div 2m^3$
  i $g^5 \times g^4$ **j** $5m^6 \div 5m^2$ **k** $8t^5 \div 2t^3$ **l** $5m^3 \times 3m^5$
  m $12q^4 \times 4q^2$ **n** $am^2 \times bm^3$ **o** $cy \times dy^3$

2 Write each of the following in fraction form.

  a m^{-1} **b** k^{-2} **c** x^{-3} **d** n^{-4}
  e $5m^{-2}$ **f** $4y^{-1}$ **g** $8x^{-3}$ **h** ab^{-1}

3 Write each of the following using a negative power.

  a $\dfrac{1}{5}$ **b** $\dfrac{1}{4}$ **c** $\dfrac{3}{x}$ **d** $\dfrac{1}{x^2}$
  e $\dfrac{1}{m^6}$ **f** $\dfrac{1}{9}$ **g** $\dfrac{5}{x^4}$ **h** $\dfrac{A}{m^3}$

4 Simplify each of the following. Your answers should not contain fractions.

  a $4x \div x^3$ **b** $7m^3 \div m^5$ **c** $n^2 \div n^5$
  d $8x^6 \div 2x^9$ **e** $8m^2 \div 2m^7$ **f** $3x \div 2x^3$
  g $5t^3 \times 3t^{-5}$ **h** $10m \div 2m^3$ **i** $g^{-5} \times g^4$

5 Simplify each of the following.

  a $x^3 \div x^{-4}$ **b** $m^4 \div m^{-3}$ **c** $n^{-2} \div n^{-4}$
  d $4x^5 \div 2x^{-3}$ **e** $9m^{-4} \div 3m^{-1}$ **f** $6x \div 2x^{-2}$
  g $4t^{-2} \times 3t^{-5}$ **h** $12m \div 2m^{-4}$ **i** $3g^{-4} \times 2g^{-1}$

6 Simplify each of the following.

a $3x^4 \times x^{-3} \times x$ b $2m^3 \times 5m^{-4} \times 3m^2$ c $4n^3 \div 2n^3 \times 3n$

d $8x^5 \div 2x^{-2} \times 3x^3$ e $10m^3 \div 5m \times 3m^{-4}$ f $4x^2 \times 3x^{-3} \times 2x^{-1}$

g $4t^5 \times 5t^{-1} \times 3t^{-1}$ h $12m^5 \div 3m^2 \times 2m^{-4}$ i $3g^6 \times g^{-4} \times 3g^{-1}$

j $7m^7 \div 7m^5 \times 4m^{-3}$ k $18t^6 \div 3t^{-4} \times 5t^{-3}$ l $6m^2 \times 4m^3 \div m^{-2}$

m $3q^5 \times 2q^3 \div q^{-4}$ n $km^2 \times pm^3 \div m^{-1}$ o $dy^3 \times ey \div y^{-4}$

Extension Work

1 Find some values of x which meet each of the following conditions.

a x^2 is always larger than x.

b x^2 is always smaller than x.

c $x^2 = x$

2 Find some values of x which meet each of the following conditions.

a x^2 is always larger than $5x$.

b x^2 is always smaller than $5x$.

c $x^2 = 5x$

Square roots, cube roots and other fractional powers

The **square root** of a given number is that number which, when multiplied by itself, produces the given number.

For example, the square root of 36 is 6, since $6 \times 6 = 36$. A square root is represented by the symbol $\sqrt{}$. For example, $\sqrt{36} = 6$.

Example 8.4

Solve $x^2 = 49$.

Taking the square root of both sides gives $x = 7$ and -7.

The negative value of x is also a solution, because $-7 \times -7 = 49$.

Note that all square roots have two solutions: a positive value and its negative.

The **cube root** of a given number is that number which, when multiplied by itself twice, produces the given number.

For example, the cube root of 64 is 4, since $4 \times 4 \times 4 = 64$. A cube root is represented by the symbol $\sqrt[3]{}$. For example, $\sqrt[3]{64} = 4$.

Example 8.5 Solve $y^3 = 216$.

Taking the cube root of both sides gives $y = 6$.

Note that the sign (+ or –) of the value is the *same* as the sign of the original number, because here $+ \times + \times + = +$. If the original number had been –216, the solution would have been –6 (because $- \times - \times - = -$).

You should be familiar with the following square roots and cube roots.

$\sqrt{1}$	$\sqrt{4}$	$\sqrt{9}$	$\sqrt{16}$	$\sqrt{25}$	$\sqrt{36}$	$\sqrt{49}$	$\sqrt{64}$	$\sqrt{81}$	$\sqrt{100}$	$\sqrt{121}$	$\sqrt{144}$	$\sqrt{169}$	$\sqrt{196}$	$\sqrt{225}$
±1	±2	±3	±4	±5	±6	±7	±8	±9	±10	±11	±12	±13	±14	±15

$\sqrt[3]{1}$	$\sqrt[3]{8}$	$\sqrt[3]{27}$	$\sqrt[3]{64}$	$\sqrt[3]{125}$	$\sqrt[3]{216}$	$\sqrt[3]{343}$	$\sqrt[3]{512}$	$\sqrt[3]{729}$	$\sqrt[3]{1000}$
1	2	3	4	5	6	7	8	9	10

Often a calculator will be needed to find a square root or a cube root. So, do make sure you know how to use the power key and root key on your calculator.

When decimal numbers are involved, solutions are usually rounded to one decimal place. For example: $\sqrt[3]{250} = 6.3$, $\sqrt{153} = 12.4$.

Expressions of the form $x^{\frac{1}{n}}$

The investigation below demonstrates how to interpret powers given as fractions.

Investigation This investigation looks at the values of expressions which are given in the form $x^{\frac{1}{n}}$. The index $\frac{1}{n}$ shows that the nth root of x is to be taken, as shown below.

You know that $\sqrt{3} \times \sqrt{3} = 3$

$3^{\frac{1}{2}} \times 3^{\frac{1}{2}}$ can be simplified to $3^{\frac{1}{2} + \frac{1}{2}}$

So, $3^{\frac{1}{2}} \times 3^{\frac{1}{2}} = 3^{\frac{1}{2} + \frac{1}{2}} = 3^1 = 3$

This means that $3^{\frac{1}{2}}$ is the same as $\sqrt{3}$.

a   Simplify $5^{\frac{1}{3}} \times 5^{\frac{1}{3}} \times 5^{\frac{1}{3}}$.

b   What does $5^{\frac{1}{3}}$ mean?

c   What meaning can be given to the expressions   i $x^{\frac{1}{4}}$ and   ii $x^{\frac{1}{5}}$?

d   Write down what you can say about the expression $x^{\frac{1}{n}}$.

Example 8.6 Find $3^{\frac{1}{4}}$ using a calculator.

Press the following keys:

$\boxed{3}$ $\boxed{x^{\frac{1}{y}}}$ $\boxed{4}$

which gives the answer 1.316, correct to three decimal places.

On some makes of calculator the root key is $\boxed{\sqrt[y]{x}}$.

1 Write down two solutions to each of the following equations.

    a $x^2 = 9$ **b** $x^2 = 36$ **c** $x^2 = 49$ **d** $x^2 = 121$

2 Jack has done his homework incorrectly. Find out on which line he has gone wrong and correct the homework from there.

    a Solve the equation $2x^2 = 50$.

        $x^2 = 2 \times 50 = 100$

        $x = 10$ and -10

    b Solve the equation $4x^2 = 36$.

        $4x = \sqrt{36} = 6$ and -6

        $x = \frac{6}{4}$ and $-\frac{6}{4}$

        $x = 1\frac{1}{2}$ and $-1\frac{1}{2}$

3 Write down the value of each of the following without using a power. Use a calculator to help you.

    a $16^{\frac{1}{2}}$ **b** $25^{\frac{1}{2}}$ **c** $81^{\frac{1}{2}}$ **d** $100^{\frac{1}{2}}$

    e $8^{\frac{1}{3}}$ **f** $1000^{\frac{1}{3}}$ **g** $(-64)^{\frac{1}{3}}$ **h** $(-125)^{\frac{1}{3}}$

    i $625^{\frac{1}{4}}$ **j** $81^{\frac{1}{4}}$ **k** $1296^{\frac{1}{4}}$ **l** $32^{\frac{1}{5}}$

    m $729^{\frac{1}{6}}$ **n** $3125^{\frac{1}{5}}$ **p** $1024^{\frac{1}{10}}$ **q** $729^{\frac{1}{3}}$

4 Estimate the square root of each of the following. Then use a calculator to find each result to one decimal place to see how close you were.

    a $\sqrt{26}$ **b** $\sqrt{55}$ **c** $\sqrt{94}$ **d** $\sqrt{109}$ **e** $\sqrt{275}$

5 Without using a calculator, state the cube root of each of the following numbers.

    a 8   **b** 1   **c** 125   **d** 27   **e** 1000

    f −64   **g** −1   **h** −1000   **i** 0.001   **j** 0.008

6 **a** Estimate the integer closest to the cube root of each of the following.

        i 86   **ii** 100   **iii** 45   **iv** 267   **v** 2000

    b Use a calculator to find the accurate value of each of the above. Give your answers to one decimal place.

    c Which numbers gave you the smallest and the largest percentage error?

7 State which of each pair of numbers is larger.

    a $\sqrt{10}$, $\sqrt[3]{50}$ **b** $\sqrt{30}$, $\sqrt[3]{150}$ **c** $\sqrt{20}$, $\sqrt[3]{60}$

    d $\sqrt{35}$, $\sqrt[3]{200}$ **e** $\sqrt{15}$, $\sqrt[3]{55}$ **f** $\sqrt{40}$, $\sqrt[3]{220}$

8 The cube root of numbers

    ● between 1 and 10 are between 1 and 2.2

    ● between 10 and 100 are between 2.2 and 4.6

    ● between 100 and 1000 are between 4.6 and 10

    a Estimate each of the following cube roots without using a calculator.

        i 45   **ii** 5   **iii** 500   **iv** 250   **v** 750

    b Use a calculator to find each of the above cube roots to one decimal place.

    c See if you are any more accurate in estimating each of the following cube roots without a calculator.

        i 65   **ii** 7   **iii** 400   **iv** 320   **v** 850

9 You can estimate the cube root of numbers greater than 1000 as shown by the following examples:

$$\sqrt[3]{5000} = \sqrt[3]{5} \times \sqrt[3]{1000} = 1.7 \times 10 = 17$$
$$\sqrt[3]{83\,000} = \sqrt[3]{83} \times \sqrt[3]{1000} = 4.4 \times 10 = 44$$

Estimate each of the following cube roots, without using a calculator.

a 35 000   **b** 7000   **c** 74 000   **d** 39 000   **e** 87 000

Extension Work

Investigate each of the following statements to see which are **i** always true and which are **ii** sometimes true. For those which are sometimes true, state when they are true.

a $\sqrt{A} + \sqrt{B} = \sqrt{(A + B)}$ **b** $\sqrt{A} \times \sqrt{B} = \sqrt{(A \times B)}$

c $\sqrt{A} - \sqrt{B} = \sqrt{(A \div B)}$ **d** $\sqrt{A} \div \sqrt{B} = \sqrt{(A \div B)}$

Quadratic graphs

A quadratic equation has the form $y = ax^2 + bx + c$. That is, it is an equation which has a square as its highest power.

Follow through Example 8.9 in which a graph is drawn from a quadratic equation. This example demonstrates that the graph of a quadratic equation is a curved line.

Example 8.7

Draw a graph of the equation $y = x^2 - 4x + 3$ between $x = -1$ and $x = 4$.

Start by constructing a table of coordinates for values of x from -1 to 4. To do this, calculate each part of the quadratic equation, then add the parts together.

x	-1	0	1	2	3	4
x^2	1	0	1	4	9	16
$-4x$	4	0	-4	-8	-12	-16
3	3	3	3	3	3	3
$y = x^2 - 4x + 3$	8	3	0	-1	0	3

Plot these points and join them with a smooth curve. The outcome is shown on the right.

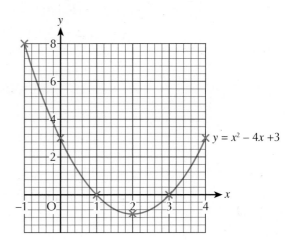

Notice that the graph has a smooth U-shape. All quadratic graphs have a similar shape, although some will be upside down.

When drawing quadratic graphs, remember the following important points:

- They have curved bottoms (or tops).
- There are *no* straight sections in the graph.
- There are *no* kinks, bulges or sharp points.

Exercise 8C

1. Copy and complete each table and use the suggested scale to draw a smooth graph of each equation.

a $y = x^2$

x	–3	–2	–1	0	1	2	3
x^2	9						9
$y = x^2$	9						9

x on the horizontal axis, scale 2 cm to 1 unit, from –3 to 3.
y on the vertical axis, scale 2 cm to 1 unit, from 0 to 9.

b $y = x^2 + 4$

x	–3	–2	–1	0	1	2	3
x^2	9						9
4	4	4	4	4			4
$y = x^2 + 4$	13						13

x on the horizontal axis, scale 2 cm to 1 unit, from –3 to 3.
y on the vertical axis, scale 2 cm to 1 unit, from 0 to 13.

c $y = x^2 + x$

x	–4	–3	–2	–1	0	1	2
x^2	16						
x	–4	–3					2
$y = x^2 + x$	12						

x on the horizontal axis, scale 2 cm to 1 unit, from –4 to 2.
y on the vertical axis, scale 2 cm to 1 unit, from –1 to 12.

d $y = x^2 + 3x - 1$

x	–4	–3	–2	–1	0	1	2
x^2	16						
$3x$	–12						
–1	–1						
$y = x^2 + 3x - 1$	3						

x on the horizontal axis, scale 2 cm to 1 unit, from –4 to 2.
y on the vertical axis, scale 2 cm to 1 unit, from –3 to 9.

2 Construct a table of values for each of the following equations. Then, using a suitable scale, draw its graph.

    a $y = 2x^2$ from $x = -3$ to 3.

    b $y = x^2 + 2x$ from $x = -4$ to 2.

    c $y = x^2 + 2x - 3$ from $x = -4$ to 2.

    d $y = x^2 + x - 2$ from $x = -3$ to 3.

3 Investigation

    a   Construct a table of values for each equation below. Then plot the graph of each equation on the same pair of axes, $x = -2$ to 2. Use a scale of 4 cm to 1 unit on the horizontal axis and 1 cm to 1 unit on the vertical axis.

        i $y = x^2$ **ii** $y = 2x^2$

        iii $y = 3x^2$ **iv** $y = 4x^2$

    b   Comment on your graphs.

    c   Sketch on your diagram the graphs with these equations:

        i $y = \frac{1}{2}x^2$ **ii** $y = 2\frac{1}{2}x^2$ **iii** $y = 5x^2$

4 Investigation

    a   Construct a table of values for each equation below. Then plot the graphs of each equation on the same pair of axes, $x = -3$ to 3. Use a scale of 2 cm to 1 unit on both the horizontal and vertical axes.

        i $y = x^2$ **ii** $y = x^2 + 1$ **iii** $y = x^2 - 1$

        iv $y = x^2 + 2$ **v** $y = x^2 - 2$

    b   Comment on your graphs.

    c   Sketch on your diagram the graphs with these equations:

        i $y = x^2 + 3$ **ii** $y = x^2 - \frac{1}{2}$ **iii** $y = x^2 + 3\frac{1}{2}$

Extension Work

1 **a**   Construct a suitable table of values and draw the graph of the equation $y = 1 - x^2$.

      b   Comment on the shape of the graph.

2 **a**   Draw the graph of $y = x^2$.

      b   Draw the reflection of the graph of $y = x^2$ on the same grid.

      c   What is the equation of this reflection?

Cubic graphs

A cubic equation is one which has a cube as its highest power. For example: $y = x^3$, $y = 4x^3 + 5$ and $y = 3x^3 + x^2$.

Example 8.8

Draw a graph of the equation $y = x^3 + 4x^2$ between $x = -5$ and $x = 2$.

Start by constructing a table of coordinates for values of x from -5 to 2. To do this, calculate each part of the cubic equation, then add the parts together.

x	-5	-4	-3	-2	-1	0	1	2
x^3	-125	-64	-27	-8	-1	0	1	8
$4x^2$	100	64	36	16	4	0	4	16
$y = x^3 + 4x^2$	-25	0	9	8	3	0	5	24

Plot these points and join them with a smooth curve. The outcome is shown on the right.

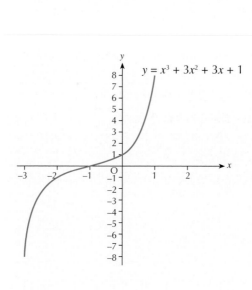

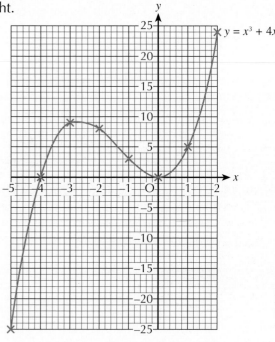

Notice that the graph is a smooth curve with two bends or turning points. All cubic graphs have a similar shape. Sometimes the two bends coincide, giving the graph a single twist instead. (One example of such a graph is given above by $y = x^3 + 3x^2 + 3x + 1$.)

Also notice that this graph starts in the third quadrant (bottom left-hand corner) and finishes in the first quadrant (top right-hand corner). Others start in the second quadrant (top left-hand corner) and finish in the fourth (bottom right-hand corner).

Exercise 8D

1 Plot the graph of the equation $y = x^3$ for values of x from -2 to 2.

2 Plot the graph of the equation $y = x^3 - 9x$ for values of x from -3 to 3.

3 Plot the graph of the equation $y = x^3 - x + 3$ for values of x from -2 to 2. You will need to include $x = -0.5$ and $x = 0.5$ in your table.

4 Plot the graph of the equation $y = x^3 - 5x^2 - 4$ for values of x from -2 to 3.

5 By drawing suitable graphs, solve the following pair of simultaneous equations:
$$x + y = 4$$
$$y = x^3 + 1$$

There is only one solution.

6 The velocity, v metres per second, of a particle moving along a straight line is given by $v = 1 + t^3$, where t is the time in seconds.

Draw the velocity–time graph for the first 3 seconds.

Extension Work

Investigate the shapes of each of the following graphs.

a $y = x^{-1}$ **b** $y = x^{-2}$ **c** $y = x^{-3}$

What you need to know for level 6

- How to find factors of expressions
- The simple rules of indices
- How to solve equations which involve square roots
- How to draw graphs from real-life situations

What you need to know for level 7

- How to find the HCF of algebraic expressions

What you need to know for level 8

- How to interpret negative and fractional indices
- How to construct quadratic and cubic graphs

National Curriculum SATs questions

LEVEL 6

1 *1999 Paper 1*

Write the values of k and m.

$$64 = 8^2 = 4^k = 2^m$$

LEVEL 7

2 *2000 Paper 1*

Look at these expressions. $n - 2$ $2n$ n^2 $\dfrac{n}{2}$ 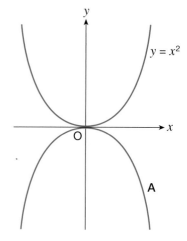 $\dfrac{2}{n}$

a Which expression gives the greatest value when n is between 1 and 2?

b Which expression gives the greatest value when n is between 0 and 1?

c Which expression gives the greatest value when n is negative?

LEVEL 8

3 *1998 Paper 1*

a The diagram shows the graph with equation $y = x^2$. Copy the graph and on the same axes, sketch the graph with equation $y = 2x^2$.

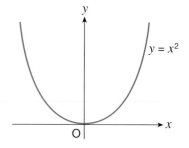

b Curve A is the reflection in the x-axis of $y = x^2$. What is the equation of curve A?

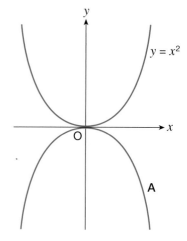

c Curve B is the translation, one unit up the y-axis, of $y = x^2$. What is the equation of curve B?

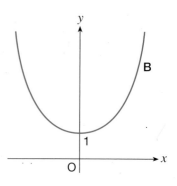

d The shaded region is bounded by the curve $y = x^2$ and the line $y = 2$. Choose two inequalities which together fully describe the shaded region.

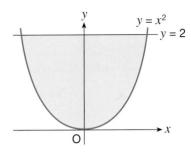

$$y < x^2 \qquad x < 0 \qquad y < 2 \qquad y < 0$$

$$y > x^2 \qquad x > 0 \qquad y > 2 \qquad y > 0$$

4 *1997 Paper 1*

Alan throws a ball to Katie, who is standing 20 m away.

The ball is thrown and caught at a height of 2.0 m above the ground.

The ball follows the curve with equation

$$y = 6 + c(10 - x)^2$$

where c is constant.

a Calculate the value of c by substituting $x = 0$, $y = 2$ into the equation. Show your working.

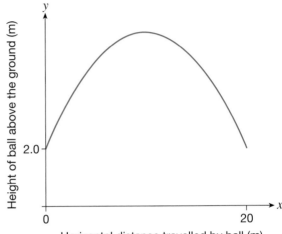

Alan throws the ball to Katie again, but this time the ball hits the ground before it reaches her. The ball follows the curve with equation $y = -0.1(x^2 - 6x - 16)$.

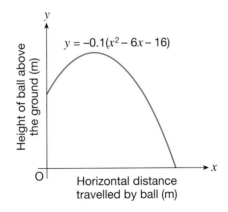

b Calculate the height above the ground at which the ball left Alan's hand. Show your working.

CHAPTER **9**   Handling Data **2**

This chapter is going to show you

- how to interpret statements about probability
- how to identify mutually exclusive outcomes
- how to solve probability problems involving mutually exclusive outcomes
- how to use tree diagrams to solve probability problems involving more than one event
- how to use relative frequency to compare the outcomes of experiments

What you should already know

- How to use a probability scale
- How to calculate probabilities for single events
- How to use a two-way table or sample space diagram to calculate probabilities
- How to compare fractions

Probability statements

You have already studied many probability situations. Check, using the tables below, that you remember how each of the probabilities is worked out.

Also, make sure that you know and understand all the **probability** terms which are used in this chapter.

Single event	Outcome	Probability
Roll a dice	5	$\frac{1}{6}$
Toss a coin	Head	$\frac{1}{2}$
Two blue counters and three green counters in a bag	Blue	$\frac{2}{5}$

Two events	Outcome	Probability
Roll two dice	Double 6	$\frac{1}{36}$
Toss two coins	Two heads	$\frac{1}{4}$
Toss a coin and roll a dice	Head and 5	$\frac{1}{12}$

Most of the combined events you have dealt with so far have been **independent events**. Two events are said to be independent when the outcome of one of them does not affect the outcome of the other event. Example 9.1 illustrates this situation.

Example 9.1 ▷ A Glaswegian girl was late for school on Friday, the day before the world record for throwing the javelin was broken in Sydney by a Korean athlete. Were these events connected in any way?

The student's late arrival at school clearly could have no effect on the Korean's performance on the Saturday. So, the two events are independent.

Now look closely at the statements in Examples 9.2 and 9.3, and the comments on them. In Exercise 9A, you will have to decide which given statements are sensible.

Example 9.2 ▷ Daniel says: 'There is a 50–50 chance that the next person to walk through the door of a supermarket will be someone I know because I will either know them or I won't.'

The next person that walks through the door may be someone whom he knows, but there are far more people whom he does not know. So, there is more chance of she/he being someone whom he does not know. Hence, the statement is incorrect.

Example 9.3 ▷ Clare says: 'If I buy a lottery ticket every week, I am bound to win sometime.'

Each week, the chance of winning is very small (1 chance in 13 983 816), so it is highly unlikely that Clare would win in any week. Losing one week does not increase your chances of winning the following week.

Exercise 9A

1 Write a comment on each of the following statements, explaining why the statement is incorrect.

   a A game for two players is started by rolling a six on a dice. Ashad says: 'I never start first because I'm unlucky.'

   b It will rain tomorrow because it rained today.

   c There is a 50% chance of snow tomorrow because it will either snow or it won't.

   d There are mint, chocolate and plain sweets in the packet, so the probability of picking out a chocolate sweet is $\frac{1}{3}$.

2 Decide whether each of the following statements is correct or incorrect.

   a I fell down yesterday. I don't fall down very often, so it could not possibly happen again today.

   b I have just tossed a coin to get a Head three times in succession. The next time I throw the coin, the probability that I will get a Head is still $\frac{1}{2}$.

   c My bus is always on time. It will be on time tomorrow.

   d There is an equal number of red and blue counters in a bag. My friend picked a counter out and it was blue. She then put it back. It is more likely that I will get red when I pick one out.

3 Here are three coloured grids. The squares have either a winning symbol or a losing symbol hidden.

   a If you pick a square from each grid, is it possible to know on which you have the greatest chance of winning?

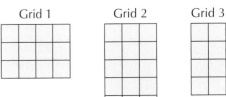

Grid 1   Grid 2   Grid 3

b You are now told that on Grid 1 there are three winning squares, on Grid 2 there are five winning squares and on Grid 3 there are four winning squares. Which grid gives you the least chance of winning?

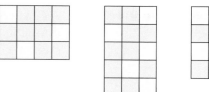

c Helen says that there are more winning squares on Grid 2, which means that there is more chance of winning using Grid 2. Explain why she is wrong.

4 Here are three events, *A*, *B*, and *C*.

    A Jonathan writes computer programs on Monday evenings.

    B Jonathan watches television on Monday evenings.

    C Jonathan wears a blue shirt on Mondays.

Which of these events are independent?

    a *A* and *B*   **b** *A* and *C*   **c** *B* and *C*

Extension Work

Draw each of the following different-sized grids:
- 5 by 5 grid with seven winning squares
- 6 by 6 grid with ten winning squares
- 10 by 10 grid with 27 winning squares

Work out which grid gives you the best chance of finding a winning square. Explain your reasoning.

Mutually exclusive events and exhaustive events

In Year 8, you looked at **mutually exclusive events**. Remember that these are events which do *not* overlap.

Example 9.4 Which of these three types of number are mutually exclusive: odd, even and prime?

Odd and even numbers are mutually exclusive. Odd and prime numbers, and even and prime numbers are not: for example, 11 and 2.

Example 9.5 There are red, green and blue counters in a bag.
- Event A: Pick a red counter.
- Event B: Pick a blue counter.
- Event C: Pick a counter that is not green.

Which pairs of events are mutually exclusive?

Events A and B are mutually exclusive because there is no overlap. A red counter and a blue counter are different.

Events A and C are *not* mutually exclusive because they overlap. A red counter and a counter which is not green could be the same colour.

Events B and C are *not* mutually exclusive because they overlap. A blue counter and a counter which is not green could be the same colour.

Example 9.6 ▶   The eight counters shown are contained in a bag.
A counter is chosen at random.

    a   What is the probability of picking a red counter?

    b   What is the probability of not picking a red counter?

    c   What is the probability of picking a green counter?

    d   What is the probability of picking a blue counter?

    e   What is the sum of the three probabilities in **a**, **c** and **d**?

a   There are three red counters out of a total of eight. This gives:

$$P(\text{red}) = \tfrac{3}{8}$$

b   Since there are five outcomes which are not red counters, this means:

$$P(\text{not red}) = \tfrac{5}{8}$$

Notice that

$$P(\text{red}) + P(\text{not red}) = \tfrac{3}{8} + \tfrac{5}{8} = 1$$

So, if you know P(Event happening), then

P(Event not happening) = 1 – P(Event happening)

c   There is one green counter, which means:

$$P(\text{green}) = \tfrac{1}{8}$$

d   There are four blue counters, which means:

$$P(\text{blue}) = \tfrac{4}{8} = \tfrac{1}{2}$$

e   The sum of the probabilities is

$$P(\text{red}) + P(\text{green}) + P(\text{blue})$$
$$= \tfrac{3}{8} + \tfrac{1}{8} + \tfrac{4}{8} = 1$$

All these events are mutually exclusive because only one counter is taken out at a time.

Also, because they cover all possibilities, they are called **exhaustive events**.

Note that the probabilities of exhaustive events which are also mutually exclusive **add up to 1**.

Exercise 9B

1   Discs lettered A, B, C, D and E, and the probability of choosing each, are shown.

   P(A) = 0.3   P(B) = 0.1   P(C) = ?   P(D) = 0.25   P(E) = 0.05

    a   What is the probability of choosing a disc with either A or B on it?

    b   What is the probability of choosing a disc with C on it?

    c   What is the probability of choosing a disc which does not have E on it?

2 A set of 25 cards is shown.

a What is the probability of choosing a card with a fish on it?

b What is the probability of choosing a card with a fish or a cow on it?

c What is the probability of choosing a card with a sheep or a pig on it?

d What is the probability of choosing a card *without* a fish on it?

3 A spinner is shown with the probabilities of its landing on red, green or blue.

What is the probability of the spinner landing on one of the following?

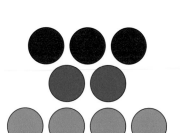

a Red or green   **b** Blue or green

c Blue, green or red   **d** Yellow

4 The discs shown right are placed in a bag. One of them is chosen at random. Here are four events:

A A red disc is chosen.

B A blue disc is chosen.

C A green disc is chosen.

D A green or blue disc is chosen.

State which events are mutually exclusive, exhaustive, both or neither.

a *A* and *B*   **b** *A* and *C*   **c** *A* and *D*   **d** *B* and *D*

Extension Work

You can work out how many times that you expect something to happen over a number of trials using this formula.

   Expected number of successes = Probability of success in each trial × Number of trials

For example, the probability of the spinner in Question **3** landing on green is 0.25. If the spinner is spun 20 times, you have:

   Expected number of times it lands on green = 0.25 × 20 = 5 times

Copy and complete the table of the expected number of successes in each case.

Probability of success	Number of trials	Expected number of successes
$\frac{1}{2}$	10	
$\frac{1}{4}$	80	
$\frac{2}{3}$	60	
0.24	100	
0.4	150	
0.75	120	

Combining probabilities and tree diagrams

There are four pets in a vet's waiting room, a white dog, a white cat, a black dog and a black cat. Two of these pets are owned by David. He has a dog and a cat. How many different possibilities are there?

Sometimes tree diagrams are used to help to calculate probabilities when there are two or more events.

Example 9.7 ▷ Dawn makes candles. The probability that a candle is damaged is 0.1. Each candle is made independently.

Dawn makes two candles. Calculate the probability that:

a Both candles are damaged.

b Only one candle is damaged.

The probabilities can be written on a tree diagram as shown.

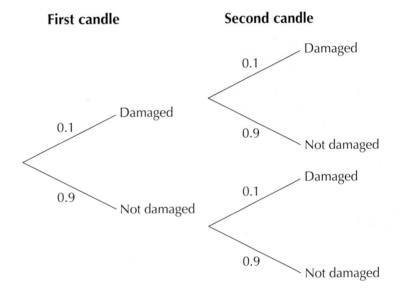

To work out the probability of one event happening and then another event happening independently, the probabilities must be multiplied together.

a The probability that the first candle is damaged and the second candle is damaged = 0.1 × 0.1 = 0.01

b There are two ways that *only one* candle could be damaged.

The first candle could be damaged and the second candle not damaged. Or the first candle could be not damaged and the second candle damaged.

The probability that the first candle is damaged and the second candle is not damaged = 0.1 × 0.9 = 0.09

The probability that the first candle is not damaged and the second candle is damaged = 0.9 × 0.1 = 0.09

This gives a total probability of 0.09 + 0.09 = 0.18.

Often, probability questions use fractions which need to be simplified.

Example 9.8 ▶

A cube is chosen from each bag. What is the probability of choosing two red cubes?

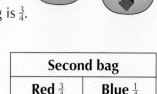

The probability of choosing a red cube from the first bag is $\frac{4}{5}$.

The probability of choosing a red cube from the second bag is $\frac{3}{4}$.

The probability of choosing red *and* red $= \frac{4}{5} \times \frac{3}{4} = \frac{3}{5}$.

Here is a two-way table showing all the different combinations.

		Second bag	
		Red $\frac{3}{4}$	Blue $\frac{1}{4}$
First bag	Red $\frac{4}{5}$	$\frac{4}{5} \times \frac{3}{4} = \frac{3}{5}$	$\frac{4}{5} \times \frac{1}{4} = \frac{1}{5}$
	Blue $\frac{1}{5}$	$\frac{1}{5} \times \frac{3}{4} = \frac{3}{20}$	$\frac{1}{5} \times \frac{1}{4} = \frac{1}{20}$

Exercise 9C

1 Two fair, six-sided dice are rolled. Copy and complete the tree diagram and use it to calculate the probability that the first dice lands on 5 or 6, and the second dice lands on an even number.

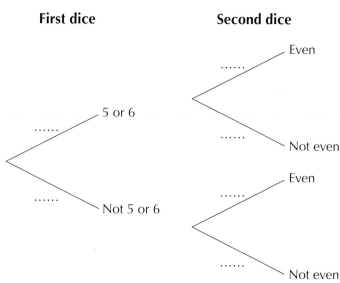

2 A woman goes to a health club. The probability that she goes on a Saturday is $\frac{1}{4}$. The probability that she goes swimming is $\frac{2}{3}$. Each event is independent. Calculate the probability for each of the following situations.

a She does not go on a Saturday.

b She does not go swimming.

c She goes on a Saturday and she goes swimming.

3 A cube is chosen from each bag.

a Copy and complete the two-way table.

		Second bag	
		Red $\frac{1}{5}$	Blue $\frac{4}{5}$
First bag	Red $\frac{1}{2}$		
	Blue $\frac{1}{2}$		

b What is the probability of choosing two red cubes?

c What is the probability of choosing one red cube and one blue cube? (Remember that it could be red and then blue *or* blue and then red.)

A player plays three games. The probability of winning each time is $\frac{2}{3}$.

a Copy and complete the tree diagram.

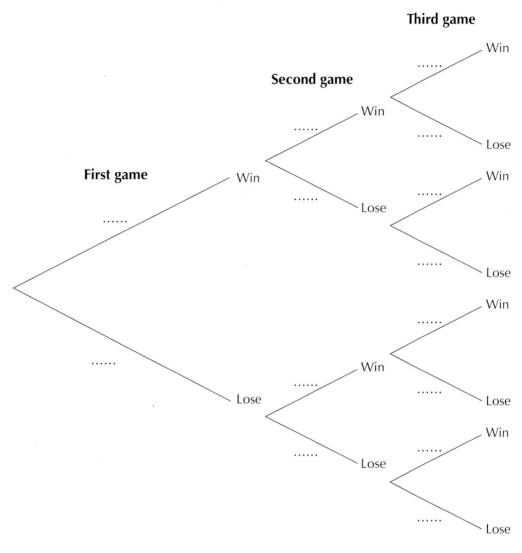

b Write down the different ways of winning at least two games.

c Work out the probability of winning at least two games.

Estimates of probability

In an experiment to test whether a dice is biased, the dice was rolled 120 times. These are the results.

Number on dice	1	2	3	4	5	6
Frequency	18	25	20	22	14	21

Do you think that the dice is biased?

Number 2 was rolled 25 times out of 120. So, an **estimate of the probability** of rolling number 2 is given by:

$$\frac{25}{120} = 0.208$$

The fraction $\frac{25}{120}$ is called the **relative frequency**.

Relative frequency is an estimate of probability based on experimental data. The relative frequency may be the only way of estimating probability when events are not equally likely.

$$\textbf{Relative frequency} = \frac{\textbf{Number of successful trials}}{\textbf{Total number of trials}}$$

Number 2 was rolled 25 times out of 120. So, for example, you would expect it to be rolled 50 times out of 240. The expected number of successes can be calculated from the formula:

Expected number of successes = Relative frequency × Number of trials

Hence, in this case, the expected number of times number 2 is rolled is given by:

$$\frac{25}{120} \times 240 = 50$$

Example 9.9 ▷

Look again at the example above.

A dice is rolled 120 times. Here are the results.

Number on dice	1	2	3	4	5	6
Frequency	18	25	20	22	14	21

a How could you obtain a more accurate estimate than the relative frequency?

b If the dice were rolled 1000 times, how many times would you expect to get a score of 2?

a A more accurate estimate could be obtained by carrying out more trials.

b The expected number of times a score of 2 is rolled in 1000 trials is given by:
$$0.208 \times 1000 = 208$$

Example 9.10 ▷

The relative frequencies of the number of times a spinner lands on red is shown in the table below.

Number of spins	10	20	50	75	100
Relative frequency of landing on red	0.3	0.25	0.28	0.24	0.26

a Plot the relative frequencies on a graph.

b Write down the best estimate of the number of times the spinner would land on red in 1000 spins.

c Do you think the spinner is fair? Explain your answer.

Example 9.10

continued

a

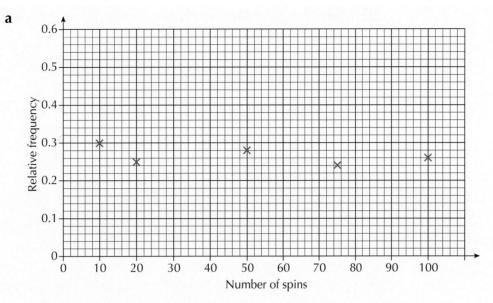

b The best estimate of the theoretical probability is 0.26 as this was the result of the most spins in the experiment. So the best estimate of the number of times the spinner would land on red is 0.26 × 1000 = 260.

c There are two out six sections of the spinner which are red, so if the spinner were fair, the theoretical probability of landing on red would be $\frac{1}{3}$. Also, in 1000 spins the spinner would be expected to land on red 333 times ($\frac{1}{3}$ of 1000). It is likely that this spinner is biased.

Exercise 9D

1 A four-sided spinner was spun 100 times. Here are the results.

Number on spinner	1	2	3	4
Frequency	20	25	23	32

a What is the estimated probability of a score of 4?

b Do you think from these results that the spinner is biased? Give a reason for your answer.

c If the spinner were spun 500 times, how many times would you expect to get a score of 4?

2 A drawing pin is thrown and the number of times that it lands point up is recorded at regular intervals and the results shown in the table.

a Copy and complete the table for the relative frequencies.

Number of throws	10	20	30	40	50
Number of times pin lands point up	6	13	20	24	32
Relative frequency of landing point up	0.6				

b What is the best estimate of the probability of the pin landing point up?

c How many times would you expect the pin to land point up in 200 throws?

3 A bag contains yellow and blue cubes. Cubes are picked from the bag, the colour recorded and the cubes replaced.

  a Copy and complete the table for the relative frequencies for the number of times a blue cube was chosen.

Number of trials	10	25	50	100
Number of times blue cube chosen	3	8	15	28
Relative frequency	0.3			

  b What is the best estimate of the probability of picking a blue cube from the bag?

  c You are now told that there are 75 cubes in the bag altogether. What is the best estimate of the number of blue cubes in the bag?

4 The number of times a coin lands on Heads is shown in the table below.

Number of throws	10	20	30	40	50
Number of Heads	7	12	18	22	28
Relative frequency of Heads	$\frac{7}{10} = 0.7$				

  a Copy and complete the table to show the relative frequency of Heads
  b Plot the relative frequencies on a graph
  c Write down the best estimate of the probability of a Head.
  d Use your estimate to predict the number of Heads in 200 throws.
  e Do you think the coin is biased towards Heads? Explain your answer.

5 The relative frequencies of the number of times a player wins a game of bowling is shown below.

Number of games	2	4	6	8	10
Relative frequency of winning	0.5	0.75	0.67	0.75	0.70
Number of wins					

  a Plot the relative frequencies on a graph.
  b Explain why it is not possible to tell from the graph whether the first game was a win.
  c Write down the best estimate of the probability of winning a game
  d Copy and complete the table to show the number of wins for 2, 4, 6, 8 and 10 games.

Here is a graph showing the relative frequency of the number of times a darts player hits the target.

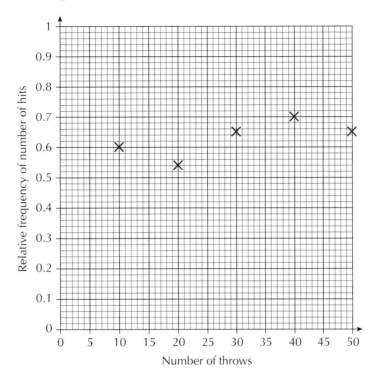

a How many times did the darts player hit the target in the first 10 throws?

b What is the best estimate of the probability of a hit?

c How many times would you expect the darts player to hit the target in 100 throws? State any assumptions that you make.

d Why is it not appropriate to use the graph to find out how many hits there were in the first 15 throws?

What you need to know for level 6

- How to identify outcomes from two events
- How to use tables and diagrams to show outcomes
- How to solve problems involving mutually exclusive events
- How to use the fact that the total probability of all mutually exclusive events of an experiment is 1

What you need to know for level 7

- How to take account of bias
- How to compare outcomes of experiments
- Understand relative frequency as an estimate of probability

What you need to know for level 8

- Understand how to calculate the probability of a compound event and use this in solving problems

National Curriculum SATs questions

LEVEL 6

1 *1996 Paper 2*

Barry is doing an experiment. He drops 20 matchsticks at random onto a grid of parallel lines.

Barry does the experiment 10 times and records his results. He wants to work out an estimate of probability.

Number of the 20 matchsticks which have fallen across a line

5	7	6	4	6	8	5	3	5	7

a Use Barry's data to work out the probability that a single matchstick when dropped will fall across one of the lines. Show your working.

b Barry continues the experiment until he has dropped the 20 matchsticks 60 times.

About how many matchsticks in total would you expect to fall across one of the lines? Show your working.

LEVEL 7

2 *2002 Paper 1*

I have a bag that contains blue, red, green and yellow counters. I am going to take out one counter at random.

The table shows the probability of each colour being taken out.

	Blue	Red	Green	Yellow
Probability	0.05	0.3	0.45	0.2

a Explain why the number of yellow counters in the bag cannot be 10.

b What is the smallest possible number of each colour of counter in the bag? Copy and complete the table.

Blue	Red	Green	Yellow

3 *1998 Paper 2*

Some students threw three fair dice.

They recorded how many times the numbers on the dice were the same.

Name	Number of throws	Results		
		All different	Two the same	All the same
Morgan	40	26	12	2
Sue	140	81	56	3
Zenta	20	10	10	0
Ali	100	54	42	4

a Write the name of the student whose data are most likely to give the best estimate of the probability of getting each result. Explain your answer.

b This table shows the students' results collected together:

Number of throws	Results		
	All different	Two the same	All the same
300	171	120	9

Use these data to estimate the probability of throwing numbers that are all different.

c The theoretical probability of each result is shown below:

	All different	Two the same	All the same
Probability	$\frac{5}{9}$	$\frac{5}{12}$	$\frac{1}{36}$

Use these probabilities to calculate, for 300 throws, how many times you would theoretically expect to get each result.

Copy the table below and complete it.

Number of throws	Theoretical Results		
	All different	Two the same	All the same
300	......	......	......

d Explain why the pupils' results are not the same as the theoretical results.

e Jenny throws the three dice twice.

Calculate the probability that she gets all the same on her first throw and gets all the same on her second throw. Show your working.

4 *2003 Paper 1*

    a   A fair coin is thrown. When it lands it shows Heads or Tails.

        Game: Throw the coin three times.

            Player A wins one point each time the coin shows a Head.

            Player B wins one point each time the coin shows a Tail.

        Show that the probability that player A scores three points is $\frac{1}{8}$.

    b   What is the probability that player B scores exactly two points? Show your working.

5 *2003 Paper 1*

    A girl plays the same computer game lots of times. The computer scores each game using 1 for win, 0 for lose.

    After each game, the computer calculates her overall mean score. The graph shows the results for the first 20 games.

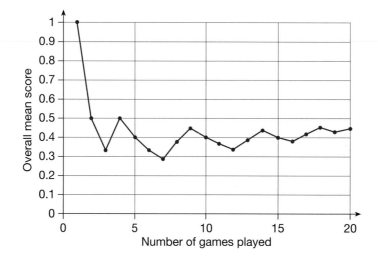

    a   For each of the first three games, write W if she won or L if she lost.

        First game ......   Second game ......   Third game ......

    b   What percentage of the 20 games did the girl win?

    The graph below shows the girl's results for the first 100 games.

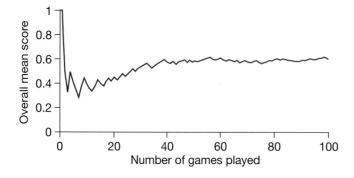

    c   She is going to play the game again. Estimate the probability that she will win.

d Suppose for the 101st to 120th games, the girl were to lose each game. What would the graph look like up to the 120th game?

Show your answer on a copy of the graph below.

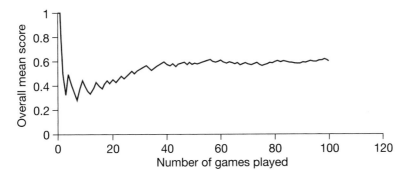

This chapter is going to show you	What you should already know
○ how to enlarge a shape by a fractional scale factor ○ how to use trigonometry to find lengths and angles in right-angled triangles ○ how to solve problems using trigonometry	○ How to enlarge a shape by a positive scale factor ○ How to recognise similar shapes ○ How to use Pythagoras' theorem

Fractional enlargements

Positive enlargement

The diagram will remind you how to enlarge triangle ABC by a **scale factor** of 3 about the centre of enlargement O to give triangle A'B'C'.

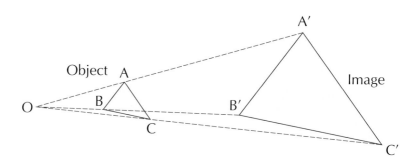

Lines called **rays** or **guidelines** are drawn from O through A, B, C to A', B', C'. Here, the scale factor is given as 3. So, OA' = 3 × OA, OB' = 3 × OB, OC' = 3 × OC. The length of each side of △A'B'C' is three times the length of the corresponding side of triangle ABC.

That is, the **object** triangle ABC is enlarged by a **scale factor** of 3 about the **centre of enlargement**, O, to give the **image** triangle A'B'C'.

The object and image are on the *same side* of O. The scale factor is positive. So, this is called **positive enlargement**.

Notice that the object and image are similar shapes, since the corresponding angles are equal and the corresponding sides are all in the ratio 1 : 3.

Fractional enlargement

In the diagram below, triangle ABC is enlarged by a scale factor of $\frac{1}{2}$ to give triangle A'B'C'.

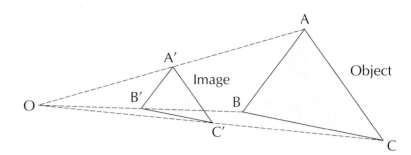

Each side of $\triangle$A'B'C' is half the length of the corresponding side of $\triangle$ABC. Notice also that OA' = $\frac{1}{2}$ of OA, OB' = $\frac{1}{2}$ of OB and OC' = $\frac{1}{2}$ of OC.

That is, the object $\triangle$ABC has been enlarged by a scale factor of $\frac{1}{2}$ about the centre of enlargement, O, to give the image $\triangle$A'B'C'.

The object and the image are on the *same side* of O, with the image *smaller* than the object. The scale factor is a fraction. This is called **fractional enlargement**.

Fractional enlargement on a grid

When fractional enlargement is on a grid, the principles are the same. The grid may or may not have coordinate axes, and the centre of enlargement may be anywhere on the grid.

The grid means that it is not always necessary to draw rays to find the image points.

Example 10.1 ▷ Enlarge $\triangle$ABC on the coordinate grid by a scale factor of $\frac{1}{2}$ about the origin (0, 0).

- Draw rays, or count grid units in the *x*- and *y*- directions, from points A, B, C to the origin.
- Multiply the ray lengths or the numbers of *x*, *y* units by $\frac{1}{2}$.
- Plot these new lengths or numbers of units to obtain points A', B', C'.
- Join these points to give $\triangle$A'B'C'.

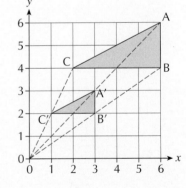

The object $\triangle$ABC has been enlarged by a scale factor of $\frac{1}{2}$ about the origin (0, 0) to give the image $\triangle$A'B'C'. Notice that we still use the term enlargement, even though the image is smaller than the object.

For a fractional enlargement about the *origin* of a grid, the coordinates of the object are multiplied by the scale factor to give the image coordinates. So here:

Object coordinates: A(6, 6)   B(6, 4)   C(2, 4)

Multiply each coordinate by $\frac{1}{2}$ to give: Image coordinates: A'(3, 3)   B'(3, 2)   C'(1, 2)

1 Draw copies of (or trace) the shapes below and enlarge each one by the given scale factor about the given centre of enlargement, O.

a Scale factor $\frac{1}{2}$

O ×

b Scale factor $\frac{1}{4}$

O ×

c Scale factor $\frac{1}{3}$

O ×

2 Draw copies of (or trace) the shapes below and enlarge each one by the given scale factor about the given centre of enlargement, O.

a Scale factor $1\frac{1}{2}$

O ×

b Scale factor $2\frac{1}{2}$

O ×

c Scale factor $-\frac{1}{2}$

× O

3 Copy the diagrams below onto a coordinate grid and enlarge each one about the origin (0,0) by multiplying the coordinates by the given scale factor. Plot your image coordinates and check them using rays.

a Scale factor $\frac{1}{2}$

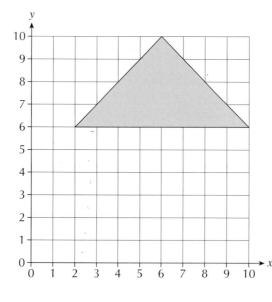

b Scale factor $\frac{1}{3}$

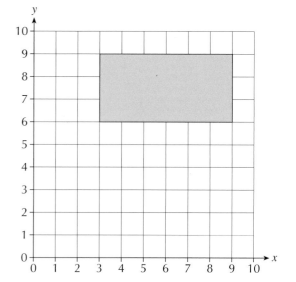

c Scale factor $\frac{1}{4}$

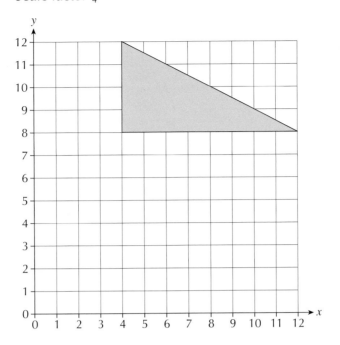

4 Copy the diagram shown onto centimetre squared paper.

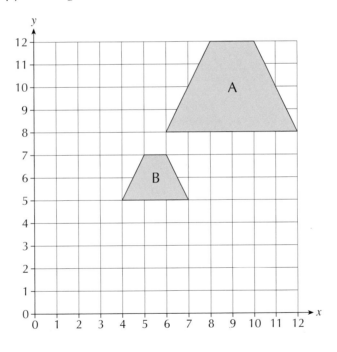

a Trapezium A is mapped onto Trapezium B by an enlargement. What is the scale factor of the enlargement?

b Find the coordinates of the centre of enlargement by adding suitable rays to your diagram.

c **i** Write down the areas of Trapezium A and Trapezium B.

  ii Use your answer to **c i** to find the ratio of the two areas in its simplest form.

d If a shape is enlarged by a scale factor of $\frac{1}{2}$, what is the area scale factor for the enlargement?

1   Working in pairs or groups, design a poster to show how the symbol on the right can be enlarged by different fractional scale factors about any convenient centre of enlargement.

2   a   i   Find the total surface area of the cuboid shown.
        ii   Find the volume of the cuboid.

    b   The cuboid is enlarged by a scale factor of 2.
        i   Find the total surface area of the enlarged cuboid and write down the area scale factor.
        ii   Find the volume of the enlarged cuboid and write down the volume scale factor.

    c   The original cuboid is now enlarged by a scale factor of 3.
        i   Find the total surface area of the enlarged cuboid and write down the area scale factor.
        ii   Find the volume of the enlarged cuboid and write down the volume scale factor.

    d   The cuboid is now enlarged by a scale factor of k.
        i   Write down the area scale factor.
        ii   Write down the volume scale factor.

3   Use ICT software, such as Logo, to enlarge shapes by different fractional scale factors and with different centres of enlargement.

Trigonometry – The tangent of an angle

Trigonometry is a branch of Mathematics that is concerned with calculating the lengths of sides and the size of angles in right-angled triangles. Its main use is in areas of engineering, navigation and surveying.

Right-angled triangles

In a right-angled triangle, such as those shown on the right:

- The side opposite the right angle (AC) is always the longest side and is known as the **hypotenuse**
- The side opposite the angle in question (labelled θ here) is called the **opposite** side (BC in the top triangle and AB in the bottom triangle)
- The side next to the angle in question is called the **adjacent** side (AB in the top triangle and BC in the bottom triangle).

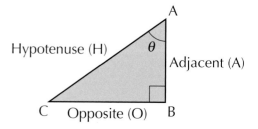

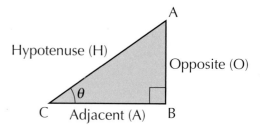

The tangent of an angle

Investigation ▶

Draw the diagram below accurately on 2mm graph paper, with AB = 3 cm, AC = 5 cm, AD = 8 cm and AE = 10 cm.

Measure the lengths of BF, CG, DH and EI to the nearest millimetre. Copy the table below and use these measurements to complete the table, giving your answers to two decimal places.

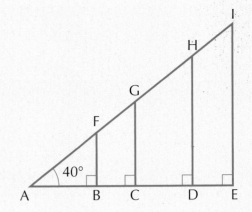

Ratio of sides	Answer to 2 dp
$\dfrac{BF}{AB}$	
$\dfrac{CG}{AC}$	
$\dfrac{DH}{AD}$	
$\dfrac{EI}{AE}$	

Using ∠A as 40°, you have found the values of the ratio of

$$\frac{\text{the opposite side}}{\text{the adjacent side}} \left(\frac{O}{A}\right) \text{ in Triangles ABF, ACG, ADH and AEI.}$$

If you have measured accurately, you should have found that the four ratios have the same value – approximately 0.84. The investigation has shown that the corresponding sides are in the same ratio. This means that the triangles are similar.

The value of the ratio you have just found is called **the tangent of angle A**, and is shortened to **tanA**. The value of the tangent of every angle is stored in your calculator.

Using your calculator

Before you start any calculations in trigonometry, you need to make sure that your calculator is in **degree mode**. You can check this by looking for D or DEG in the display.

To find the value of the tangent of an angle using your calculator, you first need to find the ⎡tan⎤ key. On some calculators you have to key in the size of the angle before you press the tan button:

⎡tan⎤ ⎡4⎤ ⎡0⎤

and on others you have to press the tan key before you key in the size of the angle:

⎡4⎤ ⎡0⎤ ⎡tan⎤

Find out how to use your calculator to find the tangent of an angle. The number on the display should be 0.839099631. Work through **Example 10.2** carefully to make sure you are using the keys in the correct order.

Example 10.2 ▷ Find the value of **i** tan20° **ii** tan32° **iii** tan72.3°. Give your answers to 3 decimal places.

i 0.364 **ii** 0.625 **iii** 3.133

The $\boxed{\text{tan}}$ key can be used to find the lengths of sides and the size of angles in right-angled triangles.

For right-angled triangles, we can use the formula $\textbf{tan}\theta = \dfrac{\textbf{Opposite}}{\textbf{Adjacent}}$.

Once you have found the value of tan θ, you will need to be able to find the value of the angle θ itself. You can use the inverse tan button function on your calculator to do this. This is usually marked above the tan key as tan⁻¹ or arctan. Depending on your calculator, you will need to press one of the following keys to access this function:

$\boxed{\text{2ndF}}$ $\boxed{\text{INV}}$ $\boxed{\text{SHIFT}}$

You will then need to press the tan key and the number keys in the same order as before. Work through **Example 10.3** carefully to make sure you are using the correct keys on your calculator.

Example 10.3 ▷ Find the value of θ if **i** tanθ = 0.3 **ii** tanθ = 0.724 **iii** tanθ = 3.764. Give your answers to 1 decimal place.

i 16.7° **ii** 35.9° **iii** 75.1°

Finding an angle

When you know the opposite and adjacent sides in a right-angled triangle, you can use tangents to calculate an angle. **Example 10.4** shows you how.

Example 10.4 ▷ Calculate the angle marked θ in the diagram below. Give your answer to 1 decimal place.

Using the formula $\textbf{tan}\theta = \dfrac{\textbf{Opposite}}{\textbf{Adjacent}}$

$$= \frac{5}{8} = 0.625$$

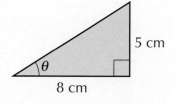

So, θ = 32.0° (1dp)

This can be done on a calculator in one sequence. This will depend on how your calculator works.

$\boxed{\text{2ndF}}$ $\boxed{\text{tan}}$ $\boxed{(}$ $\boxed{5}$ $\boxed{\div}$ $\boxed{8}$ $\boxed{)}$ $\boxed{=}$

Or, on some calculators you may have to key in

$\boxed{5}$ $\boxed{\div}$ $\boxed{8}$ $\boxed{=}$ $\boxed{\text{INV}}$ or $\boxed{\text{SHIFT}}$ $\boxed{\text{tan}}$

Finding the opposite side

You can use the same formula to calculate the length of the opposite side when you know the size of an angle and the length of the adjacent side in a right-angled triangle, as the following example shows.

Example 10.5 ▶ Calculate the length of the side marked x on the diagram below. Give your answer to 3 significant figures.

Using the formula **tan θ = $\dfrac{\text{Opposite}}{\text{Adjacent}}$**

$$\tan 42° = \frac{x}{5}$$

Multiplying both sides by 5, gives: $5\tan 42° = x$

So, $x = 4.50$ cm (3sf)

Depending on your calculator, this can be done in one sequence:

| 5 | × | tan | 42 | = | or | 5 | tan | 42 | = | or | 5 | × | 42 | tan | = |

Exercise 10B

1 Find the value of each of the following. Give your answers to 3 decimal places.

    a tan28°   **b** tan60°   **c** tan45°

    d tan9°   **e** tan37.2°   **f** tan85.1°

2 Find the value of θ for each of the following. Give your answers to 1 decimal place.

    a tanθ = 0.5   **b** tanθ = 0.23   **c** tanθ = 0.846

    d tanθ = 1.5   **e** tanθ = 2.33   **f** tanθ = 10

3 Find the value of each of the following. Give your answers to 3 significant figures.

    a 2tan37°   **b** 8tan25°   **c** 10tan45°

    d 24tan59°   **e** 3.5tan60.1°   **f** 14.8tan80.3°

4 Calculate the angle marked θ in each of the following triangles. Give your answers to 1 decimal place.

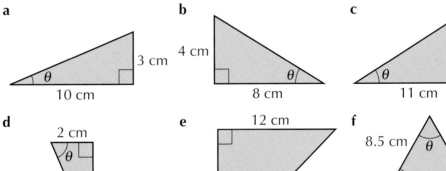

5 Calculate the length of the side marked x in each of the following triangles. Give your answers to 3 significant figures.

a

28°

8 cm

x

b

x

18°

10 cm

c

x

45°

14 cm

d

25 cm

52°

x

e

x

30°

5.7 cm

f

18.9 cm

65°

x

6 In the $\triangle PQR$, $\angle P = 90°$, $PQ = 6$ cm and $PR = 10$ cm. Find $\angle R$. Give your answer to 1 decimal place. **Hint:** Draw a sketch to help you.

7 In the $\triangle XYZ$, $\angle Z = 90°$, $\angle Y = 56°$ and $YZ = 7.2$ cm. Find the length of XZ. Give your answer to 3 significant figures. **Hint:** Draw a sketch to help you.

Extension Work

1   **Finding the adjacent side**

You can use the same trigonometric ratio to calculate the length of the adjacent side when you know the size of an angle and the length of the opposite side in a right-angled triangle, as the following example shows.

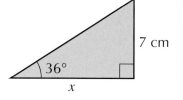

Calculate the length marked x on the diagram to the right. Give your answer to 3 significant figures.

Using the formula $\tan\theta = \dfrac{\text{Opposite}}{\text{Adjacent}}$

$$\tan 36° = \frac{7}{x}$$

Multiplying both sides by x, gives: $x\tan 36° = 7$

Dividing both sides by $\tan 36°$, gives $x = \dfrac{7}{\tan 36°}$

So, $x = 9.63$ cm (3sf)

Depending on your calculator, this can be done in one sequence:

| 7 | ÷ | tan | 36 | = | or | 7 | ÷ | 36 | tan | = |

Calculate the length of the side marked x in each of the following triangles. Give your answers to 3 significant figures.

a
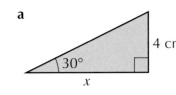
30°
4 cm
x

b
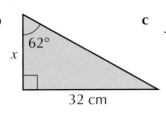
62°
x
32 cm

c
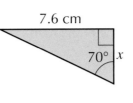
7.6 cm
70°
x

d
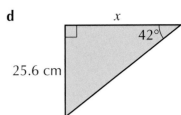
x
42°
25.6 cm

2 Angle of elevation and angle of depression

An angle of elevation is the angle measured from the horizontal when you look up to something.

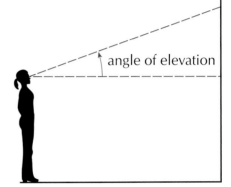
angle of elevation

An angle of depression is the angle measured from the horizontal when you look down at something.

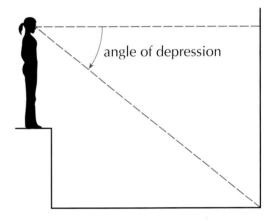
angle of depression

a The angle of elevation of the top of a tower from a point on the ground 400 m away from its base is 8°. Draw a sketch to show this and calculate the height of the tower. Give your answer to 3 significant figures.

b A boat is 250 m from the foot of vertical cliffs which are 50 m high. Draw a sketch to show this and calculate the angle of depression of the boat from the top of the cliffs. Give your answer to 1 decimal place.

Trigonometry – The sine and cosine of an angle

As you saw on page 171, for a right-angled triangle such as the one on the right, the tangent of the angle θ (tanθ) = $\frac{O}{A}$.

This is the ratio of two sides of a right-angled triangle – the opposite and the adjacent. We could just as easily have taken the ratio of any two sides such as the opposite and the hypotenuse or the adjacent and the hypotenuse.

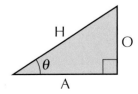
H
O
θ
A

In a right-angled triangle (such as the one above):

the value of the ratio $\dfrac{\text{Opposite}}{\text{Hypotenuse}}$ is called the **sine of the angle** θ, written as **sinθ**

the value of the ratio $\dfrac{\text{Adjacent}}{\text{Hypotenuse}}$ is called the **cosine of the angle** θ, written as **cosθ**.

The sine and cosine are used in the same way as tangent to find the lengths of sides and the size of angles in right-angled triangles when the length of the hypotenuse is either known or required.

The sin and cos keys on your calculator are used in exactly the same way as the tan key. Check that you know how to use them correctly by working through the **Examples 10.6–10.8**.

Example 10.6

1 Find the value of **i** sin25° **ii** sin38.6° **iii** cos45° **iv** cos65.3°. Give your answers to 3 decimal places.

  i 0.423   **ii** 0.624   **iii** 0.707   **iv** 0.418

2 Find the value of θ if **i** sinθ = 0.2 **ii** sinθ = 0.724 **iii** cosθ = 0.36 **iv** cosθ = 0. 895. Give your answers to 1 decimal place.

  i 11.5°   **ii** 46.4°   **iii** 68.9°   **iv** 26.5°

Example 10.7

Calculate the angle marked θ in the diagram below.
Give your answer to 1 decimal place.

The adjacent side and the hypotenuse are given, so use cosine:

$$\cos\theta = \frac{A}{H} = \frac{5}{12} = 0.416$$

So, θ = 65.4° (1dp)

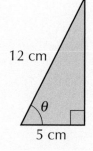

12 cm

θ

5 cm

Example 10.8

Calculate the length of the side marked x on the diagram below. Give your answer to 3 significant figures.

The angle and the hypotenuse are given, and the opposite side is required, so use sine:

7 cm

x

20°

$$\sin\theta = \frac{O}{H}$$

$$\sin20° = \frac{x}{7}$$

Multiply both sides by 7 to give: $7\sin20° = x$

So, $x = 7\sin20° = 2.39$ cm (3sf)

1 Find the value of each of the following. Give your answers to 3 decimal places.

  a sin18°   **b** sin30°   **c** sin65.8°
  d cos29°   **e** cos60°   **f** cos85.4°

2 Find the value of θ for each of the following. Give your answers to 1 decimal place.

  a sinθ = 0.1
  b sinθ = 0.53
  c sinθ = 0.855
  d cosθ = 0.4
  e cosθ = 0.68
  f cosθ = 0.958

3 Find the value of each of the following. Give your answers to 3 significant figures.

  a 3sin32°
  b 5sin45°
  c 12.2sin86°
  d 2cos9°
  e 3.8cos20.1°
  f 25cos68.9°

4 Calculate the angle marked θ in each of the following triangles. Give your answers to 1 decimal place.

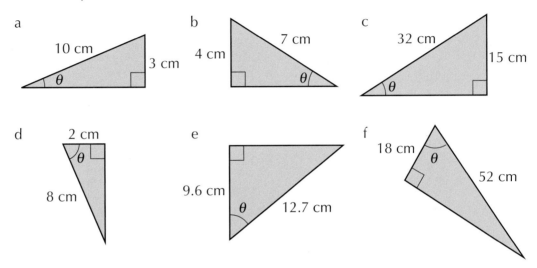

5 Calculate the length of the side marked x in each of the following. Give your answers to 3 significant figures.

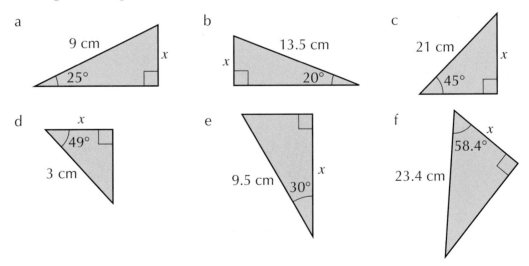

6 In the ΔABC, ∠B = 90°, ∠C = 72° and AC = 20 cm. Find the length AB. Give your answer to 3 significant figures.

7 In the ΔXYZ, ∠X = 90°, XZ = 8.6 cm and YZ = 13.2 cm. Find ∠Z. Give your answer to 1 decimal place.

1 Finding the hypotenuse

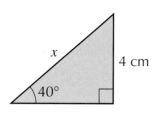

x

4 cm

40°

You can use the same trigonometric ratio to calculate the length of the hypotenuse when you know the size of an angle and the length of the opposite side or adjacent side in a right-angled triangle, as the following example shows.

Calculate the length of the side marked *x* on the diagram on the left. Give your answer to 3 significant figures.

Using the formula $\sin\theta° = \dfrac{\text{Opposite}}{\text{Hypotenuse}}$

$$\sin 40° = \frac{4}{x}$$

Multiplying both sides by *x*, gives: $x\sin 40° = 4$

Dividing both sides by $\sin 40°$, gives $x = \dfrac{4}{\sin 40°} = 6.22$ cm (3sf)

So, $x = 6.22$ cm (3sf)

Calculate the length of the side marked *x* in each of the following. Give your answers to 3 significant figures.

a

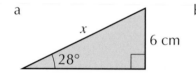

x

28°

6 cm

b

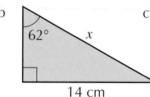

62°

x

14 cm

c

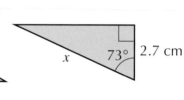

x

73°   2.7 cm

d

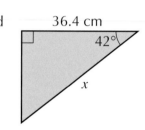

36.4 cm

42°

x

2 The graphs of $y = \sin\theta$ and $y = \cos\theta$

a Copy and complete the table below, giving your answers to two decimal places.

θ	0°	10°	20°	30°	40°	50°	60°	70°	80°	90°
sinθ										
cosθ										

b Write down anything you notice about the values of sinθ and cosθ.

c On 2 mm graph paper and using the same axes, draw the graphs of $y = \sin\theta$ and $y = \cos\theta$, for $0° \le \theta \le 90°$ and $0 \le y \le 1$.

Solving problems using trigonometry

When solving a problem using trigonometry, the following steps should be followed:

1 Draw a sketch of the right-angled triangle in the problem. Even when an illustration or diagram accompanies the problem, it is a good idea to redraw the triangle.

2 Mark on the sketch all the known sides and angles, including the units.

3   Identify the unknown side or angle by labelling it x or θ.

4   Decide and write down which ratio you need to solve the problem.

5   Solve the problem and give your answer to a suitable degree of accuracy. This is usually three significant figures for lengths and one decimal place for angles.

Example 10.10 ▷ A window cleaner has a ladder that is 8 m long. He leans it against a wall so that the foot of the ladder is 3 m from the wall. Calculate the angle the ladder makes with the wall.

1   Draw a sketch for the problem and write on all the known sides and angles:

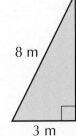

8 m

3 m

2   Identify the angle required by labelling it θ:

3   Decide and write down which ratio you need to use to solve the problem:

The opposite and hypotenuse are known, so sine should be used to solve the problem.

The ratio required is $\sin\theta = \dfrac{O}{H}$

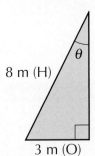

8 m (H)

θ

3 m (O)

4   Solve the problem:

$$\sin\theta = \frac{3}{8} = 0.375$$

So, $\theta = 22.0°$ (1 dp).

1 Simon places a ladder against a wall so that it makes an angle of 76° with the ground. When the foot of the ladder is 1.8 m from the foot of the wall, calculate how high up the wall the ladder reaches.

2 Veena walks for 800 m up a road that has a uniform slope of 5° to the horizontal. Calculate the vertical height she has risen.

3 Richard's slide is 7 m long and the top of the slide is 4.5 m above the ground. Calculate the angle the slide makes with the ground.

4 A ship is 8 km east and 5 km north of a lighthouse.

Calculate the bearing of the ship from the lighthouse.

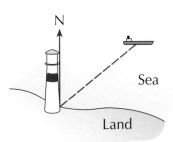

N

Sea

Land

5 Pat is flying a kite on a string that is 35 m long. She holds the string at 1 m above the ground at an angle of 42° with the horizontal. Calculate the height of the kite above the ground.

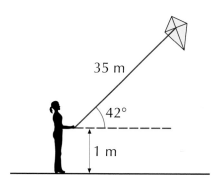

35 m

42°

1 m

6 Calculate the acute angle between the diagonals of a rectangle which has length 18 cm and width 10cm.

7 In the isosceles triangle ABC, AB = AC = 8 cm and ∠ABC = 64°. Calculate:

    a   the perpendicular height, h, of the triangle

    b   the length of BC

    c   the area of the triangle.

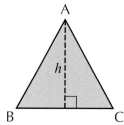

Extension Work

1 A plane flies for 200 km on a bearing of 135°. It then alters course and flies for 150 km on a bearing 135° of 040°.

    a   Calculate how far east the plane is from its starting point.

    b   Calculate how far south the plane is from its starting point.

    c   Calculate how far the plane is from its starting point.

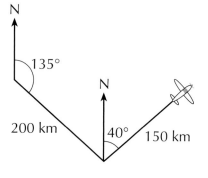

2 ABCDE is a regular pentagon of side 5 cm.

    a   Calculate the perpendicular height of ΔOCD

    b   Calculate the area of ΔOCD

    c   Hence calculate the area of the pentagon.

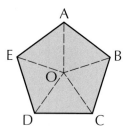

What you need to know for level 6

- How to enlarge a 2-D shape by a positive scale factor

What you need to know for level 7

- How to enlarge a 2-D shape by a fractional scale factor
- How to recognise similar shapes

What you need to know for level 8

- How to use sine, cosine and tangent in right-angled triangles
- How to solve problems using trigonometry

National Curriculum SATs questions

LEVEL 6

No questions available for topics covered in this chapter.

LEVEL 7

1 *2002 Paper 2*

The sketch shows two arrows.
The bigger arrow is an enlargement
by scale factor 1.5 of the smaller
arrow. Write down the three missing
values a, b and c. Don't forget to
include units.

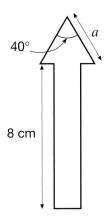

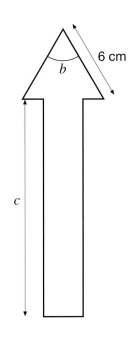

Not drawn accurately

LEVEL 8

2 *2002 Paper 1*

A picture has a board behind it. The drawings show the dimensions
of the rectangular picture and of the rectangular board.

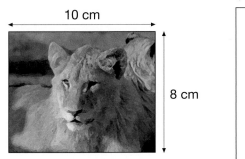

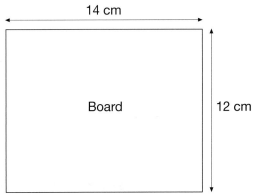

a Show that the two rectangles are not mathematically similar.

b Suppose you wanted to cut the board to make it mathematically similar to the picture.

Keep the width of the board as 14 cm. What should the new height of the board be? Show
your working.

3   *1999 Paper 2*

a   Ramps help people going into buildings.

Here are the plans for a ramp:

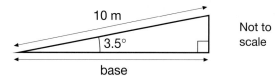

10 m

3.5°

base

Not to scale

How long is the base of this ramp? You must show your calculations.

b   The recommended gradient of a ramp is 1 in 20.

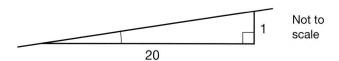

1

20

Not to scale

What angle gives the recommended gradient? You must show your calculations.

4   *1998 Paper 2*

Bargate is 6 km east and 4 km north of Cape Point.

a   Steve wants to sail directly from Cape Point to Bargate. On what bearing should he sail? Show your working.

b   Anna sails from Cape Point on a bearing of 048°. She stops when she is due north of Bargate.

How far north of Bargate is Anna? Show your working.

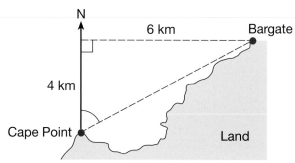

N

6 km   Bargate

4 km

Cape Point   Land

5   *2000 Paper 2*

ABC and ACD are both right-angled triangles.

a   Explain why the length of AC is 10 cm.

b   Calculate the length of AD. Show your working.

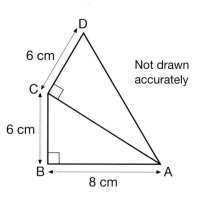

D

6 cm

C

6 cm

B   8 cm   A

Not drawn accurately

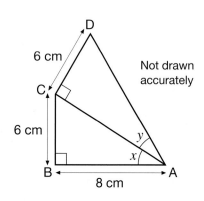

D

6 cm

C

6 cm

y

x

B   8 cm   A

Not drawn accurately

c   By how many degrees is angle x bigger than angle y? Show your working.

This chapter is going to show you	**What you should already know**
o how to expand algebraic expressions o how to factorise algebraic expressions o how to factorise quadratic expressions o how to change the subject of a formula	o How to multiply one expression by another o How to apply the simple rules of powers

Expansion

What is the area of this rectangle?

Split the rectangle into two smaller rectangles and find the area of each. Then the area of the original rectangle is the sum of the areas of the two smaller rectangles, as shown below:

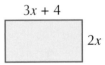

$$
\begin{array}{cc}
3x & 4 \\
2x\ \boxed{6x^2} & +\ \boxed{8x}\ 2x
\end{array}
$$

Area = $6x^2 + 8x$

This helps to illustrate the expansion of $2x(3x + 4)$, where the term outside the bracket multiplies every term of the expression inside the bracket. This is the principle of expanding brackets, which you met first in Year 8.

Take, for example, the next two expressions:

$$3(2x + 5) = 3\ \boxed{\underset{6x}{2x}}\ +\ \boxed{\underset{15}{5}}\ 3$$

$$= 3 \times 2x + 3 \times 5 = 6x + 15$$

$$t(8 - 3t) = t\ \boxed{} = t\ \boxed{\underset{8t}{8}}\ -\ \boxed{\underset{3t^2}{3t}}\ t$$

$$= t \times 8 - t \times 3t = 8t - 3t^2$$

Example 11.1 Find the two missing lengths, AB and CD, of this rectangle.

From the diagram, the length of AB is given by:

$$(2p + 7) - 3 = 2p + 7 - 3$$
$$= 2p + 4$$

Hence, the length of AB is $2p + 4$.

The length of CD is given by:

$$(5m + 6) - m = 5m + 6 - m$$
$$= 4m + 6$$

Hence, the length of CD is $4m + 6$.

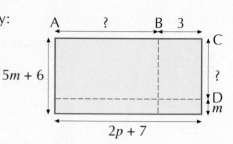

Exercise 11A

1 Expand each of the following.

a $3(x + 2)$	**b** $5(t + 4)$	**c** $4(m + 3)$	**d** $2(y + 7)$
e $4(3 + m)$	**f** $3(2 + k)$	**g** $5(1 + t)$	**h** $7(2 + x)$

2 Expand each of the following.

a $2(x - 3)$	**b** $4(t - 3)$	**c** $3(m - 4)$	**d** $6(y - 5)$
e $5(4 - m)$	**f** $2(3 - k)$	**g** $4(2 - t)$	**h** $3(5 - x)$

3 Expand each of the following.

a $4(2x + 2)$	**b** $6(3t - 4)$	**c** $5(2m - 3)$	**d** $3(3y + 7)$
e $3(3 - 3m)$	**f** $4(2 + 4k)$	**g** $6(1 - 2t)$	**h** $2(2 + 3x)$

4 Write down an expression for the area of each of the following rectangles. Simplify your expression as far as possible.

a $4t + 1$, 3 **b** $3x + 2$, 5 **c** $5x - 1$, 2 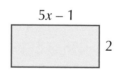   **d** $6x - 2$, 4 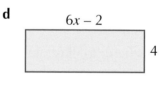   **e** 7, $4t - 2$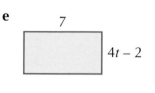

5 Expand each of the following.

a $x(x + 3)$	**b** $t(t + 5)$	**c** $m(m + 4)$	**d** $y(y + 8)$
e $m(2 + m)$	**f** $k(3 + k)$	**g** $t(2 + t)$	**h** $x(5 + x)$

6 Expand each of the following.

a $x(x - 2)$	**b** $t(t - 4)$	**c** $m(m - 3)$	**d** $y(y - 6)$
e $m(5 - m)$	**f** $k(2 - k)$	**g** $t(3 - t)$	**h** $x(6 - x)$

7 Expand each of the following.

a $x(4x + 3)$	**b** $t(2t - 3)$	**c** $m(3m - 2)$	**d** $y(4y + 5)$
e $m(4 - 5m)$	**f** $k(3 + 2k)$	**g** $t(4 - 3t)$	**h** $x(1 + 4x)$

8 Write down an expression for the area of each of the following rectangles. Simplify your expression as far as possible.

a
$2x + 3$

x

b
$5 - 3t$

t

c
$4 + 5m$

m

d
k

$7k - 2$

9 Expand and simplify each of the following.

a $3(x + 2) + 2(4 + 3x)$ **b** $4(t + 3) + 3(5 + 2t)$ **c** $4(m + 3) + 3(2 - 4m)$

d $5(2k + 4) + 2(3 - 4k)$ **e** $6(2x - 3) + 2(3 - 4x)$ **f** $5(3x - 2) + 3(1 - 2x)$

g $3(x + 4) - 2(3 + 2x)$ **h** $4(x + 5) - 3(4 + 2x)$ **i** $4(m + 2) - 3(2 - 3m)$

j $5(2m + 1) - 2(4 - 3m)$ **k** $5(2x - 1) - 2(1 + 3x)$ **l** $6(3x - 5) - 3(2 + 4x)$

m $3(x - 2) - 2(4 - 3x)$ **n** $4(2x - 1) - 3(5 - 2x)$

10 Write down the missing lengths in each of the following rectangles.

a
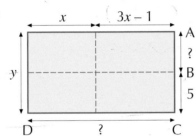

b
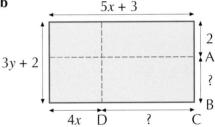

c
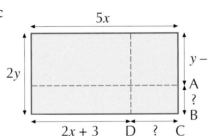

d
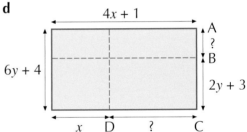

1 a Show that $\dfrac{1}{a} + \dfrac{1}{b} = \dfrac{(a + b)}{ab}$ is true for *all* values of a and b.

b Show that $\dfrac{a}{b} + \dfrac{c}{d} = \dfrac{(ad + bc)}{bd}$ is true for *all* values of a and b.

2 a Think of a number. Multiply it by 3 and add 15. Then divide the result by 3 and take away 5.

b What is the number you end up with? What do you notice? Try this with a few more numbers.

c Show by algebra that this result will *always* be the answer.

d Find another similar routine which gives a constant answer.

Factorisation

Factorisation is the opposite (inverse) process to expanding a bracket. For example, expanding $3(2x + 5)$ gives:

$$3(2x + 5) = 3 \times 2x + 3 \times 5$$
$$= 6x + 15$$

Factorisation starts with an expression, such as $6x + 15$, and works back to find the factors which, when multiplied together give that expression when simplified.

Example 11.2

Factorise $6x + 15$.

Look for a factor which will divide into each term in the expression. Here, that common factor is 3.

Now rewrite the expression using the common factor, which gives:

$$3 \times 2x + 3 \times 5$$

Insert brackets and place the common factor outside them, to obtain:

$$3(2x + 5)$$

Example 11.3

Factorise $8t - 3t^2$.

Look for a factor which will divide into each term in the expression. Here, that is t.

Now rewrite the expression using the common factor, which gives:

$$t \times 8 - t \times 3t$$

Insert brackets and place the common factor outside them, to obtain:

$$t(8 - 3t)$$

Always check your factorised expressions by expanding them. So, in the case of Example 11.2:

$$3(2x + 5) = 3 \times 2x + 3 \times 5$$
$$= 6x + 15$$

and in the case of Example 11.3:

$$t(8 - 3t) = t \times 8 - t \times 3t$$
$$= 8t - 3t^2$$

Exercise 11B

1 Factorise each of the following.

a $3x + 6$	**b** $4t + 6$	**c** $4m + 8$	**d** $5y + 10$
e $8 + 2m$	**f** $3 + 6k$	**g** $5 + 15t$	**h** $12 + 3x$

2 Factorise each of the following.

a $2x - 4$	**b** $4t - 12$	**c** $3m - 9$	**d** $6y - 9$
e $14 - 7m$	**f** $21 - 3k$	**g** $12 - 8t$	**h** $15 - 3x$

3 Factorise each of the following.

a $12x + 3$	**b** $6t - 4$	**c** $9m - 3$	**d** $3y + 6$
e $15 - 3m$	**f** $12 + 4k$	**g** $6 - 2t$	**h** $27 + 3x$

4 Write down an expression for the missing lengths of each of the following rectangles. Simplify each expression as far as possible.

a
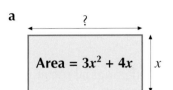

b
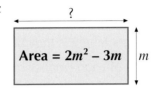

c
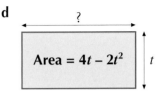

d

5 Factorise each of the following.

a $x^2 + 3x$	**b** $t^2 + 4t$	**c** $m^2 + 5m$	**d** $y^2 + 7y$
e $3m + m^2$	**f** $4k + k^2$	**g** $3t + t^2$	**h** $x + x^2$

6 Factorise each of the following.

a $x^2 - 3x$	**b** $3t^2 - 5t$	**c** $m^2 - 2m$	**d** $4y^2 - 5y$
e $2m - m^2$	**f** $4k - 3k^2$	**g** $5t - t^2$	**h** $7x - 4x^2$

7 Factorise each of the following.

a $3x^2 + 4x$	**b** $5t^2 - 3t$	**c** $3m^2 - 2m$	**d** $4y^2 + 5y$
e $4m - 3m^2$	**f** $2k + 5k^2$	**g** $4t - 3t^2$	**h** $2x + 7x^2$

8 Write down an expression for the missing lengths of each of the following rectangles.

a
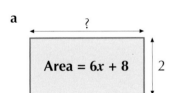

b
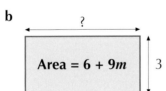

c
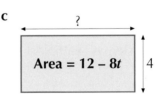

d
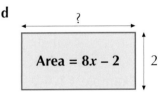

9 **a** Write down expressions for three consecutive integers, where the smallest of them is n.

b Write down an expression for the sum of these three consecutive integers. Simplify your expression as far as possible.

c Factorise this expression.

d Use your result to explain why the sum of *any* three consecutive integers is a multiple of 3.

Extension Work

a The area of a rectangle is $2x^2 + 4x$. Write down *three* different pairs of expressions for the possible lengths of two adjacent sides of the rectangle.

b Show, by substitution of $x = 1$, $x = 2$ and $x = 3$, that each pair of values generates the *same* values of areas.

c The area of another rectangle is $12x^2 + 18x$. Write down *seven* different pairs of expressions for the possible lengths of two adjacent sides of the rectangle.

Quadratic expansion

What is the area of this rectangle?

It is $(x + 3)(x + 2)$.

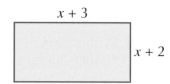

Its area can also be found by splitting each side into two sections, as shown below. The original rectangle is thus divided into four smaller rectangles.

The area of each smaller rectangle is then found, giving the area of the original rectangle as the sum of the areas of the four smaller rectangles.

	x	3	
	x^2	$3x$	x
	$2x$	6	2

The area of the four rectangles $= x^2 + 3x + 2x + 6 = x^2 + 5x + 6$

The area of the original rectangle $= (x + 3)(x + 2)$.

Hence:

$$(x + 3)(x + 2) = x^2 + 5x + 6$$

This illustrates the expansion of $(x + 2)(x + 3)$, where every term in the first bracket is multiplied by every term in the second bracket, as shown below.

$$(x + 3)(x + 2) = x^2 + 3x + 2x + 6$$
$$= x^2 + 5x + 6$$

Using this method of curved arrows makes dealing with negative signs inside the brackets much easier, as Example 11.4 shows.

Example 11.4 ▷ Expand $(x - 3)(x - 4)$.

$$(x - 3)(x - 4) = x^2 - 4x - 3x + 12$$
$$= x^2 - 7x + 12$$

Example 11.5 ▷ Expand $(x + 3)^2$.

$$(x + 3)^2 = (x + 3)(x + 3) = x^2 + 3x + 3x + 9 = x^2 + 6x + 9$$

Exercise 11C Expand each of the following expressions.

1 $(x + 3)(x + 4)$

2 $(x + 5)(x + 1)$

3 $(x + 2)(x + 7)$

4 $(x + 2)(x - 4)$

5 $(x + 4)(x - 3)$

6 $(x + 1)(x - 5)$

7 $(x - 3)(x + 2)$

8 $(x - 1)(x + 6)$

9 $(x - 4)(x + 3)$

10 $(x - 1)(x - 2)$

11 $(x - 3)(x - 6)$

12 $(x - 4)(x - 5)$

13 $(4 + x)(1 - x)$

14 $(5 + x)(2 - x)$

15 $(3 + x)(6 - x)$

16 $(x + 5)^2$

17 $(x - 3)^2$

18 $(2 - x)^2$

19 **Investigation**

a Take a square piece of card or paper and label the two adjacent sides, x.

The area of the square is x^2.

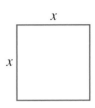

b In the unlabelled corner, draw a smaller square and label each side.

The area of the smaller square is y^2.

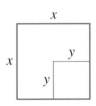

c Cut out this square of side y, and then label the remaining parts of the two sides $x - y$.

The area of this remaining shape must be $(x^2 - y^2)$.

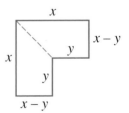

d Now cut this remaining shape diagonally, as indicated by the dashed line. Fit the two parts together, as shown.

The area remains, as before, $(x^2 - y^2)$.

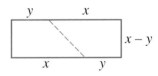

e This makes a rectangle of side $(x + y)$ and $(x - y)$.

Hence:

$$(x + y)(x - y) = x^2 - y^2$$

f It has been shown that the above identity is true geometrically. Now show it is also true algebraically.

20 The result $x^2 - y^2 = (x + y)(x - y)$ from Question **19** is called the **difference of two squares**, and can be used to solve certain arithmetic problems. For example, find the value of $32^2 - 28^2$ without squaring any numbers.

$$32^2 - 28^2 = (32 + 28)(32 - 28)$$
$$= 60 \times 4 = 240$$

Use this method to calculate each of the following.

a $54^2 - 46^2$

b $25^2 - 15^2$

c $17^2 - 3^2$

d $38^2 - 37^2$

e $29^2 - 21^2$

f $18^2 - 17^2$

g $8.1^2 - 1.9^2$

h $7.9^2 - 2.1^2$

i $999^2 - 998^2$

Expand each of the following quadratic expressions.

1 $(2x + 3)(4x + 1)$

2 $(3x + 2)(4x + 5)$

3 $(4x + 3)(2x - 1)$

4 $(5x - 2)(2x + 6)$

5 $(4x - 3)(2x - 4)$

6 $(5x - 3)^2$

Quadratic factorisation

Expansion removes brackets, so $(x + 2)(x + 4)$ gives $x^2 + 6x + 8$. Factorisation is the opposite of expansion and involves putting an expression back into the brackets from which it was derived.

This generally requires the application of what is called 'intelligent trial and improvement'.

Let's look at a few examples of factorising expressions in the form of $x^2 + Bx + C$.

Example 11.6   Factorise $x^2 + 6x + 8$.

Given the x^2 and both signs being +, the arrangement of brackets must be of the form $(x + a)(x + b)$. So, the question is what are the values of a and b?

The product ab is equal to 8. So, a and b must be a factor pair of 8. The choices are 8, 1 and 4, 2.

The sum of a and b is 6. So the pair required is 2 and 4. Hence:
$$x^2 + 6x + 8 = (x + 2)(x + 4)$$

Example 11.7   Factorise $x^2 - 9x + 20$.

Look at the signs. The second sign is a plus which means that the two signs in the brackets will be the same. The first sign is a minus which means that both signs are minuses.

From the x^2 and the signs, the arrangement of the brackets must be of the form $(x - a)(x - b)$. The question is what are the values of a and b?

The product ab is equal to 20. So, a and b must be a factor pair of 20. The choices are 20, 1; 10, 2; 5, 4.

The sum of a and b is -9. So, the pair required is -5 and -4. Hence :
$$x^2 - 9x + 20 = (x - 5)(x - 4)$$

Example 11.8 ▷   Factorise $x^2 - 5x - 24$.

Look at the signs. The second sign is a minus which means that the signs in the brackets will be different. The first sign is also a negative, which means that the larger number will need to be negative.

From the x^2 and the signs, the arrangement of the brackets must be of the form $(x + a)(x - b)$. The question is what are the values of a and b?

The product ab is equal to 24. So a and b must be a factor pair of 24. The choices are 24, 1; 12, 2; 8, 3; 6, 4.

The sum of a and b is -5. As the signs are different, this means that the *difference* of a and b is -5, with the larger number being negative. So, the pair required is 3 and -8. Hence:

$$x^2 - 5x - 24 = (x + 3)(x - 8)$$

Exercise 11D   Factorise each of the following.

1 $x^2 + 10x + 24$

2 $x^2 + 14x + 24$

3 $x^2 + 9x + 18$

4 $x^2 - 11x + 18$

5 $x^2 - 7x + 12$

6 $x^2 - 8x + 12$

7 $x^2 + 2x - 24$

8 $x^2 + 7x - 44$

9 $x^2 + 4x - 12$

10 $x^2 - 7x - 44$

11 $x^2 - 2x - 63$

12 $x^2 - x - 90$

13 $x^2 + 10x + 25$

14 $x^2 - 12x + 36$

15 $x^2 - 2x + 1$

16 $x^2 - 4$

17 $x^2 - 25$

18 $x^2 - 100$

Extension Work

Factorise each of the following. Take note of the coefficient of x^2.

1 $3x^2 + 4x + 1$

2 $3x^2 - 5x - 2$

3 $9x^2 + 12x + 4$

4 $2x^2 - 11x + 5$

5 $4x^2 - 15x - 25$

6 $6x^2 - 7x - 20$

Change of subject

The cost, in pounds sterling, of advertising in a local paper is given by the formula:

$$C = 10 + 4A$$

where A is the area (in cm^2) of the advertisement.

To find the cost of a 7cm^2 advertisement, substitute $A = 7$ into the formula to give:

$$C = 10 + 4 \times 7 = £38$$

To find the size of the advertisement you would get for, say, £60, you would take these two steps.

● Rearrange the formula to make it read $A = \dfrac{C - 10}{4}$

● Substitute $C = 60$ into this formula

When a formula is rearranged like this, it is called **changing the subject** of the formula. The subject of a formula is the variable (letter) in the formula which stands on its own, usually on the left-hand side of the equals sign. So, in this case, C is the subject in the original formula. In the rearranged formula, A becomes the subject.

To change the subject of a formula, use the same method as in solving equations. That is, do the same thing to both sides of the equals sign in order to isolate the variable which is to be the new subject. So, in this example:

$$C = 10 + 4A$$

● First, subtract 10 from both sides: $C - 10 = 4A$

● Then divide both sides by 4: $\dfrac{C - 10}{4} = A$

● Now switch the formula so that the subject is on the left-hand side:

$$A = \dfrac{C - 10}{4}$$

Hence, to find the size of an advertisement costing £60, substitute $C = 60$ to give:

$$A = \dfrac{60 - 10}{4} = 12.5 \text{ cm}^2$$

Exercise 11E

1. Change the subject of each of the following formulae as indicated.

    a   **i**   Make I the subject of $V = IR$.

        ii   Make R the subject of $V = IR$.

    b   **i**   Make U the subject of $S = U + FT$.

        ii   Make F the subject of $S = U + FT$.

        iii   Make T the subject of $S = U + FT$.

    c   **i**   Make b the subject of $P = 2b + 2w$.

        ii   Make w the subject of $P = 2b + 2w$.

    d   **i**   Make b the subject of $A = \dfrac{bh}{2}$.

        ii   Make h the subject of $A = \dfrac{bh}{2}$.

2 The formula $F = \dfrac{9C}{5} + 32$ is used to convert temperatures in degrees Celsius, C, to degrees Fahrenheit, F.

    a   Make C the subject of the formula.

    b   Use this formula to find the Celsius value of each of the following Fahrenheit temperatures. Give your answers to 1 decimal place.

        i   Temperature on the planet Corus, –65 °F.

        ii Body temperature of a reptile, 66.5 °F.

        iii Recommended temperature for a tropical fish tank, 56.5 °F.

3 The Greek mathematician Hero showed that the area A of a triangle with sides a, b and c is given by the formula:

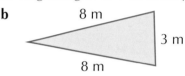

$$A = \sqrt{S(S - a)(S - b)(S - c)}$$

where $S = \dfrac{a + b + c}{2}$.

Use Hero's formula to find the area of the following triangles to 1 decimal place.

    a   **b**

5 cm   10 cm   8 m

12 cm   3 m   8 m

4 The estimated cost, £C, of making a pizza of radius r cm and depth d cm is given by:

$$C = \dfrac{r^2 d}{20}$$

    a   What is the estimated cost of making a pizza of radius 8 cm with a depth of 0.5 cm?

    b   What is the depth of a 10 cm radius pizza whose estimated cost to make is £3.75?

5 The area, A cm^2, of an ellipse is given by $A = \pi ab$. Calculate to one decimal place each of these.

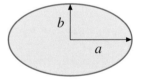

    a   The area of an ellipse with $a = 8$ cm and $b = 5$ cm.

    b   The length of a when $A = 150$ cm^2 and $b = 5$ cm.

    c   The length of b when $A = 45$ cm^2 and $a = 9.5$ cm.

6 Euler's theorem, which connects the number of nodes (N), the number of regions (R) and the number of arcs (A) of a figure, is stated as:

$$N + R - A = 2$$

Take, for example, the figure on the right. This shows 5 nodes, 3 regions (two inside and one outside the figure) and 6 arcs.

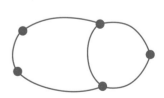

    a   Show that Euler's theorem is correct for the shape shown.

    b   Show that Euler's theorem is correct for a shape with 6 nodes and 5 regions.

    c   How many arcs will there be in a shape which has 10 nodes and 9 regions?

7 Rearrange each of the following to make y the subject.

    a $y - 2x + 3 = 0$ **b** $y - 3x + 5 = 0$ **c** $y + 2x - 9 = 0$

    d $y + 3x - 14 = 0$ **e** $y - 4x - 3 = 0$ **f** $y - 5x - 1 = 0$

8 **a**   Copy and complete the following values for each of the given equations.

     b   Use each table to draw the graph of its equation.

       i $y - 2x - 1 = 0$

x	−1	0	1	2	3
y					

      ii $y - 3x + 1 = 0$

x	−1	0	1	2	3
y					

     iii $y + 2x - 5 = 0$

x	−1	0	1	2	3
y					

9 Draw a pair of axes as shown on the right. Then, draw a graph of each of the following equations on this pair of axes.

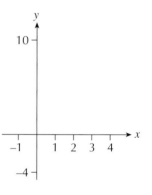

    a $y - x - 2 = 0$

    b $y - x - 5 = 0$

    c $y - x + 2 = 0$

    d $y - x + 1 = 0$

Comment on the similarities and the differences between the graphs.

10 Investigate the similarities and the differences between the following graphs.

    a $y + x - 2 = 0$ **b** $y + x + 2 = 0$ **c** $y + x - 5 = 0$ **d** $y + x + 1 = 0$

Extension Work

Investigate the similarities and the differences between the following graphs.

    a $\dfrac{y}{2} + 3x - 5 = 0$ **b** $\dfrac{y}{2} + 3x - 1 = 0$

    c $\dfrac{y}{3} + 2x - 4 = 0$ **d** $\dfrac{y}{3} + 2x - 3 = 0$

National Curriculum SATs questions

LEVEL 6/7

1 *1999 Paper 1*

a The diagram shows a rectangle 18 cm long and 14 cm wide.

It has been split into four smaller rectangles.

i Calculate the area of each small rectangle.

One has been done for you.

ii What is the area of the whole rectangle?

iii What is 18×14?

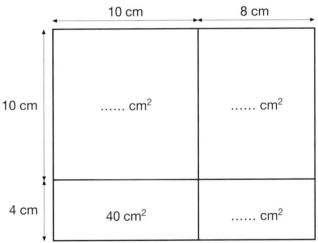

b The diagram shows a rectangle $(n + 3)$ cm long and $(n + 2)$ cm wide. It has been split into four smaller rectangles.

i Write a number or an expression for the area of each small rectangle.

One has been done for you.

ii What is $(n + 3)(n + 2)$ multiplied out?

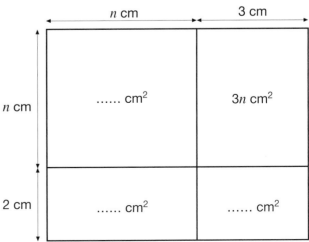

2 *2000 Paper 1*

    a   Two of the expressions below are equivalent. Write them down.

          $5(2y + 4)$ $5(2y + 20)$ $7(y + 9)$ $10(y + 9)$ $2(5y + 10)$

    b   One of the expressions below is not a correct factorisation of $12y + 24$. Which one is it? Write down your answer.

          $12(y + 2)$ $3(4y + 8)$ $2(6y + 12)$ $12(y + 24)$ $6(2y + 4)$

    c   Factorise this expression: $7y + 14$.

    d   Factorise this expression as fully as possible: $6y^3 - 2y^2$.

3 *1998 Paper 1*

    a   Find the values of a and b when $p = 10$.

$$a = \frac{3p^3}{2} \qquad b = \frac{2p^3(p - 3)}{7p}$$

    b   Simplify this expression as fully as possible:

$$\frac{3cd^2}{5cd}$$

LEVEL 8

4 *2000 Paper 1*

    a   Explain how you know that $(y + 3)^2$ is not equal to $y^2 + 9$.

    b   Multiply out and simplify these expressions.

        i $(y + 2)(y + 5)$ **ii** $(y - 6)(y - 6)$ **iii** $(3y - 8)(2y + 5)$

This chapter is going to give you practice in SATs questions about

- Number – fractions, percentages and decimals
- Number – the four rules, ratios and standard form
- Algebra – the basic rules and solving linear equations
- Algebra – graphs
- Shape, space and measures
- Handling data

Number 1 – Fractions, percentages and decimals

Exercise 12A   Do not use a calculator for the first five questions.

1 Calculate the following, giving your answers as fractions.

    a $\dfrac{3}{5} + \dfrac{1}{3}$ **b** $\dfrac{5}{9} - \dfrac{1}{6}$ **c** $2\dfrac{3}{4} + 1\dfrac{2}{5}$

2 The following method can be used to work out 12% of 320:

$$10\% \text{ of } 320 = 32$$
$$1\% \text{ of } 320 = 3.2$$
$$\underline{1\% \text{ of } 320 = 3.2}$$
$$12\% \text{ of } 320 = 38.4$$

Use a similar method or a method of your own to work out 28% of 480.

3 **a** Calculate **i** 0.2×0.4 **ii** $600 \div 0.3$

    b Estimate the answer to $\dfrac{479 \times 0.48}{0.59}$

4 **a** Which calculation below gives the answer to the question?

    In a sale, Tomb Taker III, which is priced at £45, is reduced by 15%. The sale price is then reduced by a further 10%. How much is Tomb Taker III now?

      $45 \times 0.15 \times 0.10$ $45 \times 1.15 \times 1.1$ $45 \times 0.85 \times 0.9$ $45 \times (0.85 + 0.9)$

    b What value do you multiply by to increase a quantity by 13%?

5 For each part of the question, where n is always an integer, write down the answer that is true and explain your choice.

    a When n is even, $\dfrac{n(n+1)(n+2)}{4}$ is:

        Always odd   Always even   Sometimes odd, sometimes even

    b When n is even, $\dfrac{n(n+1)(n+2)}{6}$ is:

        Always an integer   Always a fraction   Sometimes an integer, sometimes a fraction

 You may use a calculator for the rest of the exercise.

6 Some bathroom scales measure in stones and pounds, whilst others measure in kilograms. One way to change from stones and pounds to kilograms is shown below.

Number of stones	→	Multiply by 14	→	Add number of pounds	→	Divide by 2.2	→	Answer is weight in kilograms

Convert 11 stone 10 pounds to kilograms.

7 The train fare for an adult from Sheffield to London is £97. A child's fare is 35% less than this. How much is a child's fare?

8 Jack's Jackets is having a sale:

Calculate the sale price of a jacket that is normally priced at £42.60.

9 This table shows the populations (in thousands) of the eight largest towns in the United Kingdom in 1991 and in 2001. It also shows the percentage change in the populations of the towns over that 10 year period.

	London	Birmingham	Leeds	Glasgow	Sheffield	Liverpool	Manchester	Bristol
1991	6 800	1 007	717	660	529	481	439	407
2001	7 200	1 017	731	692	531	456		423
% change	5.9%	1%	2.0%	4.8%	0.3%	−5.2%	−3.2%	

    a How many more people lived in Leeds than Sheffield in 2001?

    b Calculate the population of Manchester in 2001.

    c Calculate the percentage change in the population of Bristol over the 10 years.

10 A garage records the sales of fuel in one morning.

Fuel	Number of litres sold	Takings
Unleaded	345	£262.89
Premium	180	£142.56
Diesel	422	£289.07
LP Gas	25	£12.15
Lead replacement	125	£96.25
Total	**1097**	**£802.92**

a   What percentage of the total litres sold was Unleaded?

b   What percentage of the total money taken was for Diesel?

c   Which is cheaper per litre, Unleaded or Lead replacement?

11 The table shows the number of mobile phones per thousand of the population in the USA and Britain.

	1995	2003
USA	740	830
Britain	440	

a   Between 1995 and 2003 the use of mobile phones in Britain increased by 81.8%. How many people per 1000 had mobile phones in Britain in 2003?

b   What was the percentage increase in mobile phone use in the USA between 1995 and 2003?

12 On Sunday, an Internet auction site posted some computers for sale. Each day the price of the computers is reduced by 12% of the price the day before.

a   A computer was priced at £950 on Sunday. Derek bought it on Monday. How much did he pay for it?

b   Another computer sold for £439.12 on Monday. What was its price on Sunday?

c   A computer was priced at £560 on Sunday. It was eventually sold on Friday. How much did it sell for?

d   John decides to take a chance on a computer that is priced at £1500 on Sunday, and wait until it is less than half the original price. How many days will he have to wait?

13 The following formula can be used to calculate the area of a triangle with sides a, b and c.

$$A = \sqrt{s(s-a)(s-b)(s-c)} \quad \text{where } s = \tfrac{1}{2}(a+b+c).$$

a   If a triangle has sides of length $a = 4.5$ cm, $b = 7.5$ cm and $c = 9.5$ cm, calculate the area of the triangle. Write down all the digits shown on your calculator.

b   Round off your answer to three significant figures.

Number 2 – The four rules, ratios and standard form

Exercise 12B

Do not use a calculator for the first six questions.

1 Litter bins cost £29 each. A school has a budget of £500 to spend on bins. How many bins can the school afford?

2 Alf and Bert are paid £48 for doing a job. They decide to share the money in the ratio 3 : 5. How much does Alf get?

3 Work out **a** 24×0.6 **b** $54 \div 0.6$ **c** 0.2×0.3

4 Find the values of a, b and c.

    a $81 = 3^a$ **b** $256 = 2^b$ **c** $64 = (2^2)^c$

5 Look at the six cards with numbers on below.

$(-1)^2$ 4^4 $(-2)^6$ 8^2 5^9 $(-3)^4$

    a Which card has the largest value?
    b Which two cards have the same value?
    c Which card is equal to 2^8?
    d Which cards have values that are cube numbers?

6 **a** Which of these statements is true?
        i $3^2 \times 10^3$ is smaller than $3^3 \times 10^2$
        ii $3^2 \times 10^3$ is equal to $3^3 \times 10^2$
        iii $3^2 \times 10^3$ is larger than $3^3 \times 10^2$
    b Which two numbers below are equal?
        360×10^2 3.6×10^3 36×10^2 0.36×10^5 $(3.6 \times 10)^2$
    c One of these numbers has the same value as 5.4×10^{-2}. Which one?
        0.54×10^{-3} 54×10^{-3} 0.54×10^{-1} 54×10^{-1} 540×10^{-5}

You may use a calculator for the rest of the exercise.

7 A car company wants to move 700 cars by rail. Each train can carry 48 cars.
    a How many trains will be needed to move the 700 cars?
    b Each train costs £3745. What is the total cost of the trains?
    c What is the cost per car of transporting them by train?

8 **a** A bus travels 234 miles in 4 hours and 30 minutes. What is the average speed of the bus?
    b A car travels 280 miles at an average speed of 60 miles per hour. How long was the car travelling for? Give your answer in hours and minutes.

9 Concrete is made by mixing cement and sand in the ratio 1 : 4.

  a What weight of sand is needed to mix with four bags of concrete, each weighing 25 kg?

  b Frank needs one tonne of concrete. How many 25 kg bags of cement will he need?

10 Parking tickets cost £1.25 each. In one day a ticket machine takes the coins listed in the table.

  How many tickets were sold that day?

Coin	Number of coins
£1	126
50p	468
20p	231
10p	185
5p	181

11 A litre jug contains orange squash and water in the ratio 1 : 4. A 900 ml jug contains orange squash and water in the ratio 2 : 7. Both jugs are poured into a two-litre jug. This is then topped up with water. What is the ratio of orange squash to water in the two-litre jug now?

12 The diameter of a virus is 0.000 001 cm.

  a Write this number in standard form.

  b How many viruses would fit across a full stop which has a diameter of 0.05 cm? Give your answer in standard form.

13 The table below shows the population of some areas of the world in 2000 together with their yearly population growth.

Continent	Population (2000)	Growth per year
Asia	8.25×10^8	2.5%
Australia	1.92×10^7	0.7%
Pacific Islands and New Zealand	1.4×10^7	1.1%

  a Australia, the Pacific Islands and New Zealand form the continent of Oceania. Work out the population of Oceania.

  b If the growth rate of Asia continues at the same rate, work out the population of Asia in 2003. Give your answer in standard form to three significant figures.

  c If the growth rate of Australia continues at the same rate, work out the population of Australia in 2010. Give your answer in standard form to three significant figures.

Algebra 1 – Basic rules and solving linear equations

Exercise 12C

Do not use a calculator for this exercise.

1 The diagram shows a square with sides of length $(n + 4)$ cm.

The square has been split into four smaller rectangles. The area of one rectangle is shown.

	n	4
n	......	$4n$
4	......	......

   a On a copy of the diagram, fill in the three missing areas with a number or an algebraic expression.

   b Write down an expression for the total area of the square.

2 Expand each of the following brackets and simplify each expression if possible.

   a $4(x - 5)$ **b** $3(2x + 1) + 5x$ **c** $3(x - 2) + 2(x + 4)$

   d $5(3x + 4) + 2(x - 2)$ **e** $4(2x + 1) - 3(x - 6)$

3 **a** When $x = 4$ and $y = 6$, work out the value of each of the three expressions below.

       i $3x + 9$ **ii** $4x - y$ **iii** $2(3x + 2y + 1)$

   b Solve the equations below to find the value of z in each case.

       i $5z + 9 = 24$ **ii** $\dfrac{z - 8}{2} = 7$ **iii** $5z + 9 = 3z + 7$

4 Two friends, Selma and Khalid are revising algebra.

Selma says: 'I am thinking of a number. If you multiply it by 6 and add 3, you get an answer of 12.'

Khalid says: 'I am thinking of a number. If you multiply it by 3 and subtract 6, you get the same answer as adding the number to 7.'

   a Call Selma's number x and form an equation. Then solve the equation.

   b Call Khalid's number y and form an equation. Then solve the equation.

5 For each equation below, write down the missing expression to make the equation true.

   a $\boxed{3n - 1} + \boxed{\ldots\ldots\ldots} = \boxed{5n + 3}$ **b** $\boxed{6n + 9} - \boxed{\ldots\ldots\ldots} = \boxed{5n + 3}$

   c $\boxed{6n + 1} + \boxed{\ldots\ldots\ldots} = \boxed{5n + 3}$ **d** $\boxed{8n + 2} - \boxed{\ldots\ldots\ldots} = \boxed{5n + 3}$

6 **a** You are told that $2a + 4b = 15$ and that $2b - c = 13$.

     Write down the values of:

       i $6a + 12b = \ldots$ **ii** $4b - 2c = \ldots$ **iii** $2a + 2c = \ldots$

   b Factorise each of the following:

       i $3x + 6y$ **ii** $x^2 + x$ **iii** $4ab + 6a$

7 Solve each of the following equations.

   a $3x + 7 = x + 10$ **b** $5x - 6 = 10 - 3x$ **c** $3(x + 3) = x + 8$

8 **a** Two of the expressions below are equivalent. Which ones are they?

$3(4x - 6)$ $\qquad$ $2(6x - 4)$ $\qquad$ $12(x - 3)$ $\qquad$ $6(2x - 3)$ $\qquad$ $8(4x - 1)$

b Factorise this expression:

$6y - 12$

c Factorise this expression as fully as possible:

$9y^2 - 6y$

9 Look at this sequence of fractions:

$$\frac{2}{5} \qquad \frac{4}{7} \qquad \frac{6}{9} \qquad \frac{8}{11} \qquad \frac{10}{13} \qquad \cdots$$

a What is the nth term of this sequence ?

b Another sequence has an nth term of $\dfrac{n^2}{n^2 + 1}$. The first term is $\dfrac{1}{2}$.

Write down the next three terms.

c The sequence in part **b** goes on forever and reaches a limit. What is the limit?

10 **a** Find the value of these expressions when $x = 2$.

i $\dfrac{3x^3}{8}$ $\qquad\qquad\qquad$ **ii** $\dfrac{2x^2(x + 3)}{5x}$

b Simplify the expression $\dfrac{4x^2y^3}{6xy}$.

c Simplify these expressions:

i $4(x - 3) - 3(x + 4)$ $\qquad$ **ii** $2(3y + 4x) + 3(y - 2x)$

11 Solve the following equations.

a $5 - 3y = 12 - 4y$ $\qquad$ **b** $\dfrac{7y}{y - 1} = 5$ $\qquad$ **c** $\dfrac{4}{y - 2} = y - 2$

12 Simplify these expressions:

a $(x - 4)(x - 4)$ $\qquad$ **b** $(x - 4)(x + 5)$ $\qquad$ **c** $(3x - 2)(4x + 1)$

13 The triangle and the rectangle have the same area.

Find the value of z.

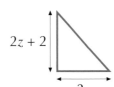 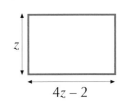

Algebra 2 - Graphs

Exercise 12D

Do not use a calculator for this exercise.

You will need graph paper or centimetre-squared paper.

For all the graphs you are asked to draw, axes the size of those in Question 4 will be large enough.

1 In a house, the hot-water tank automatically refills with cold water whenever hot water is taken out. The heating system then heats the water to a pre-set temperature.

Dad always has a shower in the morning. Mum always has a bath and the two children get up so late that all they do is wash their hands and faces.

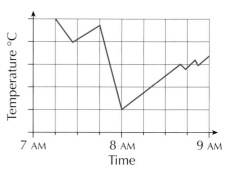

The graph shows the temperature of the water in the hot-water tank between 7 am and 9 am one morning.

a At what time did Dad have his shower?

b At what time did Mum have her bath?

c At what time did the first child wash?

d Gran likes to have as hot a bath as possible, once everyone else has left the house at 9 am. Estimate at what time the water will be back to its maximum temperature.

2 For every point on the graph of $x + y = 6$, the x- and y-coordinates add up to 6. Which of the following points lie on the line?

a **i** (3, −3)   **ii** (6, 0)
      iii (−7, −1)   **iv** (−1, 7)

b On a grid draw the graph of $x + y = 6$.

3 The prison population of Britain is increasing rapidly, as is the use of illegal drugs. These graphs show the change in prison population and drug use between 1998 and 2001.

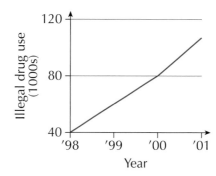 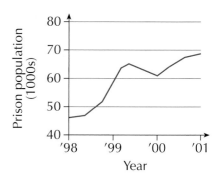

Use the graphs to decide for each of the following statements, **a**, **b** and **c**, if:

- the statement is true
- the statement is false
- you cannot be sure if it is true or false from the information given

Use only the information given in the graphs. Do not use any facts that you might already know about the subject. Explain your answers.

a There is a positive correlation between prison population and illegal drug use.

b The prison population will reach 70 000 before 2008.

c Reducing illegal drug use will decrease the prison population.

4 The graph shows the line $y = 2x + 2$.

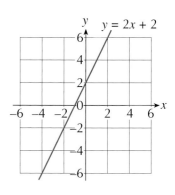

a Copy the graph and draw and label the line $y = 2x - 1$ on the same axes.

b Draw and label the line $y = x + 2$ on the same axes.

c Write down the coordinates of the point where the graphs $y = 2x - 1$ and $y = x + 2$ intersect.

5 The diagram shows a rectangle ABCD.

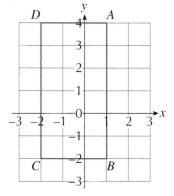

a The equation of the line AB is $x = 1$.
What is the equation of the line CB?

b The equation of the diagonal AC is $y = 2x + 2$.
What is the equation of the diagonal BD?

c Write down the equations of the two lines of symmetry of the rectangle.

6 a On the same axes, draw and label the graphs of $y = -3$, $x = 2$ and $y = 3x$.

b The three lines you have drawn enclose a triangle. Work out the area of this triangle in square units.

7 Here are the equations of six graphs.

A $y = 2x - 1$ B $y = x$ C $y = 2$ D $x = 2$

E $y = 2x + 3$ F $y = \frac{1}{2}x - 1$

a Which two graphs are parallel?

b Which two graphs are perpendicular?

c Which pair of graphs cross the y-axis at the same point?

d Which pair of graphs cross the x-axis at the same point?

8 The graph on the right shows the journey of a train from Leeds to London, stopping at Doncaster.

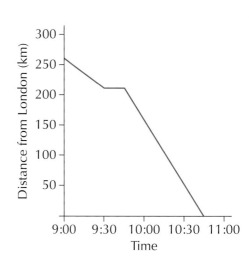

a What time did the train arrive at Doncaster?

b What was the average speed of the train for the whole journey?

9 The diagram shows two graphs, A and B.

    a   Show that the equation of line A is $x + 2y = 8$.

    b   Write down the equation of line B.

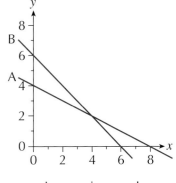

10 The graph on the right shows the equation $y = x^2 - 4$.
Use the graph to solve the equation $x^2 = 6$.

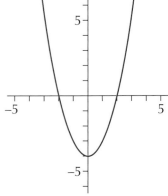

11 Copy the diagram exactly and number both axes from 0 to 4.

    a   Write down three inequalities that describe the shaded region shown on the right.

    b   Mark the region described by the following inequalities with the letter R.

$$y \geq x$$
$$y \leq 4$$
$$3 \leq x \leq 4$$

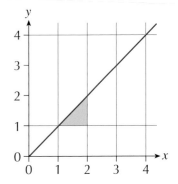

Shape, space and measures

Do not use a calculator for Questions 1 to 5.

You will find squared paper useful for Question 10.

1 Find the values of angles a, b and c in this diagram. The lines marked with arrows are parallel.

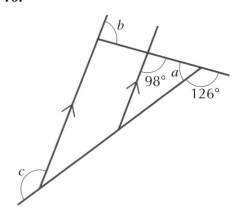

2 Calculate the area of the trapezium shown on the right.

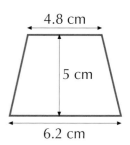

4.8 cm

5 cm

6.2 cm

3 **a** What is the volume of the prism shown on the right?
b The prism below has the same volume as the prism in part **a**. What is the cross-sectional area?

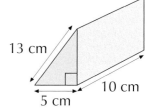

13 cm

5 cm

10 cm

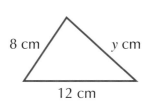

Cross section

12 cm

4 The two triangles shown are similar. Calculate the values of *x* and *y*.

8 cm

y cm

12 cm

12 cm

15 cm

x cm

5 **a** A rectangle measures 24 cm by 12 cm.
What is its area?

b The rectangle is folded in half several times until it measures 6 cm by 3 cm.
How many times was it folded?

c What is the ratio of the areas of the original rectangle and the smaller rectangle?
Give your answer in its simplest form.

12 cm

24 cm

3 cm

6 cm

You may use a calculator for the rest of this exercise.

6 This car speedometer shows speed in both miles per hour (mph) and kilometres per hour (kph). Use the speedometer to answer the following questions.

a How many kilometres are equivalent to 50 miles?

b Is someone travelling at 100 kph breaking the speed limit of 70 mph? Justify your answer.

c About how many miles is 150 kilometres? Explain your answer.

7 **a** Make an accurate construction of this triangle.

    b Measure the angle at A.

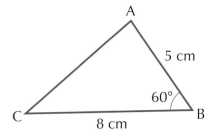

8 ABCD is an isosceles trapezium.

    a Work out the size of angles
       a, *b* and *c* in the diagram.

    b Explain how you know that BE is
       parallel to AD.

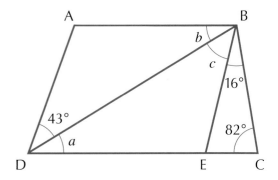

9 The diagram shows a cuboid and a triangular prism. Both solids have the same
volume. Use this information to calculate the length of the prism.

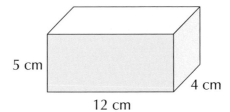

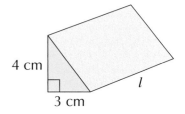

10 Copy the diagram onto squared paper
and enlarge the shape by a scale factor
of 3, using the point O as the centre of
enlargement.

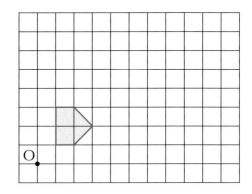

11 **a** Calculate the length of the side marked *x* in this
right-angled triangle.

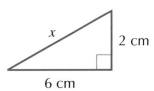

    b Calculate the length of the side marked *y* in this
right-angled triangle.

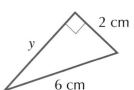

12 a What is the area and perimeter of this sector of a circle?

b A semicircle of radius 5 cm has the same perimeter as a circle of radius, r. Calculate the value of r. Give your answer to 3 sf.

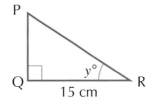

13 In the two triangles shown below, the lengths AB and PQ are equal. Calculate the value of the length x and the angle y.

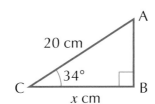

Handling data

Do not use a calculator for Questions 1 to 7.

1 A bag contains only red and blue marbles. A marble is to be taken from the bag at random.

It is twice as likely that the marble will be red as blue. Give a possible number of red and blue marbles in the bag.

2 Look at the three different spinners, P, Q and R, on the right.

 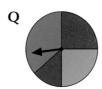 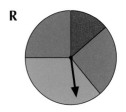

a Which spinner has the greatest chance of landing on red?

b Which spinner has an even chance of landing on blue?

c Which two spinners have an equal chance of landing on green?

3 Paul's marks for his last nine maths homeworks are:

9   3   5   4   4   7   5   8   6

a What is the range of his marks?

b What is the median mark?

c After checking his final homework, Paul realised that his teacher did not mark one of the questions. Once this had been marked, Paul's mark increased from 6 to 8.

Say whether each of the statements, **i**, **ii** and **iii** are true, false or if it is not possible to say. Explain your answers.
  i The mode of the marks has increased.
  ii The median mark has increased.
  iii The mean mark has increased.

4 The probability that a ball taken at random from a bag is black is 0.7. What is the probability that a ball taken at random from the same bag is *not* black?

5 Lee and Alex are planning a survey of what students at their school prefer to do at the local entertainment complex, where there is a cinema, a bowling alley, a games arcade and a disco.

    a Alex decides to give out a questionnaire to all the students in a Year 7 tutor group. Explain why this may not give reliable results for the survey.

    b Lee decides to include this question in his questionnaire:

        How many times in a week do you go to the entertainment complex?

        Never ☐   1–2 times ☐   2–5 times ☐   Every day ☐

    Explain why this is not a good question.

6 x is a whole number bigger than 1. For the five values on the cards below:

    a What is the median value?

    b What is the mean value?

    $\boxed{3x}$ $\boxed{2x + 1}$ $\boxed{x + 1}$ $\boxed{3x + 2}$ $\boxed{6x + 1}$

7 The diagram shows the cumulative frequency graph for the marks that 1000 students received on a GCSE maths paper.

    a Find the median mark.

    b Find the interquartile range.

    c Students who score 65 or over get a grade A. Approximately what percentage of students is this?

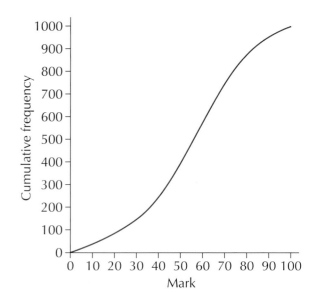

You may use a calculator for the rest of the exercise.

8 The scatter diagram shows the value and the mileage for a number of cars. The mileage is the total distance a car has travelled since new. The value of a car is given as a percentage of its value when it was new.

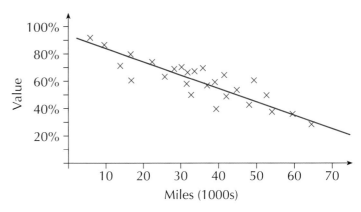

A line of best fit has been drawn on the scatter diagram.

a What does the scatter diagram show about the relationship between the value of a car and its mileage?

b A car has a mileage of 45 000. Estimate its value as a percentage of its value when new.

c A car cost £12 000 when it was new. It is now worth £7800. Use this information to estimate how many miles it has travelled.

9 The table shows the SATs Levels awarded to a class in Mathematics.

Level	3	4	5	6
Number of students	2	7	13	8

a How many students were there altogether in the class?

b Work out the mean SATs score for the class.

10 A teacher records how long it takes her class to do a test. The table shows the results.

Work out the mean time taken to do the test.

Time, t minutes	Frequency
$0 < t \le 2$	9
$2 < t \le 4$	12
$4 < t \le 6$	15
$6 < t \le 8$	3
$8 < t \le 10$	1

11 A bag contains 4 red and 6 blue marbles. A marble is taken from the bag at random and replaced. Another marble is then taken from the bag.

A tree diagram may help to answer these questions.

a What is the probability that both marbles are blue?

b What is the probability that there is one marble of each colour?

c A marble is taken from the bag. The colour is recorded and the marble is then replaced. This is done 200 times. How many red marbles would you expect to get?

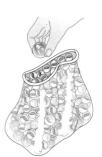

<table>
<tr><td></td><td>

This chapter is going to show you

- some of the statistical techniques you have met before
- how to make a hypothesis
- how to carry out a handling data investigation

</td><td>

What you should already know

- How to carry out a survey
- How to write a questionnaire
- How to collect data
- How to construct and interpret two-way tables
- How to construct and interpret frequency diagrams
- How to construct and interpret scatter graphs
- How to compare data
- How to draw and interpret cumulative frequency graphs
- How to calculate statistics for large sets of data

</td></tr>
</table>

Statistical techniques

This lesson will remind you of the statistical techniques that you have met before. In the next lesson you will be using these to carry out a handling data project.

The following tables show the vocabulary you should know before you start an investigation.

Handling data vocabulary

Collecting data

	Definition	Example
Questionnaire	A set of questions used to collect information from people	Here is an example of a poor question: How old are you? ☐ 0–10 ☐ 10–20 ☐ 20–30 ☐ over 30 It is poor because the categories overlap, so that both 10 and 20 are in two response sections.
Population	The set of people or objects being investigated	A school with 1000 students
Sample	Part of the whole population being used for analysis	50 students picked from the 1000 in a school
Survey	The collection of data from a sample of the population	Investigating the favourite colour of students in a school by asking 50 students

	Definition	Example
Census	The collection of data from an entire population	Investigating the favourite colour of students in a school by asking *every* student in the school
Data collection sheet or Observation sheet	A form for recording results	Favourite colours of 50 students: Blue ┼┼┼ ┼┼┼ Red ┼┼┼ ┼┼┼ ┼┼┼ |||
Tally	A means of recording data quickly	Green ┼┼┼ ┼┼┼ |||| Other ┼┼┼ |||
Raw data	Data which has not been sorted or analysed	Ages of 10 students: 12, 14, 13, 11, 12, 12, 15, 13, 11, 12
Primary data	Data that *you* have collected, usually by observation, surveys or experiments	Colours of cars on your street
Secondary data	Data collected by someone else and then used by you	Acceleration times of different cars
Two-way table	A table for combining two sets of data	(see table below)
Frequency table	A table showing the quantities of different items or values	(see table below)
Frequency diagram	A diagram showing the quantities of different items or values	(see diagrams below)

Two-way table example:

	Ford	Vauxhall	Peugeot
Red	3	5	2
Blue	1	0	4
Green	2	0	1

Frequency table example:

Weight of parcels W (kg)	Number of parcels (frequency)
$0 < W \le 1$	5
$1 < W \le 2$	7
$W > 2$	3

Journey times

HISTOGRAM

Students' favourite colours

BAR CHART

Reasons for absence
- Sick
- Dentist
- Holiday
- Unauthorised

PIE CHART

	Definition	Example
Frequency diagram *(continued)*		**Mean temperature for two cities** **LINE GRAPH**
Stem-and-leaf diagram	A way of grouping data, in order	**Recorded speeds of 16 cars** $$\begin{array}{c\|cccccc} 2 & 3 & 7 & 7 & 8 & 9 & 9 \\ 3 & 1 & 2 & 3 & 5 & 5 & 5 & 7 \\ 4 & 2 & 2 & 5 \end{array}$$ Key: 2 | 3 means 23 miles per hour
Population pyramid	A statistical diagram often used for comparing large sets of data	**Age distribution in France (2000)**
Scatter graph or scatter diagram including line of best fit	A graph to compare two sets of data	
Cumulative frequency diagram	A graph used to estimate median and interquartile range for large sets of data	

Processing data

	Definition	Example
Mode	The value that occurs *most* often	Find the mode, median, mean and range of this set of data 23, 17, 25, 19, 17, 23, 21, 23
Median	The *middle* value when the data is written in order (or the average of the middle two values)	Sorting the data into order, smallest first, gives: 17, 17, 19, 21, 23, 23, 23, 25 Mode = 23
Mean	The sum of all the values divided by the number of items of data	Median = $\dfrac{21+23}{2}$ = 22 Mean = $\dfrac{17+17+19+21+23+23+23+25}{8}$ = 21
Range	The difference between the largest and smallest values	Range = 25 − 17 = 8
Lower quartile	One quarter of the values lie below the lower quartile	From the stem-and-leaf diagram find the median and the interquartile range
Upper quartile	Three quarters of the values lie below the upper quartile	**Ages of a team of 11 footballers** 1 | 7 7 7 8 9 9 2 | 0 5 6 3 | 1 5
Interquartile range	The difference between the upper quartile and the lower quartile	Key: 1 | 7 means 17 years old There are 11 footballers Median = $\dfrac{(11+1)}{2}$ = 6th value = 19 years Lower quartile = 3rd value = 17 years Upper quartile = 9th value = 26 years Interquartile range = 26 − 19 = 7 years

---

Exercise 13A

1 Criticise each of the following questions that were used in a questionnaire about travelling to school.

    a How do you travel to school?

        ☐ Walk   ☐ Bus   ☐ Car

    b How long does your journey take?

        ☐ 0 – 5 minutes   ☐ 5 – 10 minutes

        ☐ 10 – 15 minutes   ☐ 15 – 20 minutes

    c At what time do you usually set off to school?

        ☐ Before 8.00 am   ☐ 8.00 am – 8.15 am

        ☐ 8.15 am – 8.30 am   ☐ Other

2 Below are the times taken (*T* seconds) by 20 students to run 100 metres.

Boys	13.1	14.0	17.9	15.2	15.9	17.5	13.9	21.3	15.5	17.6
Girls	15.3	17.8	16.3	18.0	19.2	21.4	13.5	18.2	18.4	13.6

a Copy and complete the two-way table to show the frequencies.

b What percentage completed the 100 metres in less than 16 seconds?

c Which is the modal class for the girls?

d In which class is the median time for the boys?

	Boys	Girls
$12 \leq T < 14$		
$14 \leq T < 16$		
$16 \leq T < 18$		
$18 \leq T < 20$		
$20 \leq T < 22$		

3 19 students take a test. The total marks available were 20. Here are the results.

17, 16, 12, 14, 19, 15, 9, 16, 18, 10, 6, 11, 11, 14, 20, 8, 12, 19, 5

a Use the data to copy and complete this stem-and leaf-diagram:

```
0 |
1 |
2 |
```
Key: ☐ | ☐ means ☐

b Work out the median mark.

c State the range of the marks.

d How many students scored 75% or more in the test?

4 Look at the population pyramid for France in the year 2000 on page 185.

a Compare the number of females and males alive in the year 2000 who were born during or before World War II, which lasted from 1939 to 1945.

b Suggest some possible reasons for the difference in the number of males and females in this age range.

5 Calculate the mode, the median and the mean for each set of data below.

a 1, 1, 1, 4, 8, 17, 50

b 2, 5, 11, 5, 8, 7, 6, 1, 4

c £2.50, £4.50, £2, £3, £4.50, £2.50, £3, £4.50, £3.50, £4, £3.50

d 18, 18, 19, 21, 24, 25

6 A school quiz team is made up of students from four different classes. The table shows the number of students in the team from each class.

a Represent this information in a pie chart.

b Holly says: 'The percentage of students chosen from class C is double the percentage chosen from class A.' Explain why this might not be true.

Class	Number of students
A	4
B	3
C	8
D	5

7 The table below shows the heights of 100 students in Year 9.

    a   Copy and complete the cumulative frequency table.

    b   Draw the cumulative frequency graph.

    c   Use your graph to estimate the median and interquartile range.

Height, h (cm)	Number of students	Height, h (cm)	Cumulative frequency
$0 < h \leq 100$	0	$h \leq 100$	
$100 < h \leq 120$	7	$h \leq 120$	
$120 < h \leq 130$	32	$h \leq 130$	
$130 < h \leq 140$	41	$h \leq 140$	
$140 < h \leq 150$	17	$h \leq 150$	
$150 < h \leq 160$	3	$h \leq 160$	

8 Use the table of data in **Question 7** to estimate the mean height of the group of Year 9 pupils.

Extension Work

It was estimated that there were 58 836 700 people living in the UK in mid 2001. This was an increase of 1.4 million people (2.4 per cent) since 1991.

The graph shows the population (in thousands) of the UK between 1991 and 2001. Explain why it may be misleading.

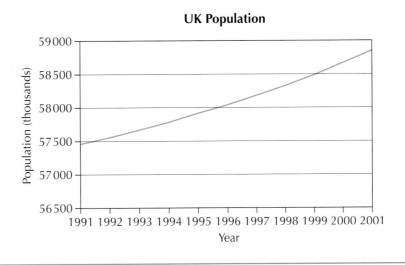

UK Population

A handling data project

In this section you are going to plan and write a handling data investigation. Look at the handling data cycle below. This shows the basic steps in an investigation.

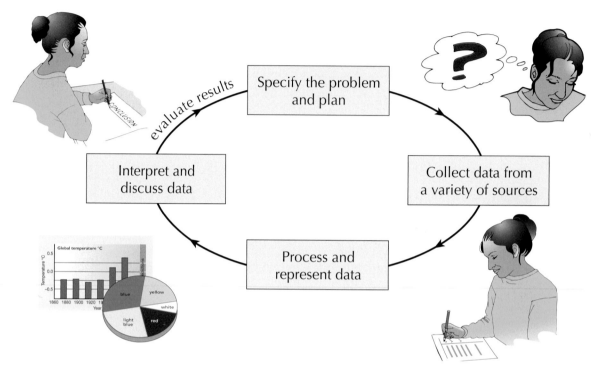

More detail is given about each step below. Follow this checklist when doing your investigation and writing your report.

- **Specify the problem and plan**
  - statement of problem or topic to investigate
  - hypothesis stating what you think the investigation will show
  - how you will choose your sample and sample size
  - any practical problems you foresee
  - identify any sources of bias and plan how to minimise them
  - how you will obtain your data
  - identify what extra information may be required to extend the project

- **Collect data from a variety of sources**
  - follow initial plan and use a suitable data-collection sheet

- **Process and represent data**
  - analysis of your results using appropriate statistical calculations and diagrams

- **Interpret and discuss data**
  - comparison of results with your original hypothesis
  - list of any factors which might have affected your results and how you could overcome these in future
  - consider the limitations of any assumptions made
  - a final conclusion

In small groups investigate one of the following topics.

1 Compare people's hand-span with their shoe size.

2 Compare the reaction times of two different groups of people: for example, girls and boys.

3 Investigate the ability of people to estimate the lengths of lines (straight or curved) and to estimate the size of angles.

4 Compare the word lengths in a newspaper with those in a magazine, or compare the word lengths in two different newspapers.

5 Choose your own investigation.

Extension Work

Choose one of the following tasks.

1   Working individually, write a report of your investigation using the checklist. Look again at the limitations of your investigation. Think how you could overcome these: for example, by increasing your sample size or choosing your sample using a different method.

2   In your small group, create a display which can be used as part of a presentation to show the other groups in your class how you carried out your investigation and what results you obtained. Look again at the limitations of your investigation. Think how you could overcome these: for example, by increasing your sample size or choosing your sample using a different method.

3   If you have completed your report, then consider a different problem from the list in Exercise 13B. Write a plan of how you would investigate it, including how to overcome any problems encountered in your first project.

CHAPTER 14 Shape, Space and Measures 4

This chapter is going to show you	**What you should already know**
o some of the methods already met to determine shapes and their properties o how to carry out a shape and space investigation o how to carry out a symmetry investigation	o How to find the surface area of 2-D shapes o How to find the volume of 3-D shapes o How to use reflective and rotational symmetry

Shape and space revision

Before starting an investigation into shape and space, you must be familiar with all the formulae and terms which you have met so far.

This section provides a checklist before you start your investigation.

Perimeter and area

Square	Rectangle	Parallelogram	Triangle	Trapezium	Circle

 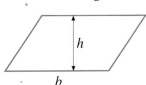 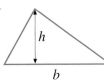 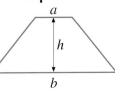

$P = 4l$	$P = 2l + 2w$	$A = bh$	$A = \frac{1}{2}bh$	$A = \frac{1}{2}(a + b)h$	$C = \pi d = 2\pi r$
$A = l^2$	$A = lw$				$A = \pi r^2$

Volume and surface area

Cube	Cuboid	Prism	Cylinder

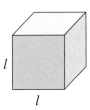 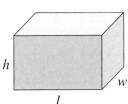 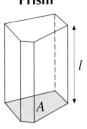 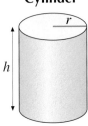

$V = l^3$	$V = lwh$	$V = Al$	$V = \pi r^2 h$
$A = 6l^2$	$A = 2lw + 2lh + 2hw$		

1 Find **i** the perimeter and **ii** the area of each of the following shapes.

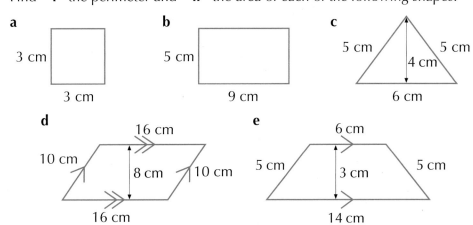

a

3 cm

3 cm

b

5 cm

9 cm

c

5 cm   5 cm

4 cm

6 cm

d

16 cm

10 cm

8 cm   10 cm

16 cm

e

6 cm

5 cm   5 cm

3 cm

14 cm

2 Calculate **i** the circumference and **ii** the area of each of the following circles. Take $\pi = 3.14$ or use the π key on your calculator. Give your answers to one decimal place.

a

3 cm

b

4.5 cm

c

10 cm

d

12.6 cm

3 Calculate **i** the surface area and **ii** the volume of each of the following 3-D shapes.

a

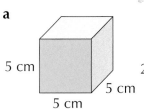

5 cm

5 cm

5 cm

b

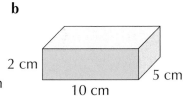

2 cm

10 cm

5 cm

c

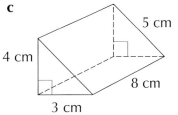

5 cm

4 cm

8 cm

3 cm

d

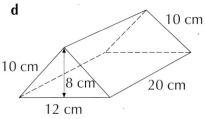

10 cm

10 cm

8 cm   20 cm

12 cm

4 Calculate the volume of each of the following cylinders. Give each answer to three significant figures. (Take $\pi = 3.142$ or use the π key on your calculator.)

a

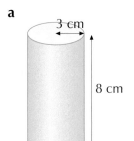

3 cm

8 cm

b

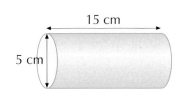

15 cm

5 cm

c

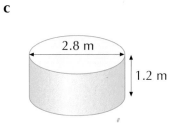

2.8 m

1.2 m

5 A circle has a circumference of 20 cm.

    a   Calculate the diameter of the circle.

    b   Calculate the area of the circle.

Take $\pi = 3.14$ or use the $\boxed{\pi}$ key on your calculator. Give each answer to one decimal place.

6 A cylinder has a volume of 200 cm³ and a height of 5 cm. Calculate the diameter of the cylinder. Give your answer to one decimal place.

Extension Work

Calculate the perimeter and the area of the shape below.

Take $\pi = 3.14$ or use the $\boxed{\pi}$ key on your calculator. Give your answers to three significant figures.

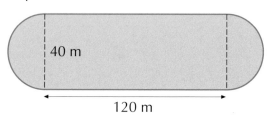

40 m

120 m

Shape and space investigations

When undertaking an investigation, you should carry out the following:

- Draw some easy examples first, making all diagrams clear with all measurements shown.
- Put your results in a table with suitable headings.
- Look for any patterns among the entries in the table.
- Describe and explain any patterns you spot.
- Try to find a rule or formula to explain each pattern.
- Try another example to see whether your rule or formula does work.
- Summarise your results with a conclusion.
- If possible, extend the investigation by introducing different questions.

Exercise 14B

Working in pairs or small groups, investigate one of the following.

1 Investigate whether the perimeter and the area of a square can have the same value. Extend the problem by looking at rectangles.

2 For the growing squares on the grid below, investigate the ratio of the length of a side to the perimeter and the ratio of the length of a side to the area.

3 A coin is stamped from a square sheet of metal. Investigate the percentage waste for coins of different sizes.

4 The diagram below represents a 6 × 2 snooker table with a pocket at each corner, A, B, C and D.

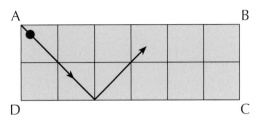

A snooker ball is hit from the corner at A at an angle of 45° and carries on bouncing off the sides of the table until it goes down one of the pockets.

a How many times does the ball bounce off the sides before it goes down a pocket?

b Down which pocket does the ball go?

c Investigate for different sizes of snooker tables.

Symmetry revision

Before starting an investigation into symmetry, you must be familiar with terms which you have met so far.

This section provides a checklist before you start your investigation.

There are two types of symmetry: **reflection symmetry** and **rotational symmetry**.

Some 2-D shapes have both types of symmetry, while some have only one type.

All 2-D shapes have rotational symmetry of order 1 or more.

Reflection symmetry

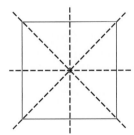

A square has 4 lines of symmetry

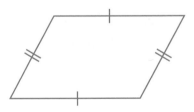

A parallelogram has no lines of symmetry

Remember that tracing paper or a mirror can be used to find the lines of symmetry of a shape.

Rotational symmetry

A 2-D shape has rotational symmetry when it can be rotated about a point to look exactly the same in its new position.

The **order of rotational symmetry** is the number of different positions in which the shape looks the same when rotated about the point.

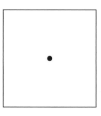 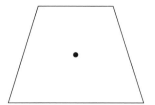

A square has rotational symmetry of order 4

This trapezium has rotational symmetry of order 1

Remember that tracing paper can be used to find the order of rotational symmetry of a shape.

Planes of symmetry

A **plane of symmetry** divides a 3-D shape into two identical parts. Each part is a reflection of the other in the plane of symmetry.

A cuboid has three planes of symmetry, as shown below.

  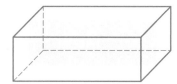

Each plane of symmetry is a rectangle.

Exercise 14C

1 Copy each of these shapes and draw its lines of symmetry. Write below each shape the number of lines of symmetry it has.

a   b   c   d   e

2 Write down the number of lines of symmetry for each of the following shapes.

a   b   c   d

3 Copy each of the following diagrams and write the order of rotational symmetry below each one.

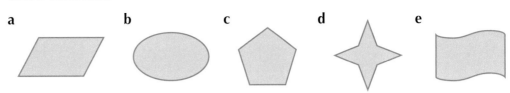

a   b   c   d   e

4 Write down the order of rotational symmetry for each of the following shapes.

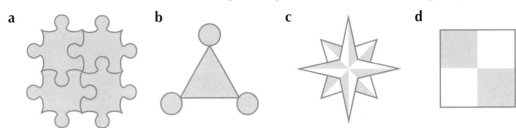

a   b   c   d

5 Write down the number of planes of symmetry for each of the following 3-D letters.

a   b   c   d

6 Draw a 3-D shape that has five planes of symmetry.

Extension Work

Find pictures in magazines which have reflection or rotational symmetry.

Make a poster of your pictures to display in your classroom.

Symmetry investigations

When undertaking a symmetry investigation, you should carry out the following:

- Draw some easy examples first, showing any lines of symmetry and/or stating the order of rotational symmetry on the diagrams.
- Explain anything you notice from the diagrams.
- Describe and explain any patterns which you spot.
- Summarise your results with a conclusion.
- If possible, extend the investigation by introducing different questions.

Working in pairs or small groups, investigate one of the following.

1 Three squares are shaded on the 3 × 3 tile shown so that the tile has one line of symmetry.

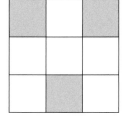

  a Investigate the line symmetry of the tile when three squares are shaded.

  b Investigate the line symmetry when different numbers of squares are shaded.

Extend the problem by looking at different sizes of tiles.

2 Pentominoes are shapes made from five squares which touch edge to edge. For example:

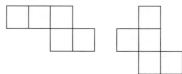

Investigate line symmetry and rotational symmetry for different pentominoes.

Extend the problem by looking at hexominoes. These are shapes made from six squares which touch edge to edge.

3 In how many ways will the T-shape fit inside the 3 × 3 grid?

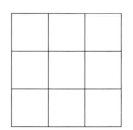

Investigate the number of ways the T-shape will fit inside a 10 mm square grid of any size.

4 The **symmetry number** for a 3-D solid is the number of ways the solid can be placed through a 2-D outline of the solid.

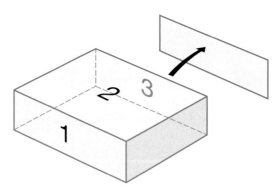

For example, the outline of a cuboid is a rectangle and the cuboid can be 'posted' (so that it fits exactly) through the rectangle in four different ways. These are:

  side 3 first, with side 2 facing up (shown above)
  side 3 first, with 2 facing down
  side 1 first, with 2 facing up
  side 1 first, with 2 facing down

So, the symmetry number for a cuboid is 4.

Investigate the symmetry number for other 3-D solids.

Handling Data **4**

This chapter is going to show you	**What you should already know**
<ul><li>different topics within probability</li><li>how to use probability to make a hypothesis</li><li>how to carry out a handling data investigation using experimental and theoretical probabilities</li></ul>	<ul><li>Probabilities are numbers between 0 and 1</li><li>How to work out simple probabilities</li><li>How to calculate probabilities for two or more outcomes using sample spaces</li><li>How to calculate probabilities for two or more outcomes using tree diagrams</li><li>The difference between experimental and theoretical probability</li><li>The vocabulary of probability</li></ul>

Revision of probability

Make sure that you are familiar with the vocabulary of probability, which is listed in the table below.

Probability vocabulary

	Example
Probability scale Chance/likelihood Equally likely Certain Uncertain Very likely Unlikely Fifty–fifty chance/evens	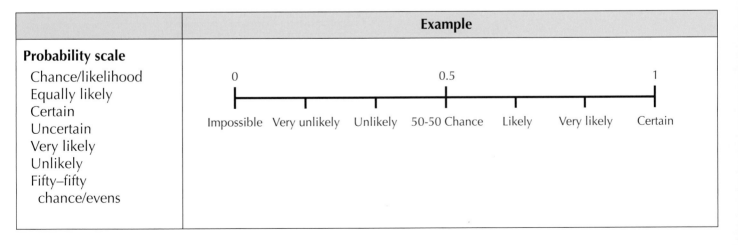

Example

Probability

Event
Outcome
Random
Experimental probability
Theoretical probability
Relative frequency
Expectation
Bias
Fair

Example 1

A fair spinner is numbered 1, 2, 3.

a The spinner is spun twice.
List all the outcomes.

b How many possible outcomes are there if the spinner is spun 3 times?

a 1, 1   1, 2   1, 3   2, 1   2, 2   2, 3   3, 1   3, 2   3, 3

b $3 \times 3 \times 3 = 27$

Example 2

A six-sided dice is rolled 60 times.
It lands on 6 fifteen times.

a What is the experimental probability of landing on a 6?

b If the dice were rolled 300 times, how many times would you expect it to land on 6?

c If the dice were fair, what would be the theoretical probability of landing on 6?

a $\frac{15}{60} = \frac{1}{4}$

b $\frac{1}{4} \times 300 = 75$ times

c $\frac{1}{6}$

Probability diagram

Sample
Sample space

Example 3

A coin is thrown and a dice is rolled.

a Draw a sample space diagram.

b Write down the probability of getting a head and a 6.

a

		Dice					
		1	2	3	4	5	6
Coin	Head	H,1	H,2	H,3	H,4	H,5	H,6
	Tail	T,1	T,2	T,3	T,4	T,5	T,6

b $\frac{1}{12}$

Tree diagram

Example 4

The probability that it rains on one day = 0.6

a Draw a tree diagram to show the probabilities of rain on two consecutive days.

b Use the tree diagram to calculate the probability that it rains on only one of the two days.

	Example

a

1st day	2nd day

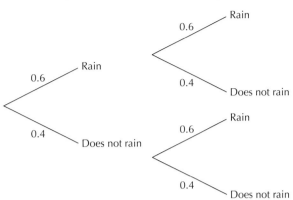

          0.6 — Rain
    Rain
  0.6   0.4 — Does not rain

  0.4   0.6 — Rain
    Does not rain
          0.4 — Does not rain

b   Probability of rain on only one day is given by:

P(Rain on 1st day and does not rain on 2nd day) OR
P(Does not rain on 1st day and rains on 2nd day)

$= 0.6 \times 0.4 + 0.4 \times 0.6$

$= 0.24 + 0.24$

$= 0.48$

Estimate of probability (relative frequency)

Example 5

The number of times a javelin successfully sticks in the ground is shown.

Number of throws	10	20	30	40	50
Number of successes	8	19	27	36	45
Relative frequency of success	$\frac{8}{10}$ $= 0.8$				

a   Complete the table to show the relative frequency of success.

b   Plot the relative frequencies on a graph.

c   Write down the best estimate of the probability of success.

d   Use your estimate to predict the number of times a javelin successfully sticks in the ground in 500 throws.

a

Number of throws	10	20	30	40	50
Number of successes	8	19	27	35	45
Relative frequency of success	$\frac{8}{10}$ $= 0.8$	$\frac{19}{20}$ $= 0.95$	$\frac{27}{30}$ $= 0.9$	$\frac{35}{40}$ $= 0.875$	$\frac{45}{50}$ $= 0.9$

	Example
Estimate of probability (relative frequency) *(continued)*	**b** **c** Best estimate of probability = 0.9 (50 throws) **d** 0.9 × 500 = 450 successes
Event Exhaustive Independent Mutually exclusive	**Example 6** In a raffle there are blue, green and yellow tickets. The table shows the probability of each colour being chosen. **a** What is the probability of picking a blue or a yellow ticket? **b** What is the probability of picking a green ticket? **a** $\frac{1}{2} + \frac{1}{8} = \frac{5}{8}$ **b** $1 - \frac{5}{8} = \frac{3}{8}$
Probability notation P(Event)	P(Green) = $\frac{3}{8}$

Table within Example 6:

Ticket colour	Probability
Blue	$\frac{1}{2}$
Green	?
Yellow	$\frac{1}{8}$

1 Three coins are thrown.

   a How many different outcomes are there? Make a list to show all the possibilities.

   b Work out the probability of getting no Heads.

   c Work out the probability of getting exactly one Head.

   d Work out the probability of getting at least one Head.

2 Matthew is either late, on time or early for school. The probability that he is late is 0.1 and the probability that he is on time is 0.3.

   a What is the probability that he is late or on time?

   b What is the probability that he is early?

3 A group of 50 students are told to draw two straight lines on a piece of paper. Seven students draw parallel lines, twelve draw perpendicular lines and the rest draw lines which are neither parallel nor perpendicular.

Use these results to estimate the probability that a student chosen at random has:
a Drawn parallel lines.
b Drawn perpendicular lines.
c Drawn lines that are neither parallel nor perpendicular.

4 A five-sided spinner is spun 50 times. Here are the results.

Number on spinner	1	2	3	4	5
Frequency	8	11	10	6	15

a Write down the experimental probability of the spinner landing on the number 4.
b Write down the theoretical probability of a fair, five-sided spinner landing on the number 4.
c Compare the experimental and theoretical probabilities and say whether you think the spinner is fair.
d How many fours would you expect if the spinner were spun 250 times?

5 Geoff is building a wall. The probability that Geoff completes the wall by Saturday is $\frac{4}{5}$.

Andy is building a patio. The probability that Andy completes the patio by Saturday is $\frac{1}{3}$. Calculate the probability that by Saturday:

a Both the wall and the patio are completed.
b The wall is completed but the patio is not completed.
c Neither the wall nor the patio are completed.

6 The relative frequencies of the number of wins of a football team are shown in the table below.

Number of games	5	10	15	20	25
Relative frequency of wins	0.8	0.7	0.67	0.75	0.76
Number of wins	4				

a Plot the relative frequencies on a graph.
b Explain why it is not possible to tell from the graph whether the first game was a win.
c Write down the best estimate of the probability of winning the next game.
d Copy and complete the table to show the number of wins for 10, 15, 20 and 25 games.

1   State whether each of the following pairs of events are independent or not independent. Explain your answers.

    a   Rolling a dice and getting 6;
        Rolling the dice a second time and getting 6.

    b   Picking out a winning raffle ticket;
        Picking out a second winning raffle ticket.

    c   It raining in London on Monday;
        It raining in London on Tuesday.

2   State whether each of the following pairs of outcomes are mutually exclusive or not mutually exclusive. Explain your answers.

    a   An ordinary, six-sided dice landing on an even number;
        The dice landing on a prime number.

    b   Two coins being thrown and getting at least one Head;
        The two coins being thrown and getting two Tails.

    c   Two coins being thrown and getting at least one Tail;
        The two coins being thrown and getting two Tails.

3   State whether each of the following outcomes are exhaustive or not exhaustive. Explain your answers.

    a   A dice landing on an odd number;
        The dice landing on a multiple of 2.

    b   A spinner numbered 1, 2, 3, 4, 5 landing on a number greater than 3;
        The spinner landing on a number less than 3.

    c   A spinner numbered 1, 2, 3, 4, 5 landing on a number greater than 2;
        The spinner landing on a number less than 4.

A probability investigation

Look again at the handling data cycle.

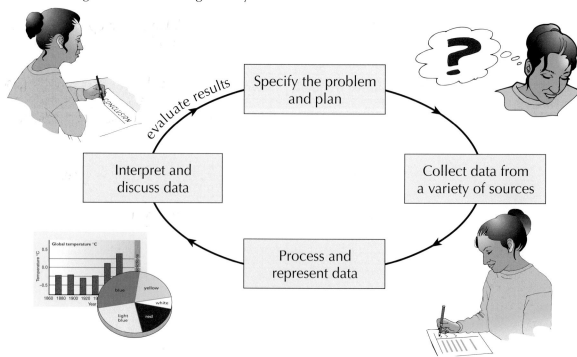

Use the handling data cycle to help you when completing your probability investigation. More detail is given about each step below.

- **Specify the problem and plan**
  - statement of problem or topic to investigate
  - hypothesis stating what you think the investigation will show
  - how you will choose your sample and sample size
  - any practical problems you foresee
  - identify any sources of bias and plan how to minimise them
  - how you will obtain your experimental data
  - identify what extra information may be required to extend the project

- **Collect data from a variety of sources**
  - follow initial plan and use a suitable data-collection sheet

- **Process and represent data**
  - analysis of your results using appropriate statistical calculations and diagrams

- **Interpret and discuss data**
  - comparison of results with your original hypothesis
  - list of any factors which might have affected your results and how you could overcome these in future
  - consider the limitations of any assumptions made
  - a final conclusion

Exercise 15B

In small groups carry out an experiment to investigate one of the following.

1 Organise a class lottery. Get each person to choose ten numbers, from 1 to 20. Have ten separate draws and record who has a winning number each time (there may be more than one winner for each draw). Compare the theoretical and experimental probabilities of each player winning.

2 Investigate whether a drawing pin will land point up more often than point down. Use different-sized drawing pins to test whether the results are always the same.

3 Ask a member of your group to put ten coloured cubes in a bag, so that the rest of the group do not know what the colours are. Investigate how many times you need to pick a cube out and replace it in order to be able to predict accurately the contents of the bag.

4 Some people are luckier than others when rolling a dice.

5 A playing card usually lands face-up when dropped.

Choose one of the following tasks.

1   Working individually, write a report of your experiment using the checklist. Look again at the limitations of your experiment and think how you could overcome these: for example, by increasing your sample size or choosing your sample using a different method.

2   In your small group, create a display which can be used as part of a presentation to show the other groups in your class how you carried out your experiment and what results you obtained. Look again at the limitations of your experiment and think how you could overcome these: for example, by increasing your sample size or choosing your sample using a different method.

3   If you have completed your report, then consider a different problem from the list in Exercise 15B. Write a plan of how you would investigate it, including how to overcome any problems encountered in your first project.

This chapter is going to

○ Get you started on your GCSE course

Solving quadratic equations

Example 16.1 ▷ Substitute into the quadratic expression $x^2 - 5x + 6$

    a $x = 2$ **b** $x = 3$

    a $(2)^2 - 5(2) + 6 = 4 - 10 + 6 = 0$
    b $(3)^2 - 5(3) + 6 = 9 - 15 + 6 = 0$

The values 2 and 3 are known as the roots of the quadratic equation $x^2 - 5x + 6 = 0$ since they solve the equation exactly.

Example 16.2 ▷ **a** $p \times q = 0$. What are the possible values of p and q?
       b $(x - 2)(x - 3) = 0$. What are the possible values of x?

    a   Either $p = 0$, so $0 \times q = 0$, or $q = 0$, so $p \times 0 = 0$.
    b   Either $x - 2 = 0$, so $0 \times (x - 3) = 0$, in which case $x = 2$; or $x - 3 = 0$,
         so $(x - 2) \times 0 = 0$, in which case $x = 3$.

To solve a quadratic equation, firstly **factorise** the left hand side.

For example, solve $x^2 - 5x + 6 = 0$.

Factorising the left hand side gives $(x - 2)(x - 3) = 0$.

The values of the brackets multiplied together can only give 0 if one or the other brackets equals 0. So either $x - 2 = 0$ or $x - 3 = 0$.

Therefore the roots of $x^2 - 5x + 6 = 0$ are $x = 2$ or $x = 3$.

Example 16.3 ▷ Solve these quadratic equations using the above rule.

    a $(x - 5)(x + 2) = 0$ **b** $x^2 + 5x - 14 = 0$ **c** $x^2 - 4x + 4 = 0$

    a   Either $x - 5 = 0$, so $x = 5$; or $x + 2 = 0$, so $x = -2$.
       The roots are $x = 5$ or $x = -2$.

    b $x^2 + 5x - 14 = 0$ factorises into $(x + 7)(x - 2) = 0$.
       Either $x + 7 = 0$, so $x = -7$; or $x - 2 = 0$, so $x = 2$.
       The roots are $x = -7$ or $x = 2$.

Sometimes the roots of a quadratic equation are the same.

    c $x^2 - 4x + 4 = 0$ factorises into $(x - 2)(x - 2) = 0$.
       As both brackets are the same, $x - 2 = 0$, so $x = 2$.
       Hence the quadratic equation has just one root, $x = 2$.

1 Solve these equations.

a $(x + 1)(x - 1) = 0$ b $(x - 2)(x + 5) = 0$ c $(x - 3)(x + 6) = 0$

d $(x + 4)(x + 3) = 0$ e $(x + 2)(x + 7) = 0$ f $(x - 3)(x - 8) = 0$

g $(x - 8)(x + 1) = 0$ h $(x + 3)(x + 3) = 0$ i $(x - 4)(x - 4) = 0$

2 First factorise then solve these equations.

a $x^2 + 3x + 2 = 0$ b $x^2 + 11x + 30 = 0$ c $x^2 + 6x + 8 = 0$

d $x^2 - 5x + 6 = 0$ e $x^2 - 7x + 10 = 0$ f $x^2 - 5x + 4 = 0$

g $x^2 + 10x + 25 = 0$ h $x^2 - 8x + 16 = 0$ i $x^2 - 2x - 15 = 0$

j $x^2 + 2x - 15 = 0$ k $x^2 - 2x - 24 = 0$ l $x^2 - x - 6 = 0$

m $x^2 - 10x + 9 = 0$ n $x^2 - 3x - 18 = 0$ p $x^2 + 2x + 1 = 0$

Quadratic expressions of the form $ax^2 + bx + c$

Example 16.4 ▷ Expand these brackets.

a $(2x + 3)(x - 1)$ b $(3x - 4)(2x + 3)$ c $(3x - 2)^2$

a $(2x + 3)(x - 1) = 2x(x - 1) + 3(x - 1) = 2x^2 - 2x + 3x - 3 = 2x^2 + x - 3$

b $(3x - 4)(2x + 3) = 3x(2x + 3) - 4(2x + 3) = 6x^2 + 9x - 8x - 12 = 6x^2 + x - 12$

c $(3x - 2)^2 = (3x - 2)(3x - 2) = 9x^2 - 6x - 6x + 4 = 9x^2 - 12x + 4$

Example 16.5 ▷ Factorise:

a $3x^2 + 7x + 2$ b $6x^2 - 17x + 12$

a We know that there will be 2 brackets. The factors of 3 are 3 and 1, so the brackets must start $(3x \quad)(x \quad)$. The factors of 2 are 2 and 1. Now it is a matter of finding a combination of both sets of factors to give $7x$. By trial we can find that $(3x + 1)(x + 2)$ works.

b Factors of 6 are 1 and 6 or 3 and 2. Factors of 12 are 1 and 12, 2 and 6 and 3 and 4.

We now have to find a pair of factors of 6 that combine with a pair of factors of 12 to give -17.

Factors of 6		Factors of 12		
1	2	1	2	3
6	3	12	6	4

We can see that combining the following factors gives $(2 \times -4) + (3 \times -3) = -17$.

$$\begin{matrix} 2 & & 3 \\ & \times & \\ 3 & & 4 \end{matrix}$$

So, the factorisation is $(2x - 3)(3x - 4)$.

1 Expand the brackets into quadratic expressions.

a $(2x + 1)(x + 5)$ **b** $(3x - 3)(x + 4)$ **c** $(2x - 5)(2x - 4)$

d $(3x + 3)(2x - 7)$ **e** $(2x + 6)^2$ **f** $(3x - 4)^2$

g $(2x - 8)(3x + 1)$ **h** $(4x - 1)(2x + 3)$ **i** $(2x - 1)(2x + 1)$

2 Factorise these quadratic expressions.

a $2x^2 + 7x + 3$ **b** $2x^2 + 9x + 10$ **c** $3x^2 + 13x + 4$

d $2x^2 - x - 1$ **e** $6x^2 + 7x + 2$ **f** $2x^2 - x - 6$

g $2x^2 + 3x - 9$ **h** $4x^2 + 4x + 1$ **i** $4x^2 + 7x - 2$

j $5x^2 + 11x + 2$ **k** $3x^2 + 2x - 1$ **l** $8x^2 + 6x + 1$

m $3x^2 - 5x - 2$ **n** $6x^2 + x - 1$ **p** $4x^2 - 11x - 3$

q $4x^2 + 4x - 15$ **r** $2x2 - 9x - 35$ **s** $2x^2 - 5x - 25$

t $3x^2 + 14x - 5$ **u** $9x^2 + 6x + 1$ **v** $10x^2 + 13x - 3$

Quadratic equations

Example 16.6

Solve these equations.

a $2x^2 + 7x + 3 = 0$ **b** $4x^2 + 4x - 15 = 0$

a $2x^2 + 7x + 3 = 0$ factorises to $(2x + 1)(x + 3) = 0$.

Either $2x + 1 = 0$ so, $x = -\frac{1}{2}$ or $x + 3 = 0$ so, $x = -3$.

The solutions are $x = -\frac{1}{2}$ or $x = -3$.

b $4x^2 + 4x - 15 = 0$ factorises to $(2x - 3)(2x + 5) = 0$.

Either $2x - 3 = 0$ so, $x = 1\frac{1}{2}$, or $2x + 5 = 0$ so, $x = -2\frac{1}{2}$.

The solutions are $x = 1\frac{1}{2}$ or $x = -2\frac{1}{2}$.

Example 16.7

Solve the following equations.

a $x^2 + 6x = 7$ **b** $2x(x + 2) = 3(x + 1)$

a This equation is not in the correct form to factorise and solve. It needs to be rearranged.

$x^2 + 6x = 7$.

So, $x^2 + 6x - 7 = 0$.

Factorising gives $(x + 7)(x - 1) = 0$.

So, $x = -7$ or $x = 1$.

b Expanding and rearranging the brackets gives $2x^2 + 4x = 3x + 3$.

So, $2x^2 + x - 3 = 0$.

Factorising gives $(2x + 3)(x - 1) = 0$.

So, $x = -1\frac{1}{2}$ or $x = 1$.

1 First factorise then solve these equations.

a $2x^2 - 7x + 3 = 0$ b $3x^2 - 5x - 2 = 0$ c $2x^2 + 7x - 4 = 0$

d $4x^2 + 4x - 3 = 0$ e $2x^2 + 11x - 6 = 0$ f $4x^2 + 7x - 2 = 0$

g $6x^2 + 17x + 5 = 0$ h $6x^2 + x - 1 = 0$ i $4x^2 + 12x + 9 = 0$

j $20x^2 - 9x + 1 = 0$ k $6x^2 - 19x + 10 = 0$ l $9x^2 + 6x + 1 = 0$

m $4x^2 - 4x + 1 = 0$ n $6x^2 - x - 5 = 0$ p $3x^2 - x - 10 = 0$

2 Solve these equations.

a $x^2 + x = 2$ b $x(x - 1) = 1 - x$ c $2x(x - 1) = 1 - x$

d $3x^2 = x + 2$ e $4x(x - 1) = 5x - 2$ f $4x(4x - 3) = 4(x - 1)$

g $x(x + 5) = 5x + 25$ h $6x(x - 1) = x - 4$ i $1 - x = 20x^2$

The quadratic formula

Another way to solve quadratic equations in the form $ax^2 + bx + c = 0$ is by using the following formula:

$$x = \frac{-b \pm \sqrt{b^2 - 4ac}}{2a}$$

This formula is used when quadratic equations do not factorise, although it will work with any quadratic equation. The symbol '±' means that you firstly add the values to find one root to the equation, and then subtract the values to find the other root.

Example 16.8 ▷ Solve these equations.

a $2x^2 + 7x + 3 = 0$ b $x^2 - 16 = 0$

a First, identify a, b and c.

For this equation, $a = 2$, $b = 7$ and $c = 3$.

Substitute these values into the formula $x = \dfrac{-(7) \pm \sqrt{(7)^2 - 4(2)(3)}}{2(2)}$

Now evaluate the square root $x = \dfrac{-(7) \pm \sqrt{25}}{4} = \dfrac{-(7) \pm 5}{4}$

So the solutions are $x = \dfrac{-7 + 5}{4} = \dfrac{-2}{4} = -\dfrac{1}{2}$ or $\dfrac{-7 - 5}{4} = \dfrac{-12}{4} = -3$

b For this equation, $a = 1$, $b = 0$ and $c = -16$.

Substitute into the formula $x = \dfrac{-(0) \pm \sqrt{(0)^2 - 4(1)(-16)}}{2(1)}$

Now evaluate the square root $x = \dfrac{0 \pm \sqrt{64}}{2} = \dfrac{\pm 8}{2}$

So the solutions are $x = 4$ or -4.

Example 16.9 ▶ Solve these equations.

a $2x^2 + 3x - 4 = 0$, giving your answer to 2 decimal places

b $3x^2 - 4x - 1 = 0$, giving your answer in **surd** form. Surd form means leaving square roots in your answer.

These equations will not factorise. The 'clue' is that you are asked for your answers to 2 decimal places or in surd form.

a In this equation, $a = 2$, $b = 3$ and $c = -4$.

Substituting into the formula gives $x = \dfrac{-(3) \pm \sqrt{(3)^2 - 4(2)(-4)}}{2(2)}$

Therefore $x = \dfrac{-(3) \pm \sqrt{41}}{4} = \dfrac{-3 \pm 6.4031}{4}$

So the answers are $x = 0.85$ and -2.35.

b In this equation, $a = 3$, $b = -4$ and $c = -1$.

Substituting into the formula gives $x = \dfrac{-(-4) \pm \sqrt{(-4)^2 - 4(3)(-1)}}{2(3)}$

Therefore $x = \dfrac{4 + \sqrt{28}}{6}$ or $\dfrac{4 - \sqrt{28}}{6}$

Exercise 16D

1 Solve these equations using the quadratic formula. All of the answers are whole numbers or fractions.

a $x^2 + 2x - 24 = 0$ **b** $x^2 + 6x - 7 = 0$ **c** $2x^2 + 3x - 2 = 0$

d $2x^2 + 3x - 20 = 0$ **e** $x^2 + 5x = 0$ **f** $x^2 - 36 = 0$

2 Solve these equations, giving your answers to 2 decimal places.

a $2x^2 + 3x - 6 = 0$ **b** $3x^2 - x - 6 = 0$ **c** $x^2 + 4x - 7 = 0$

d $2x^2 - 4x - 1 = 0$ **e** $x^2 + 6x - 1 = 0$ **f** $2x^2 + 5x - 1 = 0$

g $3x^2 - 6x + 1 = 0$ **h** $2x^2 - 3x - 3 = 0$ **i** $x^2 - 5x + 2 = 0$

3 Solve these equations, giving your answer in surd form.

a $x^2 - 3x + 1 = 0$ **b** $x^2 + 4x - 1 = 0$ **c** $x^2 + 4x + 1 = 0$

d $x^2 + 6x + 1 = 0$ **e** $x^2 + 10x + 2 = 0$ **f** $x^2 + 2x - 1 = 0$

Completing the square

Another way of factorising quadratic expressions is called **completing the square**. This is based on the expansion $(x + a)^2 = x^2 + 2ax + a^2$, which can be rearranged to:

$$x^2 + 2ax = (x + a)^2 - a^2$$

Example 16.10 ▷ Complete the square for these quadratic expressions.

    a $x^2 + 4x$ **b** $x^2 - 10x$

    To find the value that goes with x inside the bracket, halve the x coefficient (the coefficient is the number in front of a letter), and then subtract the square of this.

    a   In this expression, half of 4 is 2.
          So, $x^2 + 4x = (x + 2)^2 - 2^2 = (x + 2)^2 - 4$.

    b $x^2 - 10x = (x - 5)^2 - 5^2 = (x - 5)^2 - 25$.

Example 16.11 ▷ By completing the square, rewrite these quadratic expressions.

    a $x^2 + 6x - 4$ **b** $x^2 - 4x + 1$

    Firstly, complete the square for the x^2 and x term. Then 'tidy up' the rest of the expression.

    a $x^2 + 6x - 4 = (x + 3)^2 - 9 - 4 = (x + 3)^2 - 13$
    b $x^2 - 4x + 1 = (x - 2)^2 - 4 + 1 = (x - 2)^2 - 3$

Example 16.12 ▷ Solve these quadratic equations by completing the square.

    a $x^2 + 6x - 1 = 0$ **b** $x^2 - 2x - 15 = 0$

    a $x^2 + 6x - 1 = 0$

Complete the square	$(x + 3)^2 - 9 - 1 = 0$
Tidy up	$(x + 3)^2 - 10 = 0$
Take constant term to right hand side	$(x + 3)^2 = 10$
Square root both sides	$x + 3 = \pm \sqrt{10}$
Make x the subject	$x = -3 \pm \sqrt{10}$

    So, the answer is $x = -3 + \sqrt{10}$ and $x = -3 - \sqrt{10}$.
    The answer should be left in surd form.

    b $x^2 - 2x - 15 = 0$

Complete the square	$(x - 1)^2 - 1 - 15 = 0$
Tidy up	$(x - 1)^2 - 16 = 0$
Take constant term to right hand side	$(x - 1)^2 = 16$
Square root both sides	$x - 1 = \pm 4$
Make x the subject	$x = +1 \pm 4$

    So, the answer is $x = 5$ or $x = -3$.

Exercise 16E

1   Complete the square for these quadratic expressions.

    a $x^2 + 8x$ **b** $x^2 - 2x$ **c** $x^2 - 12x$
    d $x^2 - 14x$ **e** $x^2 + 4x$ **f** $x^2 + 2x$

2 By completing the square, rewrite these quadratic expressions.

a	$x^2 + 8x - 1$	**b**	$x^2 - 2x + 3$	**c**	$x^2 - 12x + 5$
d	$x^2 - 14x + 7$	**e**	$x^2 + 4x - 3$	**f**	$x^2 + 2x - 5$
g	$x^2 + 6x - 2$	**h**	$x^2 + 10x - 9$	**i**	$x^2 - 6x + 3$

3 Solve these quadratic equations by completing the square method.

a	$x^2 + 8x - 1 = 0$	**b**	$x^2 - 2x - 3 = 0$	**c**	$x^2 - 12x + 5 = 0$
d	$x^2 - 14x + 7 = 0$	**e**	$x^2 + 4x - 5 = 0$	**f**	$x^2 - 6x - 2 = 0$
g	$x^2 - 10x + 1 = 0$	**h**	$x^2 - 6x + 4 = 0$	**i**	$x^2 - 8x + 5 = 0$
j	$x^2 - 2x - 1 = 0$	**k**	$x^2 + 2x - 5 = 0$	**l**	$x^2 + 12x - 7 = 0$

The difference of two squares

Example 16.13

Expand these brackets.

a $(x + 3)(x - 3)$ **b** $(a - b)(a + b)$

a $(x + 3)(x - 3) = x(x - 3) + 3(x - 3) = x^2 - 3x + 3x - 9 = x^2 - 9$

b $(a - b)(a + b) = a(a + b) - b(a + b) = a^2 + ba - ba - b^2 = a^2 - b^2$

Example 16.13 demonstrates the rule known as the difference of two squares. Reversing the result in part **b** gives:

$$a^2 - b^2 = (a - b)(a + b)$$

Example 16.14

Factorise these expressions.

a $x^2 - 16$ **b** $x^2 - 4y^2$ **c** $9x^2 - 4$

Once you know the above rule, you can use it to factorise expressions like these.

a $x^2 - 16 = x^2 - 4^2 = (x - 4)(x + 4)$

b $x^2 - 4y^2 = x^2 - (2y)^2 = (x - 2y)(x + 2y)$

c $9x^2 - 4 = (3x)^2 - 2^2 = (3x - 2)(3x + 2)$

Exercise 16F

1 Expand and simplify these brackets into quadratic expressions.

a	$(x + 1)(x - 1)$	**b**	$(x - 5)(x + 5)$	**c**	$(x - y)(x + y)$
d	$(2x + 1)(2x - 1)$	**e**	$(x + 2y)(x - 2y)$	**f**	$(2x - 3y)(2x + 3y)$

2 Factorise these quadratic expressions.

a	$x^2 - 100$	**b**	$x^2 - 4$	**c**	$x^2 - 36$
d	$x^2 - 81$	**e**	$x^2 - 64$	**f**	$x^2 - 121$
g	$x^2 - z^2$	**h**	$4x^2 - 25$	**i**	$x^2 - 9y^2$
j	$16x^2 - 9$	**k**	$4x^2 - 25y^2$	**l**	$25x^2 - 64$
m	$9 - x^2$	**n**	$4x^2 - 36$	**p**	$36x^2 - 1$

An investigation into $y = ax^2 + bx + c$

In the next two years, during your GCSE course, you will have to complete two pieces of coursework. One of these will be an investigation into Algebra or Shape and Space. The following investigation will give you practice in coursework and could be used as one of your pieces.

By using the facts you have learnt in the rest of Chapter 16 you will be able to do the following investigation.

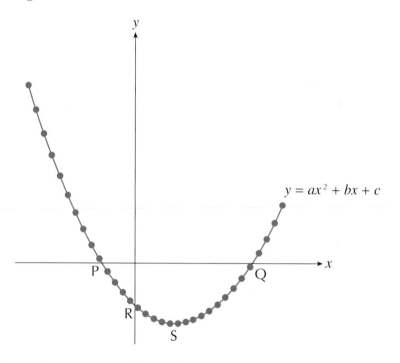

The graph of a quadratic equation has a characteristic shape called a **parabola**.

Investigate the relationship between the values a, b and c in the graph $y = ax^2 + bx + c$ and the points P, Q (where the graph crosses the x-axis), the point R (where the graph crosses the y-axis) and the point S (the **vertex** or *turning point* of the graph).

You should use a graph plotting program or a graphical calculator to help you.

You will not gain any credit for spending a lot of time drawing graphs accurately. You will gain credit for a systematic investigation into the effect of a, b and c on the graph.

GCSE past-paper questions

1 Solve the equation $x^2 - 5x = 0$.

AQA (SEG), Question 9c, Paper 10, June 2001

2 i Factorise $x^2 - 6x + 8$.

ii Hence solve this equation.

$x^2 - 6x + 8 = 0$

OCR, Question 3d, Paper 5, June 2001

3 a Factorise

i $3pq - 6r$

ii $c^2 - 9c + 20$.

b Solve the equation

$(x + 7)(x - 2) = 0$.

AQA (SEG), Question 6, Paper 39, June 2001

4 a Factorise $3p^2 + 16p + 5$.

b Hence, or otherwise, simplify

$$\frac{p^2 - 25}{3p^2 + 16p + 5}$$

AQA (SEG), Question 14, Paper 39, June 2001

5 Solve the equation $x^2 + 4x - 10 = 0$.

Give your answers to 2 decimal places.

Show your working.

AQA, Question 20, Paper 2, June 2003

6 a Simplify $(3xy^3)^2$.

b Solve the equation $2x^2 - 5x - 4 = 0$.

Give your answers correct to two decimal places.

OCR, Question 13, Paper 6, June 2001

7 Solve the equation $2x^2 - x - 2 = 0$.

Give your answer to an accuracy of two decimal places.

AQA (SEG), Question 10, Paper 10, June 2001

8 You are given that $(3x - b)^2 - 9 = ax^2 - 12x + c$, for all values of x.

Find the values of a, b, and c.

AQA (SEG), Question 14, Paper 9, June 2001

9 Find the values of a and b such that

$x^2 - 10x + 18 = (x - a)^2 + b$.

AQA, Question 21, Paper 1, June 2003

10 For all values of x,

$x^2 + 4x = (x + p)^2 + q$.

Find the values of p and q.

EDEXCEL, Question 20, Paper 6, June 2001

Published by HarperCollins*Publishers* Limited
77–85 Fulham Palace Road
Hammersmith
London
W6 8JB

Browse the complete Collins catalogue at
www.collinseducation.com

10 9 8 7 6
ISBN-13 978 0 00 713878 4
ISBN-10 0 00 713878 4

British Library Cataloguing in Publication Data
A Catalogue record for this publication is available from the
British Library

Edited by John Day
Design and typesetting by Jordan Publishing Design
Project Management by Nicola Tidman
Covers by Tim Byrne
Illustrations by Nigel Jordan and Tony Wilkins
Proofreading by Amanda Whyte and Jenny Wong
Production by Sarah Robinson
Printed and bound by Printing Express, Hong Kong

The publishers would like to thank the many teachers and
advisers whose feedback helped to shape *Maths
Frameworking*.

The publishers thank the Qualifications and Curriculum
Authority for granting permission to reproduce questions from
past SAT papers for Key Stage 3.

AQA (NEAB)/SEG AQA examination questions are reproduced
by permission fo the Assessment and Qualifications Alliance.

You might also like to visit:
www.harpercollins.co.uk
The book lover's website